TECHNOLOGY, MANAGEMENT AND MARKETS

TECHNOLOGY, MANAGEMENT AND MARKETS

An Investigation of R&D and
Innovation in Industrial Organizations

Ove Granstrand

Foreword by Christopher Freeman

St. Martin's Press
New York

© Ove Granstrand 1982

All rights reserved. For information, write:
St. Martin's Press, Inc., 175 Fifth Avenue, New York,
New York 10010
Printed in Great Britain
First published in the United States of America in 1982
ISBN 0-312-79007-4

Library of Congress Cataloging in Publication Data
   Granstrand, Ove, 1944-
    Technology, management and markets.

   Bibliography: p. 213
   Includes index.
   1. Research, Industrial. I. Title.
T175.G66   1982   658.5′7   82-16804
ISBN 0-312-79007-4

CONTENTS

List of Figures and Abbreviations . . . . *viii*
List of Tables and Corporations Studied . . . . *ix*
Foreword . . . . *xi*
Preface . . . . *xiii*
Acknowledgements . . . . *xiv*

1 INTRODUCTION   1

1.1 The Problem Context 1; **1.2 Purpose and Method** 1; **1.3 Concepts** 4; 1.3.1 A note on concept formation 4; 1.3.2 Concepts 4

2 HISTORY OF INDUSTRY AND LARGE CORPORATIONS IN SWEDEN   9

2.1 Introduction 9; **2.2 Empirical Findings and Discussions** 10; 2.2.1 Industrialization at the national level 10; 2.2.2 Rise of Large Corporations, 11; **2.3 Conclusions** 18

3 R&D, CORPORATE GROWTH AND DIVERSIFICATION   20

3.1 Introduction 20; **3.2 Empirical Findings** 20; 3.2.1 History of corporate growth and diversification 20; 3.2.2 History of corporate R&D 25; 3.2.3 Cases of R&D and diversification 28; 3.2.4 Situation in the 1970s 32; **3.3 Discussion** 39; 3.3.1 Empirical Summary 39; 3.3.2 Relationships between R&D and corporate growth 40; 3.3.3 Relationships between R&D and corporate diversification 43; **3.4 Conclusions** 44

4 R&D AND CORPORATE INTERNATIONALIZATION   46

4.1 Introduction 46; **4.2 Empirical Findings** 46; 4.2.1 History of R&D and corporate internationalization 46; 4.2.2 The situation in the 1970s 49; **4.3 Discussion** 54; 4.3.1 Empirical summary 54; 4.3.2 Corporate internationalization 55; 4.3.3 Internationalization of R&D 56; **4.4 Conclusions** 58

5 R&D AND CORPORATE POLICY MAKING   60

5.1 Introduction 60; **5.2 Empirical Findings** 61; 5.2.1 Corporate policies 61; 5.2.2 R&D policies 64; 5.2.3 Policy making 67; **5.3 Discus-**

sion 73; 5.3.1 Empirical summary 73; 5.3.2 Corporate Goals and Policies 73; 5.3.3 Policy making 75; **5.4 Conclusions** 77

6 R&D AND STRATEGIC DECISION MAKING 79

6.1 Introduction 79; **6.2 Empirical Findings** 80; 6.2.1 Strategic decision making in corporate histories 80; 6.2.2 R&D decision making 85; **6.3 Discussion** 87; 6.3.1 Empirical summary 87; 6.3.2 Strategizing and R&D decision making 87; **6.4 Conclusions** 90

7 R&D AND CORPORATE MANAGEMENT 92

7.1 Introduction 92; **7.2 Empirical Findings** 93; 7.2.1 The board and R&D 93; 7.2.2 Top management relations to R&D 93; 7.2.3 Working roles of R&D managers 101; **7.3 Discussion** 108; 7.3.1 Empirical summary 108; 7.3.2 Top management relations to R&D 109; 7.3.3 Working roles of R&D managers 111; **7.4 Conclusions** 114

8 R&D AND CORPORATE ORGANIZATION 116

8.1 Introduction 116; **8.2 Empirical Findings** 118; **8.3 Discussion** 124; 8.3.1 Empirical summary 124; 8.3.2 Corporate organization 124; 8.3.3 R&D organization 126; **8.4 Conclusion** 128

9 TECHNOLOGICAL CHANGE AND SUBCULTURES 130

9.1 Introduction 130; **9.2 Empirical Findings** 131; 9.2.1 Subcultures within science and technology 131; 9.2.2 Subcultures within marketing 136; **9.3 Discussion** 139; 9.3.1 Empirical summary 139; 9.3.2 Cultural structure 139; 9.3.3 Cultural change 141; **9.4 Conclusions** 144

10 CONFLICTS RELATED TO R&D AND INNOVATION
   IN LARGE CORPORATIONS 145

10.1 Introduction 145; **10.2 Empirical Findings** 146; 10.2.1 Groups of encountered conflicts 146; 10.2.2 Dynamics in typical significant conflict relations 147; 10.2.3 Dynamics in relations among significant actors 150; **10.3 Discussion** 154; 10.3.1 Empirical summary 154; 10.3.2 Conflicts and their effects 154; 10.3.3 Causes of conflicts 155; **10.4 Conclusions** 158

Contents

11 SOURCES OF IDEAS AND BARRIERS TO INNOVATION IN LARGE CORPORATIONS — 159

11.1 Introduction 159; **11.2 Empirical Findings** 159; 11.2.1 Sources of ideas 159; 11.2.2 Barriers to innovation 162; **11.3 Discussion** 170; 11.3.1 Empirical summary 170; 11.3.2 Pluralism, competition and cooperation 171; **11.4 Conclusions** 173

12 DISCUSSION — 175

12.1 Introduction 175; **12.2 Empirical Summary** 175; **12.3 Technology and Management** 177; 12.3.1 Technological and managerial innovation 177; 12.3.2 Management of R&D and technological innovation 182; **12.4 Management and Markets** 186; 12.4.1 Review of Williamson's work on markets and organizations 186; 12.4.2 Review of Phillips' work on markets, organizations and R&D 187; 12.4.3 Findings in the present study regarding management and markets 188; **12.5 Managerial Implications** 200; 12.5.1 A pluralistic R&D organization 201; 12.5.2 Temporalistic R&D organization 204; 12.5.3 A final comment 205

13 CONCLUSIONS — 206

13.1 Conclusions Regarding R&D and Innovation in Large Corporations 206; **13.2 Conclusions Regarding Technology, Management and Markets** 210

REFERENCES — 213

INDEX — 217

LIST OF FIGURES

Figure 1.1	Organizational structure of the book	3
Figure 3.1	Correlations between displaced time series for sales and R&D	41
Figure 4.1	Historical patterns of corporate internationalization	47
Figure 4.2	Patterns of Corporate Internationalization and Diversification 1965–1975	50
Figure 5.1	Elements of concept formation in policy making	61
Figure 8.1	Example of a divisionalized corporate organization	117
Figure 10.1	Simplified sociogram of significant actors with respect to R&D and innovation in the X-corporation	152
Figure 12.1	Organizational structures for R&D and innovation	202
Figure 12.2	Innovation and business development paths	203

LIST OF ABBREVIATIONS

CMD	Corporate managing director
MNC	Multinational corporation
R&D	Research and development
S&T	Science and technology

LIST OF TABLES

Table 3.1	Main historical features of corporate growth and diversification	21
Table 3.2	Main historical features of corporate R&D	26
Table 3.3	Examples of statistics on product R&D	33
Table 3.4	Aggregate figures of the situation of the corporations studied in 1975	34
Table 5.1	Emphasis in corporate policies 1975	62
Table 5.2	Written corporate goals and strategies in KemaNobel 1975	63
Table 5.3	Inventory of policies/strategies for the procurement and exploitation of technology	66
Table 5.4	Status of Strategic planning/policy making at the corporate and R&D level 1975	68
Table 6.1	Essential composition of principal R&D management bodies in SKF	86
Table 7.1	Summary of working roles of R&D managers in large corporations	109
Table 8.1	Corporate organizations in 1975	119
Table 8.2	Summary of corporate organization of R&D resources in 1975	120
Table 8.3	Summary of corporate organization of R&D management in 1975	121
Table 9.1	Examples of subcultural transformations	140
Table 10.1	Factors affecting conflicts related to R&D and innovation in the corporations studied	156
Table 12.1	Examples of major managerial innovations	181
Table 12.2	Examples of major technological innovations	182
Table 12.3	Examples of innovations in R&D management	183
Table 12.4	Summary of indications found in the present study that management and internal organization may be superior to market organization with respect to R&D and innovation	189

Table 12.5	Summary of indications of failures and limits to organization and management with respect to R&D and innovation as found in the present study	193
Table 12.6	Some indications of limits to organization and management with respect to R&D and innovation as reported in literature	193
Table 12.7	Summary of indications found in the present study of quasi-integrated forms of organization with respect to R&D and innovation	197

LIST OF CORPORATIONS STUDIED
(Main sectors of industry within parentheses)

Alfa-Laval (metal products and machinery)
Astra (pharmaceuticals)
   Astra-Hässle (subsidiary of Astra)
Boliden (mining, non-ferrous metals and industrial chemicals)
Iggesund (pulp, paper products, wood, steel and industrial chemicals)
KemaNobel (industrial chemicals and other chemical products)
Philips (electro-technical products)
   Philips-Sweden (subsidiary of Philips)
SKF (metal products, machinery and steel)
Volvo (transport equipment and machinery)
   Volvo Flygmotor (subsidiary of Volvo)

Currency conversion rate used: One $US (US Dollar) = 4.15 SEK (Swedish Crowns)

FOREWORD

During the twentieth century one of the most important changes in the structure and management of industry has been the rise of corporate R&D in large companies. Although some economists, such as Schumpeter and Galbraith, have recognized the significance of this change, it has received very inadequate attention in the general economics literature. Very frequently, the models of company behaviour, implicitly or explicitly adopted in such literature, ignore the change altogether.

Although such attitudes cannot be justified, they are understandable, because of the lack of good information about management behaviour in relation to R&D and innovation more generally. Moreover, the issues are complex, since company behaviour changes over time and can only be understood in a long-term historical context. It is much simpler to make drastic simplifying assumptions, which may sometimes give satisfactory results in the interpretation of short-term market situations. In the longer term, however, this approach completely fails to explain the dynamics of competition, both at the company level and at the international level. An understanding of Schumpeterian technological competition is absolutely essential for any realistic interpretation of these longer term changes.

It requires immense patience and subtlety to explore these longer-term aspects of company behaviour. It cannot be done simply by 'desk research', nor yet by the endless refinement of mathematical formulae as a substitute for delving into what is really going on. To make progress in this area requires a combination of the skills of the historian, the economist and the technologist, together of course with the ability to use mathematics in such a way as to summarize and illuminate the real processes of change. It also requires the ability to talk to people at all levels of responsibility in companies and to gain their confidence and cooperation in exploring and interpreting the evidence. As Schumpeter pointed out, very often the evidence of company reports and technical journals may be more important than official national statistics, which may conceal more than they reveal, because of the problems of aggregation.

All this means that to acquire evidence in this field and to make sense of its interpretation is a challenging and time-consuming task, and I am not in the least surprised by the final comment in Granstrand's own preface to this book. Only an exceptionally determined researcher with a great deal of originality and flair could succeed. For this reason there are very few good studies of corporate management behaviour in relation to R&D strategy and technical innovation. There are scarcely any which go beyond the level of case studies of individual companies or innovations, yet have an adequate and realistic base for generalization at the national and international level. Consequently, I am delighted to commend this considerable achievement unreservedly to the reader.

Christopher Freeman
June, 1982

PREFACE

This book builds on an investigation of the management of R&D and innovation in industrial organizations. The presentation is adapted to the needs of practitioners and moderate specialists in industry, government and academia.

The original idea to conduct a study of the management of R&D and technological innovation was formed while I was spending a year at Stanford University and benefiting, among other things, from Dr. Stewart Blake's instruction. During the course of the study, I have received much help and criticism, which cannot possibly be acknowledged in full. First, I would like to thank Professor Holger Bohlin, Dr. Gunnar Broman and Professor Sven Söderberg. Professor Bohlin's role has been crucial to the study and without his arrangements for empirically well-founded studies and institutional support the study would neither have taken off nor landed. Many people in the corporations and organizations studied have contributed most generously in various ways with their time, knowledge and interest. Often their information and insight have contributed not only to the study per se, but to my learning in a more personal way.

I would also like to thank Ms Karin Ahlberg, Professor Albert Danielsson, Dr. Pierre Guillet de Monthoux, Dr. Devendra Sahal and Professor Sven Söderberg for stimulating discussions. Discussions with Professor Christopher Freeman have provided valuable stimuli, intellectual as well as emotional, to present the original material for wider publication.

Gerd Eng has assisted in language matters, and her careful and competent work has improved clarity in numerous cases. Ulla Larsson, Marianne Sihlén, Marie Rosenhoff and Lotta Lundin have been engaged in typing the manuscript during the many years of the study. Final typing was done conscientiously by Kerstin Knutson and Ulla Martinsson. Thomas Wahlberg helped with the layout and drawings. Sverker Alänge, Sören Sjölander and Gun Åkerman assisted in proofreading. To all of you and many others at Chalmers who have shown interest and indulgence I express my sincere thanks.

Financial travel aid has been received from Knut and Alice Wallenbergs Stiftelse and Perstorp AB. The main part of the investigation has been funded by internal sources at Chalmers University of Technology.

A final reflection is that this study would have probably never been undertaken had I full knowledge at the outset of what it would mean in painstaking effort. Perhaps this conveys something about the nature of research planning.

ACKNOWLEDGEMENTS

An earlier version of Chapter 3 has been published in Sahal, Devendra (ed.): *Research, Development and Technological Innovation* in the Lexington Books program of D.C. Heath and Company and is copyrighted by D.C. Heath and Company 1980, reprinted in revised form here with their permission. Quotations on pages 181, 190 from Williamson, Oliver: *Markets and Hierarchies* are reprinted by permission of Macmillan Publishing Company, Inc., copyright 1975 by Macmillan Publishing company. The quotation on pages 55, 113 from Steele, Lowell. W.: *Innovation in Big Business* is reprinted by permission of Elsevier North Holland, Inc., copyright 1975 by Elsevier North Holland, Inc.

Chapter 1
INTRODUCTION

1.1 THE PROBLEM CONTEXT

Today, an increasing amount of managerial attention around the world deals with the problem of increasingly technology based international competition. Four inter-related phenomena are of particular relevance in this context:

(a) technological levelling among a growing group of actors (nations, companies) on the international scene;
(b) increasing international technology flows and technology sharing;
(c) rising research and development (R&D) costs, increasing R&D times, and often technological substitution at an accelerating rate;
(d) a slow-down of economic growth and an increasing struggle for market shares.

The tendency to opt for high technology and innovation might very well lead to decreasing industry-average returns on investments in new technology, at least for some time to come. On the other hand, waves of investment opportunities in some particular new technologies may increasingly differentiate profits and growth arising from investments in R&D. The pressures are mounting on nations and companies to be not only innovative but efficiently so but there is a dilemma. Large corporations constitute the backbone in the economy of many nations. At the same time it is said that large corporations tend to stifle parts of the innovation process.

Large corporations in a small nation such as Sweden often depend heavily on foreign output markets and a foreign supply of technology. Such corporations have been inclined to develop an international organization and maintain a specialized technological leadership based on the absorption of foreign technology in combination with internal R&D. Large corporations in a large nation such as the United States are accustomed to large domestic output markets and a large domestic supply of technology. Such corporations may find it increasingly necessary to have a more internationally oriented outlook on technology and markets.

1.2 PURPOSE AND METHOD

The management of R&D and innovation processes in a large corporation requires a great deal of insight into the nature of these processes whether one is a policymaker, a general manager, a functional manager or a project manager. The principal purpose of this book is to explore the processes of R&D and innovation systematically and to provide empirical insight into the management and organization of these processes in large corporations.

An attempt has been made to integrate technological, economic and behavioural perspectives. Corporate behaviour in relation to R&D and innovation is viewed from the inside out, based on in-depth studies of a medium-sized sample of corporations. In this way it is hoped the work will in some small respects be complementary to works on micro- and macro-levels of economic theory and organization theory.

The data have been collected through documents and several hundred interviews with people in R&D, marketing, and top management positions in eight large multinational corporations. A small number of supplementary interviews have been made, covering half a dozen other companies, three co-operative or collective research institutes and three universities.

The study has mainly been explorative and a wide variety of aspects of the history, strategy, structure, and behaviour of these corporations have been covered. Four criteria governed the design of the sample of eight corporations studied:

(a) the corporations should be large, industrial corporations;
(b) the corporations should represent different technologies and sectors of industry;
(c) if possible, not all of the corporations should be Swedish;
(d) the sample should be medium-sized and permit both case studies and some aggregate statistical analysis.

The largest Swedish corporations in the main industrial sectors were then approached. However, the largest corporation in the electrical engineering field and the largest one in the pulp and paper industry declined to participate in the study. The largest foreign-owned subsidiary in Sweden, Philips-Sweden, a subsidiary of Philips in Holland, which is in the electronics industry, and another large corporation in the pulp and paper industry, Iggesund, were then chosen, and these corporations agreed to participate in the study.

Naturally, one has to be cautious in generalizing from an explorative study of such a small sample drawn in this way from various industries. However, the high degree of concentration of industry and industrial R&D in Sweden means that the sample accounts for a substantial amount of the total industrial production and R&D in Sweden. Around 30 per cent of the total industrial R&D in Sweden was performed by the corporations in the sample.

The sample was not designed to contrast successes and failures, which makes it difficult to formulate firm implications for management. On the other hand, the corporations in the sample have survived a long time in international competition, and, for example, Volvo and SKF have successfully met competition from Japan, although through different strategies.

Empirical observations are presented in Chapters 2 to 11. Each of these chapters, which have the same structure, treats different aspects in a self-contained way. Thus, the chapters may be read independently, although some cross references exist. The book is organized in the same way as Chapters 2 to 11

Introduction

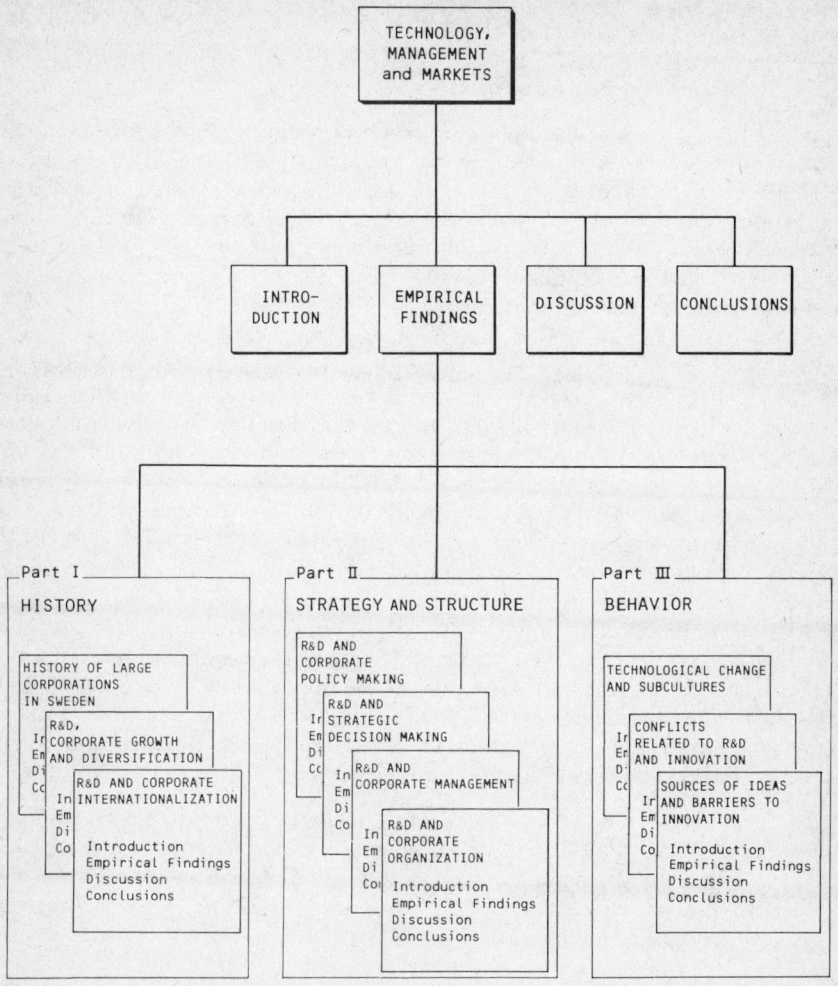

Figure 1.1 Organizational structure of the book

and constitutes a presentation of the results of the entire study. This structure is similar to a multidivisional structure in a corporation, as shown in Figure 1.1.

The introduction to each chapter defines the central concepts used in this study. The sections on empirical findings and the discussion sections constitute the body of the study. In Chapter 12 a further analysis and synthesis are presented and these are the overall contribution of the study at a higher level of aggregation. Finally, some managerial implications have been developed.

1.3 CONCEPTS

1.3.1 A note on concept formation

Penetrating studies and insights into a field are required for the formulation of useful definitions. Some problems in concept formation will be illustrated below.

There are many advocates of the view that technological innovations constitute 'the prime mover' in an economy. An extreme view is that these innovations emanate solely from scientific research. For the authors who simply define technology as applied science this is true by definition. On the other hand, several empirical studies, which do not use such a definition, claim that technology is not based solely on science. Some authors even claim that science owes more to technology than technology owes to science, that is to say, that technology applied in science characterizes the relation between science and technology rather than the reverse. Thus, the use of a conceptual connection between science and technology influences the discovery of an empirical connection and vice versa.

In definitions of both research and innovation, a basic requirement is that something new should be produced. But this is not what the linguistic construction of the terms suggests. The prefix 're-' means 'again'. Thus research has an original connotation 'to search for again'. ('Search', in turn, derives from 'circus', meaning circle, which suggests a further element of repetition.) 'Innovate' has as an original connotation 'to renew'. Thus, the etymological evolution of a concept may reveal very little about its preferred contemporary connotations.

This has been said in order to emphasize the importance of concept formation in the following descriptions and discussions. It is also a reminder that discussion of this field has to allow for a flexibility in the interpretation of many basic terms. To quote Jewkes, Sawers and Stillerman (1969, p. 25):

> There can be no doubt that an over-rigid insistence upon definition would immediately bring all discussion of invention, and of the part it plays in changes in ways of living, to a dead stop. The choice must be between discussing these matters with concepts that are necessarily somewhat vague and not discussing them at all.

1.3.2 Concepts

(a) Science, technology, research, development and related concepts

'Technology' usually stands for a branch of knowledge that deals with industrial arts, applied science, engineering etc. A common distinction is made between techniques and technology and in the language of Freeman, technology 'is simply a body of knowledge about techniques' (Freeman, 1974, p. 18). The word 'technique' here refers to arts, skills, methods, procedures and so on and derives from the Greek *téchné* meaning art, skill. Besides, the distinction between technology and techniques is related to the distinction between the 'soft' and 'hard' side of technology. The phrase 'technological knowledge', which is actually tautological, is used to emphasize the fact that physical manifestations are not referred to.

Some authors broaden the concept of technology and go beyond knowledge

Introduction

pertaining to the natural sciences, engineering and traditional inventiveness and include, for instance, the social sciences. According to Jantsch (1967, p. 15):

> Technology denotes the broad area of purposeful application of the contents of the physical, life, and behavioral sciences. It comprises the entire notion of technics as well as the medical, agricultural, management, and other fields with their total hardware and software contents.

Usually 'technology' is not used in such a broad sense but rather in accordance with Freeman's definition above. Technology then refers to knowledge about industrial products and processes and include knowledge from, for example, medical or agricultural fields but not knowledge about management.

'Science' and 'technology' often appear together, in some texts abbreviated as S&T. 'Science' has a similar connotation of knowledge as 'technology' but not specifically referring to industrial products and processes.

Another pair of basic terms that is frequently used is 'research' and 'development', often appearing as 'R&D'. These terms have diverse interpretations. A simple view is to look upon science and technology as a state of knowledge, research (basic and applied) as a systematic and methodical search for knowledge, and development as the application of knowledge and ideas to new industrial products and processes. This view underlies many official definitions of R&D. However, R&D also have many additional meanings. These are often more important in meaning than formal definitions and are therefore discussed below.

First, the concept of research and development often corresponds to the abbreviation R&D itself in the sense that 'R' always appears together with 'D' and moreover precedes 'D'. That is to say that development, according to this view, is always based on research. The connotation of R&D then is coloured by the connotation of 'R', sometimes to the extent that much inventive engineering work is not included in R&D at all. A similar view exists concerning science and technology (S&T) that is a link from 'S' to 'T' is assumed. Strong opposition against these views has been articulated, especially by Price (1973). On the other hand, there are definitions of technology as the application of science, which render truth to a linkage from 'S' to 'T'. Some authors also emphasize the conceptual continuum between 'R' and 'D'. Doubts about the usefulness of distinguishing between basic 'R' and applied 'R' exist as well.

Secondly, the rationalistic notion that R&D activities have to be systematic would — in the minds of many people — exclude much work behind innovations or technological advances because of the way this work is actually carried out. The notion of a beginning and an end of such work may sometimes be a useful simplification, but the notion of an ordered process in between is misleading.

Thirdly, 'R&D', and especially the 'R'-part, connotes together with 'science' a great deal of goodwill to some people. This connotation has to do with notions that R&D is performed by highly competent professionals, using their abilities of intelligence and creativity in solving problems requiring advanced solutions, which — correctly used — will be of benefit. Admittedly, there are vital elements of this sort in R&D, but there is also a tendency to take advantage of such notions and use the label 'R&D' generously. However, 'everything that is done by people in white coats is not research' to quote an R&D-manager. Conversely, R&D may very well be performed in a non-prestigious setting.

The need to operationalize the concept of R&D, if for nothing else than budgeting and accounting purposes, leads to the fourth point. In some cases R&D is highly integrated with other types of activities; in other cases it is not. If an organization creates departments or hires individuals to do R&D, as in large corporations or in universities, R&D will be recognized, and the idea of R&D will be influenced accordingly. When this is not the case, for example, in certain parts of industry or among independently working individuals, R&D tends to gain less attention as a concept and to be underestimated, both as a resource sink and as a source of innovations.

R&D should be viewed in a broad sense and ought to include inventive work not necessarily based on research or on scientific results or methods. As far as industrial R&D is concerned, the abbreviation is misleading in still another respect because industrial R&D is mostly 'D.' (In this case R&D ought to be written r&D instead.) Furthermore, R&D may include non-routine design, engineering, trouble-shooting and similar activities contributing to technological advances although distinguished from direct technical assistance to production or marketing. One may also draw attention to the fact that 'research' and 'development' literally refer both to activities or stages in a process and to the outcome, result or 'product' of this process.

(b) Management, entrepreneur and related concepts

Linguistically the word 'management' derives from the Latin word for hand, *manus*. 'Management' also has a connotation of doing, or influencing others to do. A typical textbook definition would include a list of so-called managerial functions such as planning, decision making, directing, organizing, co-ordinating, controlling, staffing, motivating, evaluating, communicating, goal-setting, initiating. These functions (or activities, provided these are functional) are moulded in a managerial process for purpose-oriented transformation of material and human resources. This process is considered to be carried out mostly by certain specialized individuals, although any individual can perform acts of management. The term 'management' is often associated with business and sometimes also with the business leaders as a class, although managerial processes are just as prevalent, for example, in government, universities, the church, banks, the army or labour unions.

Although technological change and industrial management have existed for centuries, the nineteenth-century economists, with Marx as a notable exception, were remarkably ignorant of these factors. Joseph A. Schumpeter is the scholar to whom has been ascribed the first more extensively articulated emphasis on technological change through a distinctive function exercised by certain individuals. His emphasis is on the concepts of innovations and entrepreneurs. About the entrepreneur concept, Schumpeter simply states, 'For actions which consist in carrying out innovations we reserve the term Enterprise; the individuals who carry them out we call Entrepreneurs'. (Schumpeter, 1939, p. 102).

Moreover, Schumpeter distinguishes between entrepreneurial and managerial functions, the latter being connected to 'the mere head or manager of a firm who runs it on established lines . .'. These functions may be exercised by the same individual or by a collective of individuals, but it may be difficult to recognize an entrepreneur or entrepreneurial activities in a corporation or in a given situation. Although Schumpeter tries to distinguish the entrepreneurial functions from those of management or administration, he has no objection to equating 'entrepreneur' with 'business leader' or 'innovator' and writes that 'The essential thing is the recognition of the distinct agent we envisage and not the word' (Schumpeter, 1951, p. 254). However, he distinguishes between an entrepreneur and a capitalist. The latter bears a risk, while 'risk bearing is no part of the entrepreneurial function'. (Schumpeter, 1939, p. 254). An obstacle the entrepreneur has to overcome is raising the necessary capital for carrying out innovations, but his entrepreneurial function does not include risk bearing. Schumpeter consequently also distinguishes between leadership and ownership.

In this study 'management' will be used in a wide sense, including the role as an entrepreneur. For further discussion, see Chapter 7.

(c) Innovation and related concepts

'Innovation' typically denotes something new but also something renewed or altered according to the Latin origin of the term. Again, the term may refer to activities in a process as well as the outcome of that process. In an industrial or wider economic setting, the normal meaning of innovation has to include some element of introduction of something new on a market or in an application. In that respect, innovation has to be distinguished from invention as solely a creation of something new. Invention is also distinguished from discovery of something that already exists (in some sense) in the physical world. The parallel to innovation in the case of discovery of, for instance, an ore deposit would be the economic utilization of the deposit. As long as an invention or a discovery is not introduced into economic life, yielding transactions, its economic relevance is nil. Innovation is thus not merely change and, in particular, not merely technological change. An innovation must possess some degree of novelty and success in application. How much of each is often discussed in patent matters. All combinations of incremental/radical novelty with small/big success occur with relevance to both industrial products and processes. The degree of 'newness' or novelty of an innovation may be considered with respect to a certain context such as a firm, a market, or a nation. It must be emphasized that with a short-hand definition of 'innovation' as 'an invention introduced on a market' nothing is said about the profitability or economic feasibility of an innovation. Also, the distinction between major innovations usually refers to the 'size' of the change involved rather than the economic outcome over a period of time.

One may also talk about financial innovations, managerial innovations, innovations in art etc., as well as innovations in the form of new industrial products or processes, which are mostly then referred to as technological innovations.

A distinction between innovation and diffusion is common. Diffusion refers to the spread of an innovation after the first market introduction or the first adoption by a user in general. The future course of an innovation in economic life may substantially involve new market introductions and alterations. Thus the processes of innovation and diffusion may be intertwined and there is seldom a simple process of first innovation and then diffusion.

The concept of diffusion is sometimes also used almost synonymously with transfer. In order for technology transfer to take place, some boundary line has to be crossed by a flow of technology. When such a crossing is connected to an economic and/or legal transaction, one may speak of technology trade, as in licensing. However, the majority of technology transfers take place without such transactions, for example, exchange or diffusion of technical information in general. The boundary line in technology transfer may pertain to structures of different kinds, such as internal departmental structures in a company, disciplinary structures in a university system, the phase structure of an innovation process, sector structures in industry, or the structure of different nations.

(d) Market and related concepts

The concept of a market is closely related to innovation. 'Market' originally meant a place for an exchange of products and economic transactions. In modern use the term has been abstracted and has several connotations. Thus, there are several ways to characterize and classify markets, for instance with respect to geography, demography, products, suppliers, customers, sectors of industry or regulations. In general, however, a market denotes a location or a group of sellers and/or buyers with actual or potential interest in making economic transactions in connection with an exchange of products, services, or knowledge.

(e) Corporation and related concepts

Such seemingly simple concepts as company, corporation, business firm, industrial organization, and enterprise may be subjected to thorough discussions in economic, legislative, sociological and political terms.

This concept will be discussed in different contexts, but for the present purpose it is enough to point out that the word 'corporation' will be used in this study to denote a company (or firm) in industry, sufficient in size and complexity to be considered (not necessarily legally) as a group of companies. A 'large corporation' generally means a corporation with 5000 or more employees. The corporations include their majority-owned companies.

Chapter 2
HISTORY OF INDUSTRY AND LARGE CORPORATIONS IN SWEDEN

2.1 INTRODUCTION

This chapter is concerned with the history of Swedish industry in general and especially with the history of the large corporations listed on the Stockholm Stock Exchange. The primary aim is to describe the rise of large corporations and to analyse the role of technology and significant actors in this process. A secondary aim is to present a short description of the history of industrial development in Sweden. This description gives the broader context of the development of the corporations in the sample studied in detail in the following chapters.

With a small domestic output market and a substantial domestic supply of raw materials, Sweden has developed both a highly internationalized and a diversified industry. Sweden is neither absolutely nor relatively a big spender on R&D. Of the world's total R&D, Sweden accounts for approximately 1 per cent. R&D performed by industry in Sweden amounted to about $855 million in 1975. This is of the same magnitude as R&D performed by General Electric or Siemens. In relation to the gross national product (GNP), total R&D in Sweden was 1.8 per cent in 1975, which was about the average of that of OECD-countries. However, there has been a substantial increase of industrial R&D in Sweden during the 1970s, also in relation to GNP. Direct government assistance to industry is lower in Sweden than in most nations with which she competes. Defence spending in the aircraft industry has, however, so far been substantial. Industrial R&D in Sweden is also financed by industry to a high degree (89 per cent in 1979) as compared with other nations, which leads to a strong dependence of industrial R&D on industrial economic results and competitive performance. On the other hand, education and research at universities and other institutions of higher learning are only financed in a very limited degree from private funds as compared with many other nations. Thus, the government mostly finances industrial R&D in an indirect way through higher education and the procurement of products.

Industrial R&D in Sweden, as elsewhere, is skewly distributed. A few large corporations in the electrical, chemical and mechanical industries account for a large part of industrial R&D. Typically these corporations have a high density of engineers, and it is notable that engineers are found in R&D, production, marketing, and general management positions (i.e., in all the main functions in the innovation process).

Since the latter part of the 1970s there has been a strong feeling of crisis in Swedish industry due to an economic recession of exceptional proportions. Financial and political involvement in industry by the government has increased and the concern for the technology factor, R&D, inventors and entrepreneurs has grown considerably among most parties involved.

2.2 EMPIRICAL FINDINGS AND DISCUSSION

2.2.1 Industrialization at the national level

Industrialization in Sweden started late but progressed rapidly. The introductory phase dates back to the 1850s and 1860s, and the pick-up started in the 1870s. Among other things the decades before World War I brought:

— a breakthrough for exports of iron ore and pulp;
— an expansion within engineering industry;
— build-up of consumer industries;
— cessation of capital imports;
— build-up of inter-organizational structures.

At the time of World War I Swedish industry was to a large extent established. Within about two generations Swedish society had been transformed at a rate of unparalleled structural changes, also in comparison with later times. The period between the wars, encompassing about one generation, also witnessed a high rate of change but mostly along already established lines. Some features of industrial development in Sweden during this period were:

— rapid industrial growth and growing diversification;
— breakthrough for cars and the utilization of electricity and related products;
— rationalization of work operations and distribution;
— increased government intervention.

The rapid industrialization placed demands on the financial institutions. Capital was imported until just before World War I when industry became nationally self-financing. A certain immigration of management took place before the twentieth century, but no substantial migration occurred in any period. Foreign influences on management have, however, been substantial. Before World War I, influences came mainly from England and Germany. Between the wars influences from the United States became important and grew to predominance after World War II.

Although technology originated mostly from abroad during the period of industrialization, domestic technological contributions grew. The latter have continued to grow, and industrial science and technology capacities have developed, but foreign technological influences and transfer still dominate in most fields today.

Basic domestic assets in forests and ores have continually been subjected to export of products with varying degrees of refinement. Hydroelectric energy became important in connection with electrification.

Internally there have been many changes accompanying the industrial developments. We may summarize by saying that the development on the whole has progressed without severe imbalances and with few disruptive events and especially without war involvements. Socially, politically and economically steady and continuous developments have predominated in spite of initial conditions of marked agrarian poverty and social inequalities. Welfare, population and social mobility have grown in parallel with the growth of industry and the

History of industry and large corporations

public sector. Close links have been maintained between significant groups of actors and institutions (banks, industry, labour, higher education and politics).

The pattern of a delayed industrialization with a rapid pick-up once started, invites to explanations in terms of effects of barriers, critical thresholds and the like, followed by advantages of backwardness, reinforcement, positive feedback and similar mechanisms. Dahmén (1970) follows this explanatory path concerning industrialization in Sweden. In relation to traditionally recognized explanatory factors, he emphasizes the role of development blocks and development imbalances. ('Development block' refers to a cluster of contingent partial developments — for example, parts of the industrial infrastructure.) Some factors causing the delay in industrialization commonly mentioned are:

— shortage of capital;
— social structure with a small base for recruitment of entrepreneurs;
— late liberalization of trade and industry;
— small domestic markets.

Factors contributing to the high rate of industrialization in Sweden, once started, are as follows (see Dahmén, 1970):

— innovations in banking and financing;
— enlarged recruitment base for entrepreneurs, especially among technologists;
— improved foreign contacts;
— increased purchasing capacity;
— improved transportation;
— passage of critical thresholds for development blocks.

Naturally, lists of factors like these derive from a biased selection from a multitude of interacting factors, which one has to penetrate in much more detail in order to obtain a picture of the dynamics of development. However, it should be noted that while conditions pertaining to capital, labour, and management are frequently mentioned, technological and raw material conditions are not directly referred to. An attempt will be made here to shed some light on the role of these factors in the formation of today's large corporations.

2.2.2 Rise of large corporations

A natural starting point is to focus on a list of corporations, original business ideas, technological innovations and significant actors. By doing so, one tends to emphasize discrete events and individual efforts. As a first approximation it may, however, be illuminating to take a closer look at such lists.

One may characterize corporations according to different combinations of productive factors at the time the original part of these corporations was established. The specific combination or mix of productive factors must have exhibited some unique competitive advantages on some input and output markets. Sometimes it is possible to discern factors of decisive importance for the establishment phase (such as assets in the form of raw materials, production and marketing capabilities, technology, labour, management) and capital or external relations (for example, to suppliers, customers, financiers, or local authorities) and finally circumstances such as location. In most cases, however, there is a complex of decisive factors, which is only partially linked to a pre-conceived business idea. It almost goes without saying that temporary restrictions of different kinds on input and output markets give an opportunistic character to the establishment phase of a business corporation.

2.2.2.1 Dominant elements in the original business idea

A large corporation consists of many parts established under different circumstances. Their legal status, names and structure as an industrial group of companies have changed, and in many cases it is hard to identify a birth of operations constituting the corporation. Many corporations were formally founded as joint-stock companies after this form of limited liability became permitted in 1849.

Most corporations on the A-list of the Stockholm Stock Exchange in 1977 fall into two large groups. One group consists of corporations that had the exploitation of sources of raw materials as a dominant element in their original business idea. Examples are Boliden, Höganäs, Iggesund and Stora Kopparberg. The second group consists of corporations that had the exploitation of a product or process invention as a dominant element in their original business idea. Examples are AGA, Alfa-Laval, ASEA, Bahco, ESAB, Ericsson, Nife Jungner, Nitro Nobel, SKF, Sandvik, Swedish Match and IRO. It is important to note that these two groups of corporations, which will be described as 'raw-material based' and 'invention based' for short, may in fact overlap since elements of business ideas cannot exist in isolation.

In addition, there are corporations that to a large extent were originally based (mostly after World War II) on providing general management and financial services (for example, Beijerinvest, Incentive, Independent Leasing), providing management of real estate (Diligentia, Drott, Hufvudstaden), or providing more purely financial management (the investment corporations). Another group consists of corporations originally based on distribution and trade services (for instance, Broströms, NK-Åhlén). Corporations in the latter groups may originally be based on innovations in finance (for example, Independent Leasing) or innovations in distribution (for instance, the Åhlén part in NK-Åhlén).

One group of corporations originated from basic local conditions with simple and 'natural' business ideas and technology. Examples are Atlas Copco, Bofors and Husqvarna, although their subsequent corporate development has involved business ideas of other types. In fact, much of the engineering industry in the nineteenth century was based on simple ideas pertaining to local conditions but with foreign influences. It is also worthwhile to note in this context that industry in general has been established rather with connections to trade and banking than with connections to handicraft (Dahmén, 1970).

The dominating elements in the original business idea often constitute a more complex picture than is displayed by a grouping like the one above. As a rule, there are combinations of several business idea elements and circumstances. Moreover, there are usually small margins for survival, and the interplay between business ideas and necessary adaptions to initial circumstances is hard to grasp in retrospect.

2.2.2.2 Roles of technological innovation

It is customary to refer to technology-based corporations as a special breed, including invention-based corporations as being based on mainly internally generated technology. Concerning the original technology base in the above cases, one may ask about the importance of:

— product versus process technology;
— radical versus incremental technological change;
— domestic versus foreign technology;
— technology versus market conditions.

Several corporations often said to be based on raw materials can be more accurately described as being based on combinations of technology and raw materials. This brings in the first issue of the relationship between product and process technology. Boliden, for example, utilized a new electric ore-prospecting technology in discovering the original deposits. This was, in fact, a rather simple application of technology, resulting from a generally growing interest in and experimentation with electromagnetism. The prospecting was initiated because of metal shortages after World War I. The refinement and melting of the poor and complex ores found, however, required the development of new and partially unique process technology. The utilization of ores and the development of technology for it have been characteristic of Boliden ever since. Although it may be correct as a first approximation to talk about Boliden as being raw-material-based, it obscures the fact that technology has played several important roles in the company's early corporate development. It is true that technological developments in raw-material-based corporations mostly concern processes. However, advances in product and process technologies are sometimes hard to separate meaningfully. An example of this is provided by the former paper mill in Östanå, one of the original parts of Iggesund. In 1751 this paper mill was the first in Sweden to produce paper out of wood instead of linen. This involved both a process and a product innovation, as would clothes made out of paper. Because the notion of raw-material-based corporations is often attached to a notion of lacking innovativeness, the incremental and intertwined elements of product and process innovation in this type of corporation should be recognized.

Export at some degree of refinement has for a long time been an important element in the business ideas of raw-material-based corporations. The extent to which export was an original idea element is hard to assess, often because the industrial operations go back to before the nineteenth century. (The idea of exporting unrefined iron ore is, however, of recent date.) It may also be added that regulations prohibited direct investments in raw-material sources in Sweden by foreign companies.

The invention-based corporations are a glamorous group. This brings up the second issue of radical versus incremental technological innovation, the answer to which is dependent upon what area and what period are considered in an innovation or diffusion-process. Here the group consists of corporations that are based on inventions which are traditionally recognized as 'big' Swedish innovations. It must, however, be kept in mind that the present concern is inventions in connection with the establishment of a corporation. Several of the corporations listed on the stock exchange have largely benefitted from inventions in later stages of their development as have the originally invention-based ones. The two main streams of corporate developments and technological developments often interplay without having common starting points.

Many, but far from all, of the inventions in the group are inventions regarding products in the form of pieces of hardware, for example, the continuously working separator (Alfa-Laval), adjustable tools (Bahco), coated welding electrodes (ESAB), telephones (Ericsson), accumulators (Nife Jungner), explosives (Nitro Nobel), ball bearings (SKF) and textile machinery components (IRO). Needless to say, the manufacturing of these new products mostly involved the development of process technology. Cases with less of a character of product invention involve Sandvik, which was based on significant developments by G. F. Göransson of an acquired patent right of the Bessemer process. Swedish Match was founded in a giant merger of match companies by Ivar Kreuger in 1917. The production of safety matches involved several inventions, some of which were typical process inventions. Swedish Match is also an example of a corporation which became integrated from raw materials to consumer markets.

Inventions of a systems nature, involving several coherent product inventions roughly at the same time, are rare but AGA with its lighthouse system and ASEA with its electric systems may be classified as more typically based on a system of inventions than the other corporations.

The third issue to be dealt with is the relationship between the invention-based corporations on one hand and foreign industry and the state of technology on the other. This issue is also related to the question of whether the inventions were radical or incremental in some sense.

The idea of using foreign technology or patterns in combination with domestic capabilities and demand underlies the establishment of many corporations, for instance, the original part of KemaNobel, Monark, Volvo and Saab-Scania. Although usually the domestic state of technology was thereby advanced, the change could be incremental as in the case of Volvo in relation to earlier automobile production in Sweden. A special case is the part of the pharmaceutical industry that was formed on the basis of a change in legislation, permitting the use of available technology.

One feature of most of the originally invention-based corporations is that their inventions were preceded by a sequence of earlier external developments. Moreover, from an international viewpoint, the establishment of many of these corporations took place in an industrial context already fairly well developed in the corresponding technology or product area. The latter two statements hold, for example, for Alfa-Laval, ASEA, Ericsson and SKF. Now, it may correctly be argued that if one is looking for previous developments, there will always be some of relevance; the question is to what extent a particular technological contribution led to a significant advance. A thorough assessment of each case cannot be done here, but at least one may conclude that in most, if not all, cases the invention led to an improvement of already existing products. For example, wrenches existed before Johansson made them adjustable, separators existed before de Laval invented a continuously working version, bearings and also ball bearings existed before Wingqvist made them self-aligning, and matches and explosives existed before Pasch and Nobel, respectively, made them safer. This was not typical only for Sweden but also for technological innovation in many fields in the industrialized world. Thus the invention-based corporations were mostly based on improvements of already existing products with existing companies operating in these product areas in an overall industrial context.

Similarly, concerning the proportions of foreign and domestic contributions to the particular inventions, it is easy to find foreign influences if one is looking for them. In some cases, the foreign connection is obvious — as when foreign patents were acquired. In others, the extent of foreign influence is much more difficult to assess. A common feature is, however, the international orientation of significant actors in connection with the establishment of the invention-based corporations. Although acquired foreign patents in some cases, for example, Sandvik and AGA, were connected to development work in the establishment phase, the foreign influence was mainly transferred via the significant actors in a more elusive way. Thus, it is hard to be conclusive about the proportions between foreign and domestic contributions without detailed studies of the significant actors.

The fourth issue considered here concerns the relation between market conditions and the inventions and corporations under consideration. A striking feature, then, is the concern about international marketing displayed in many of the invention-based corporations. Part of the reason was that the inventions led to a global advance of technology and another was that the significant actors had an international orientation. The fact that the domestic market was small contributed to this orientation. Most of the inventions appeared between 1860 and World War I, which was a period of rapid industrialization in Sweden. The producer markets grew rapidly on an average and most of the inventions were linked to the development of different parts of industry. Few of the inventions were directly related to consumer markets.

2.2.2.3 Roles of significant actors

It is possible to discern many individuals, roles and types of actors of importance in Swedish industrial development. The focus will here be limited to traditionally recognized inventors and entrepreneurs in connection with the establishment phase of the large industrial corporations listed on the stock exchange. The following skills and orientations of the significant actors have so far emerged as important personality dimensions in this context:

— entrepreneurial skill;
— inventive skill;
— multiproblem orientation;
— international orientation;
— science and technology orientation;
— market orientation.

The initially small base for recruitment of entrepreneurs was broadened later on to include a larger proportion of technologists and skilled workers. The rise of a community of technologists and industrialists with a growing influence and with a growing demand for influence was an important feature during the decades around the turn of the century.

The distinction between roles of entrepreneurs and roles of inventors is no doubt applicable and important in this context. To group the significant actors in the corresponding groups is, nevertheless, only a rough first approximation. As in the case of elements in business ideas, some more dimensions of the roles of significant actors will be discerned and exemplified as a second step of approximation, while a third step of quantification remains to be taken.

Concerning the basic distinction here between entrepreneurial and inventive contributions, the degree to which these different types of contributions was integrated is important to consider. The degree of integration of entrepreneurial and inventive skills within the single individual ranges from 'pure' inventors, such as John Ericsson to 'pure' entrepreneurs, such as Ivar Kreuger — who was actually a technologist by education. In between (or rather in the upper right-hand corner of a two-dimensional graph with entrepreneurial skill and inventive skill on the axes), one finds persons such as Wingqvist (SKF), Carlsson (KemaNobel), de Laval (Alfa-Laval and other companies), and Nobel (Nitro Nobel and other companies).

The integration of entrepreneurial and inventive skills at an interpersonal level is easy to exemplify with pairs of significant actors. The entrepreneurial and inventive roles are, however, differentiated and also differ over time as the corporations develop. The roles of financing, inspiration, and moral support, active management, initial marketing, the building of a sales organization, production, acquisitions, and continued process and product development all appear to different extents and in different combinations. It is therefore not surprising that, for example, inventors with integrated entrepreneurial skills or vice versa still appear in combination with other individuals. Some typical pairs of entrepreneurial and inventive actors are:

— A.R. Nordvall/G. Dalén (AGA)
— O. Lamm/G. de Laval (Alfa-Laval)
— L.J. Hierta/O. Carlsson (KemaNobel)
— A. Carlander/S. Wingqvist (SKF)
— A. Gabrielsson/G. Larsson (Volvo)
— B.A. Hjorth/J.P. Johansson (Bahco)

In the continued corporate development, significant actors similarly appear and play important roles, although they have not been granted the same recognition and glory as the founders.

Another important dimension of the significant actors may be described as their versatility or multiproblem orientation or inclination towards diversified (or divergent) intellectual and financial engagement. Looking at those with inventive skills, one finds persons such as Johansson and Wingqvist, who all their lives were occupied within more or less one technological problem area. On the other hand, inventors such as Dalén and de Laval, were active in many fields. It is interesting to note that the large invention-based corporations were seldom diversified early, while they internationalized early (see Chapters 3 and 4). Of the four most internationalized Swedish corporations in 1914 — AGA, Alfa-Laval, Ericsson, and SKF — only AGA was diversified early. This pattern of early corporate development also corresponds to some extent to features of the significant actors. For Ericsson and SKF the significant actors were entrepreneurially gifted technologists, who engaged in internationalization but not diversification. De Laval made contributions in diverse technological fields but was also entrepreneurially gifted and engaged in internationalization as well as the establishment of more than one corporation. Dalén, on the other hand, concentrated upon technological developments, while Nordvall engaged in internationalization. One corporation that 'missed' a splendid opportunity to internationalize early was KemaNobel. The well-integrated technologist and manager Oskar Carlsson was also internationally oriented and experienced but concentrated for some unknown reason upon domestic exploitation of his basic invention and subsequent diversification.

The roles and relations of significant actors may, of course, only partially explain the different patterns of corporate development. The nature of the different technologies, the likelihood of spin-offs etc., are important as well as external business conditions in general. Still, it seems as if internationalization and diversification are two features of early corporate development that may considerably be explained by the behaviour of one or two significant actors.

Concerning relations of inventions and inventors to science and technology, it is again possible to exemplify both very close and very loose connections. As concluded above, most inventions were improvements, although they have commonly been referred to as radical in popular histories. However, their scientific base in the form of theories and calculations was often weak, for example, for mechanical engineering inventions in the fields of bearings, separators and welding. In chemistry and electrical engineering the theoretical base was maybe more developed in some sense, but not necessarily known to the inventors. Oskar Carlsson with his invention in electrochemistry is an example of inventive abilities in combination with a confluence of science, in the form of the dissociation theory of Arrhenius in 1884, and technology, in the form of newly installed electricity in Carlsson's factory in 1889. In the subsequent attempts to exploit the invention commercially, Carlsson also engaged Arrhenius as a scientific expert, a kind of relation between industry and science that later on has become common. Another kind of relation between science and inventors concerns their mode of operation. With reasonable interpretations of the traditional requirements on scientific method as a combination of creativity, conceptualizing and systematic experimentation, many of the inventors seem to have worked scientifically, although they did not necessarily have a basis of scientific results. The entrepreneurship of Nobel is maybe the earliest and most outstanding example of how scientific methods — and in his case also scientific results — were used and generated in R&D operations integrated with industrial exploitation. Carlsson provides a similar example, although on a smaller scale. The hardship involved in integrating technological and business ambitions has a dramatic expression in the deaths of these two persons, partially because of overwork.

As far as the orientation of significant actors towards user needs and marketing is concerned, the inventors usually had a direct familiarity with a user situation. The full market potential was, however, not always initially comprehended. It is usual to refer to overestimations in this respect on the part of inventors, but sometimes they underestimated the market potential since their familiarity initially concerned a special user situation. In this sense some inventions were initially stimulated from a narrow conception of a problem or a need, but later on expansion was stimulated by renewed conceptualizations of users and their needs and technological opportunities in combination.

The marketing aspects, which include identification and education of users, the build-up of an organization for sales and technical service and so on are partially included under entrepreneurial roles. The active part of many inventors and entrepreneurs in international marketing of typical product inventions has already been mentioned. A notable feature is also the use of foreign direct investment as a marketing strategy. Sometimes this was a natural thing to do in cases of protectionism and a need for close contacts with the market, but in general this kind of entrepreneurial achievement was remarkable, considering the tradition in Swedish export and the influence of merchants and traders. Important targets for these investments before World War I were large nations, such as England, Germany, Russia, and the United States. In the absence so far of comprehensive historical studies of marketing behaviour in Swedish industry, one might hypothesize that the achievements in international marketing have been just as important for Swedish industrial development as the traditionally recognized technological achievements. The former achievements were, of course, dependent upon the latter, but the international marketing orientation of rather few significant actors, many of whom were technologists, seems to be an underemphasized aspect in common explanations of Swedish industrial development and the radical nature of the 'classical' inventions seems to be overemphasized.

2.3 CONCLUSIONS

Within a century or so, Sweden has developed an industry based to a great extent on domestic raw materials and technological advancements, the latter to a considerable degree being of foreign origin. Also, since World War II managerial influences—at least in big industry—have been of foreign origin, especially Anglo-American. Progress has been favoured by continuity in development, an international outlook, relative cultural homogeneity, and socio-political stability. Industry, government and other institutions have performed a compact communication network with many close links.

According to the dominant element in the original business idea, there are two large groups of corporations, raw-material-based and invention-based ones. These groups slightly overlap. Other groups of corporations originated in connection with the provision of management and financial services, distribution and trade, and in some cases based on innovations in finance and distribution. A final group originated from basic local conditions.

The roles of technology vary in the different groups of corporations regarding product versus process technology, radical versus incremental technological change, domestic versus foreign technology, and technology versus market conditions. Several corporations are based on combinations of process technology and raw materials. Acquisition of and impulses from foreign technology have, in general, been highly important. Major Swedish product innovations were significant product improvements rather than radically new products. The rise of large corporations based on these innovations resulted to a large extent from managerial achievements, especially in international marketing, in which foreign direct investment was an early strategy in several cases. Integration of inventive and entrepreneurial skills took place on an individual level in a few cases but mostly on a team level. Diversification and internationalization in the early corporate development corresponded to some extent to features of the significant actors, such as multiproblem orientation and international orientation. The international orientation of significant actors, in general, concerned both foreign markets and foreign technology. The inventors were often well-educated, and there are several examples of links to science in early corporate developments, the strongest link, however, being to scientific modes of operation rather than to scientific results.

Chapter 3
R&D, CORPORATE GROWTH AND DIVERSIFICATION

3.1 INTRODUCTION

The aim of this chapter is to explore the relationship between a corporation's R&D operations and its growth and diversification. The study is mainly qualitative, although available data in some cases have made quantitative calculations possible. Only rough first approximations concerning degrees of diversification have been made and further studies are required to develop more accurate measures of diversification and continuity in corporate and technological development.

'Growth' in this context is taken in a narrrow sense to mean growth in total sales unless otherwise specified. The term 'diversification' is used for the expansion of the variety of a corporation's products. Thus, the sales of an old product on a new foreign market are treated not as a case of diversification but as a case of internationalization. Diversification is also used for R&D operations to denote expansion of competencies into different technological fields.

Diversification of a corporation is difficult to specify and measure. The concept pertains to both similarities and dis-similarities among product characteristics and to the structure of sales of different products in the corporation. With respect to product characteristics, diversification has been specified on three levels: on sector level, product area level and on product line level. These levels are sometimes diffuse as are most conceptualizations of technologies, products and markets; but 'sector' refers roughly to the highest level of a standard industry classification, 'product line' to a parameterizable set of products, and 'product area' to a set of product lines associated to one another in some dimension and lying within a sector. Another way of specifying diversification is to relate it to the position of the corporation in the industrial input or output-system and talk about horizontal integration, vertical integration, backwards and forward, and finally conglomerate diversification.

The degree of diversification with respect to the structure of sales is roughly measured here as the proportion of sales outside the largest product area to total sales, as defined by the product divisionalization of the corporation. This is but a rough indicator of quantitative extent of diversification. However, most of what is said and discussed is not very sensitive to these quantifications.

3.2 EMPIRICAL FINDINGS

3.2.1 History of corporate growth and diversification

The corporations studied show a wide variety of patterns of development. Table 3.1 is a summary of the main features of this variation.

R&D, corporate growth and diversification

Table 3.1 Main historical features of corporate growth and diversification

KemaNobel	Founded in 1871. Based on foreign technology and domestic lag in a promising industry (fertilizers). Radical process invention initiated diversification but not internationalization. Continued growth and diversification parallel to technological development. Hydroelectric energy a common denominator. Severe decline in inter-war years. Entrance into plastics in the mid 1940s. Marked diversification together with change in raw material base in the 1960s. Concentration and movement into light chemicals in the 1970s together with increased internationalization.
Philips	Founded in 1891. Based on product invention (lamps). Continued technological developments. Diversification into several new product areas during and after World War I. Build-up of international organization. Serious break caused by World War II. Rapid post-war development with diversification, growth, internationalization, and strengthening of science and technology-base.
Alfa-Laval	Founded in 1883. Based on product invention (separators). Early internationalization. Strengthening of technological position. Extension of areas of product application. Post-war growth and diversification. Transition from components to systems in the 1960s. Concentration to main areas in the 1960s through acquisitions and disinvestments.
SKF	Founded in 1907. Based on product invention (bearings). Early internationalization. Integration backwards and horizontally. Diversification through concentrated R&D effort around 1920. Extension of areas of product application. Profitably post-war growth until the mid-1960s. Late synergistic diversification.
Boliden	Based on discovery of ore deposits in the mid 1920s (copper, gold). Securing of mines and development work for utilization of ore content and subsequent diversification have been continual features. Integration forwards into heavy chemicals in the 1960s and continued diversification in the 1970s. Increasing internationalization in the 1970s.
Iggesund	Manufacturing of paper and iron dates back to the seventeenth century. Shifts in emphasis on iron and wood products until pulp began to dominate in the early twentieth century. Some diversification in the 1950s. Integration forwards in the 1960s. Securing of raw materials and process developments have been continual features.
Astra	Founded in 1913 in connection with a change in legislation for pharmaceuticals. Initial expansion favoured by World War I. Acquired 1918. Nationalized and privately reconstructed in the 1920s. Break-even in the 1930s. Important product innovation in the 1940s. Internationalization and strengthening of R&D since the 1950s. No substantial diversification.
Volvo	Founded in 1915 as a subsidiary to SKF. Start of design and production of passenger cars in the mid 1920s and later on of trucks. Separation from SKF in the mid 1930s. Integration backwards and other diversification. Post-war boom with heavy investments until the mid 1950s. Growth of exports in the 1960s and growing internationalization in the 1970s. Relative growth of heavy vehicles in the 1970s. Marginal diversification in the 1970s.

In the initial phase of development a corporation is sensitive to many specific external conditions. It is not surprising, therefore, to find a variety of initial development patterns. Some corporations were slow starters and then picked up while others grew fast and then experienced a period of stagnation; some had to wait several years for profits, while others were profitable from the start; some could internationalize at an early stage, while others had to diversify. A period of successful development could be followed unexpectedly by stagnation or severe decline, and so on. The initial sensitivity of a corporation to external conditions yields many small margins and rapid changes and thus challenges the versatility of top management. Together with random factors, the characteristics of a small group of leading actors in the corporations therefore provide quite a few explanations of initial corporate development (see Chapter 2).

Although the corporations develop within many dimensions, there are often discernible time periods or phases during which development within one dimension or in one particular respect dominates. Such a period in the growth process is often characterized by bottlenecks. Thus the development of Alfa-Laval may roughly be described as consisting of periods in which the sequence of production, financing, marketing and R&D were dominating problem areas. This sequence results in a kind of sequential problem solving applied to different organizational functions. The periods of a particular orientation sometimes span more than a decade.

All corporations studied experienced World War II, and all except Boliden and Volvo also experienced World War I. With the exception of Philips (during World War II) these wars favoured both growth and diversification; World War II particularly favoured long-term growth. Diversifications, due to shortages of supply and the production of defence material, were mostly temporary, although some technological substitutions were retained after the war as well as some permanent acquisitions made because of the war. The post-World War II demand, in combination with the preparations for it during World War II, was highly significant for the growth of most of the corporations. A growth in sales has been sustained ever since among the corporations, with inflation as a significant additional factor in the 1970s. The number of employees is, however, levelling off in several cases, thus yielding growth also with respect to sales per employee.

3.2.1.1 Diversification on different levels

Regarding diversification on sector level, none of the corporations studied has completely changed its sector of industry; KemaNobel is still in chemistry, Alfa-Laval is still in engineering, and so on. Some corporations have at some time left or entered some other sector of industry, and some corporations have diversified permanently into some additional industry. At some time during its three centuries of existence Iggesund left the iron industry and SKF entered the steel industry early; Boliden recently entered and left the engineering industry, but it has also entered the chemical industry (probably permanently).

The historical continuity on product area level is also high. The original product areas remain; KemaNobel still produces fertilizers, Philips light bulbs, Alfa-Laval separators, SKF ball bearings, Boliden copper, Iggesund steel manufacture and wood products, Astra heart medicines and Volvo passenger cars. With respect to proportion of total sales, there have been shifts in the largest product area positions of KemaNobel, Philips, Iggesund and Volvo, although the shift was temporary in Volvo. These shifts of largest product area happen over long periods of time; at the same time the second largest product area may still be going strong. In Astra, with highly R&D-based products, the largest product is still growing after thirty years on the market, although it will probably be passed in the next few years.

Examples of temporary or non-remaining diversifications are sheet metal (Alfa Laval), jewelery and vermouth (SKF through compensatory business in the 1930s), lead batteries (Boliden), packaging machines (Iggesund — a new attempt at integration into packaging was done through an acquisition in 1975), sweeteners (Astra during World War II) and ventilation equipment (Volvo). Examples of remaining diversifications are plastics (KemaNobel), radios (Philips), heat exchangers (Alfa-Laval), fertilizers (Boliden), bleaching chemicals (Iggesund), penicillin (Astra) and jet engines (Volvo).

On product line level technological substitutions and product differentiations become more frequent and continuity decreases. Although all the original product areas of the corporations remain, the original product types and variants do not unless they have become standardized bulk products, such as standard chemicals, metals and pulp. Separators, bearings, light bulbs, heart medicines and cars have changed. Product ranges have grown in different technical parameters, components and materials have developed, performance has improved in different respects, new product generations have emerged and so on. To describe patterns of technological and market changes on this level would lead too far astray, but a few observations may be made. First, product life cycles are commonly considered as becoming shorter and shorter. This holds true in electronics, for example, but not in pharmaceuticals because of increased societal control, which also affects chemicals used as fertilizers. Second, there are technical parameters such as size, effect, speed, reliability and purity along which product technology has developed more or less continuously. Third, product and process changes involve to an increasing extent many different technologies. Technologies and scientific disciplines in turn differentiate and amalgamate, but their identities as coherent intellectual fields are connected to the university system and do not change as fast. Thus, many corporations find themselves working in a conglomerate of technologies. Fourth, there are differences with respect to the characteristics of technological change affecting different product areas. The electronics field is characterized by rapid change in interaction with changes in many other fields such as solid state physics, chemistry, optics and mathematics. Pharmaceutical research is often accidental, and the discovery of new pharmacological principles may lead to indications for several diseases. Within traditional process industries, technological change is not so rapid and significant long-range trends occur, for example, transitions from sulphite to sulphate pulp or transitions from basic to acid steel. (On a corporate level the changes may be drastic when the installation of new process equipment is required.)

Finally, the relationship between product changes and process changes differs both over time and among product areas. Disregarding, for the moment, the possible faults in the product/process-distinction—depending on which step in a refinement chain one is considering—one can generally say about standard chemicals, bearings and passenger cars that products have changed less than the way they are produced. Production technologies also change continually in the engineering industry with respect to parameters such as size, operation times, degree of automation and reliability. It almost goes without saying that products subjected to different patterns of technological change are an integral part of most production processes.

3.2.1.2 Strategies used for diversification

Most corporations have employed mixed strategies for diversification over time. Acquisition of companies was the dominant means of diversification in all corporations, except Philips and Astra, which are also the most R&D-intensive (see Table 3.4 in Section 3.2.4.1). Acquisitions of companies have often come about as a result of planning in which diversification has sometimes been a side effect, since the acquired company has contained products that were not the primary target of the transaction. In some cases the acquisition took place as the result of an offer to acquire or a perceived threat that a competitor would make the acquisition. If there is a real choice between diversification through acquisitions or internal R&D, important factors include the availability of external technology and internal R&D resources, technological and competitive positions, synergies, and, not least, the experience and preferences of top management. Both methods are difficult and explanations of successes and failures are not generally applicable. There are examples of over-optimism regarding possibilities of diversifying through both acquisitions of companies and internal R&D. Mixed strategies of some kind seem to have greater prospects of success. The strategies may be mixed in several modes. KemaNobel and Alfa-Laval throughout their histories have been talented acquirers of patents and know how, and Astra has been good at co-operating with universities and other companies. Another way to mix strategies is to acquire small, innovative companies at the correct stage of development, after they have passed the risky years of initial development but before they become stable. When a company is acquired with R&D overlapping internal R&D it is often hard to achieve R&D synergies with an acquired company if R&D projects or R&D people are transferred; but if firm co-ordination is not applied at once, fruitful internal R&D competition may result.

3.2.1.3 Patterns of diversification

The patterns of diversification differ greatly among the corporations. Diversification in the pharmaceutical field at Astra has proceeded along several lines. With the exception of the initiation of these lines, diversification has been rather coherent within pharmaceuticals, although new competencies have been added and new areas of disease have been worked on. Raw-material-based corporations such as Boliden and Iggesund integrate mainly forward and backward and mainly through acquisitions of assets, companies and technology. The raw-material base has remained the same for Boliden and Iggesund, although locations of mines and forests have changed and even become slightly internationalized, while the raw-material base of KemaNobel has changed completely. The securing and utilization of raw materials and by-products in production have been marked features of diversification at least at Boliden and KemaNobel. The composition of ores and other raw materials and available chemical processes, in combination with economy, have then largely determined the course of diversification.

Diversification at KemaNobel and Philips has been largely multidirectional. One way to explain this is to refer to the combinatorial nature of the corresponding technologies, the wide applicability of products and knowledge, and the high R&D-intensity. On the other hand, the products of Alfa-Laval and SKF also had a wide applicability, with many opportunities for diversification outside the product area. However, these products were sold on oligopolistic producer markets, while Philips initially operated on consumer markets. SKF has had opportunities to integrate forward, but there has been internal resistance to it, and qualified buyers present external resistance to integration forward. Alfa-Laval, on the other hand, has integrated forward through becoming systems oriented. This was stimulated by an increased systems orientation among some customers, and Alfa-Laval, in some early cases took the opportunity to supply the buyers with an extended range of components and know how. Volvo has diversified in a reverse way to a systems orientation (i.e., it worked originally only with the systems technology of design and assembly of cars, and then integrated backward into R&D and production of central components). All the engineering corporations have also integrated horizontally, in the sense that the original product line has been supplemented with additional but closely related product lines for new markets (e.g., ball and roller bearings, centrifugal separators and decanter centrifuges, passenger cars and trucks).

Vertical integration forward always poses the problem whether to deliver to competitors or compete with customers. This problem may restrain both marketing operations for intermediate products and integration forward. For example, SKF had a splendid opportunity to integrate forward into car production in the 1930s with the aid of Volvo, which was then a subsidiary of SKF. For several reasons, one of which was to avoid competition with customers, this opportunity to diversify was not taken. Instead, Volvo was literally given away to its shareholders. (The Corporate Managing Director of SKF did not 'believe in' Volvo and was about to sell it to an American automobile company but was persuaded not to by the Corporate Managing Director of Volvo, who was a former sales manager at SKF.) Volvo has, in turn, confronted the issue of integrating forward—for example, into shipbuilding—but has refrained on similar grounds.

3.2.2 History of corporate R&D

A summary with respect to history of corporate R&D is given in Table 3.2. It is difficult to summarize, considering the many parts of a corporation that emerge and the many small on-going improvements, for example, in production technologies. In-house R&D has existed more or less from the start in all the corporations, except at KemaNobel, Iggesund and Astra. The nature and intensity of R&D operations varied, of course, and some work would hardly qualify for the label R&D by more rigorous standards. A kind of continuous 'grass-roots R&D', (not often recognized or organized) has played an important role in many corporations, however. Continuous technological development is not so easily

Table 3.2 Main historical features of corporate R&D

KemaNobel	Research laboratory started in 1889. Since then R&D has continued with varying intensity. R&D strengthened in the late 1940s. Large project failed in the 1950s. In-house R&D in a transitional stage in the early 1960s with strengthening and concentration in the late 1960s and the 1970s.
Philips	Strong R&D tradition. Early product development. Research laboratory started in 1914. Strengthened and diversified R&D in inter-war years. Diversification during World War II and continued growth and widespread diversification since World War II.
Alfa-Laval	Early product development with test facilities for continuing improvements. Application orientation in inter-war years. R&D was strengthened and left the stage of materials laboratory and test shop after World War II. Further strengthening and diversification in the 1960s with increased emphasis on customer processes. Short period of stagnation followed by growth and diversification of R&D in the 1970s.
SKF	Materials laboratory started in 1911. Successful large R&D effort around 1920. Application orientation in inter-war years. Stagnation and concentration of R&D in the 1950s and the early 1960s. Strengthening and diversification of R&D in the late 1960s and 1970s.
Boliden	Continuing process developments almost from the beginning. Central R&D laboratory started in late 1940s. Product development oriented around utilization of by-products. Process developments stimulated integration forwards into chemistry in the early 1960s. Marketing of process know how in the 1970s.
Iggesund	Continuing process developments. Start of collective R&D in early 1940s. No internal product R&D until a small laboratory was started in the late 1960s.
Astra	R&D started in the early 1930s and strengthened during World War II. Substantial growth and diversification of product R&D initiated in the 1950s and strengthened in the 1960s. Continued growth but no diversification of R&D in the 1970s.
Volvo	Internal design from the start. Reliance upon suppliers' R&D. R&D around central components successively internalized. Some diversification in the 1950s and 1960s. Central R&D strengthened in the late 1960s but declined shortly afterwards. R&D integrated with other operations.

recognized or assessed and is the result of small achievements by technologists in many positions in a corporation. The production function at Boliden, Kema-Nobel, and the engineering corporations and the marketing function at Alfa-Laval and SKF have traditionally attracted many good technologists, and much R&D work has been done without being organized into an R&D department or the like.

To a large extent, earlier R&D work was a consequence of existing products, production facilities and raw materials. Organized R&D efforts for corporate growth and diversification are sometimes thought of as a new role for industrial

R&D, having emerged after World War II. In the corporations studied, however, R&D efforts yielding significant diversifications apart from continuing improvements were made before World War II in at least KemaNobel, Philips and SKF. On the other hand, World War II was followed by significant changes in the way industrial R&D was organized and regarded. Most corporations extended their engagements in R&D during and after the war. At least six of the eight corporations built new laboratories and intensified R&D during the 1940s, four corporations made significant R&D advances during the 1940s, and as a result of the war R&D also grew in the foreign subsidiaries.

Although R&D in general has grown and diversified since World War II, there are variations among the corporations. Periods of intensified R&D have been followed by stagnation or decline and then by renewal. At KemaNobel in the 1950s much hope and many management commitments were connected with a large project. After a new corporate managing director came, the project was stopped. R&D resources were transferred to other areas, and R&D was in a transition for several years. The wave of divisionalizations in the late 1960s in some cases caused a temporary decline in R&D. In the engineering corporations, periods of stagnation have occurred in the established product areas, in the sense that R&D has become increasingly oriented around some parameters for improvements. This phenomenon seems to depend more on the R&D management and staff than on the product or technology.

Since World War II the status of R&D as an organizational function, on a par with production and marketing, has increased. R&D management and organization philosophies have varied over time. In the 1950s and the early 1960s, R&D was often believed to be an almost sure generator of valuable results for corporate growth and diversification. These beliefs were later followed by pressures to control R&D more firmly and integrate it more closely with other functions, especially marketing. The preferences for centralized or decentralized R&D, large or small R&D units, internal or co-operative R&D, have changed. R&D management and organization philosophies also vary greatly among sectors of industry and among corporations.

An overall historical pattern is that corporate R&D becomes larger, more diversified, and more internationalized as the corporation grows, diversifies, and internationalizes. On the one hand, R&D is a consequence of products and processes employed in the corporation: as soon as production is established, there will be growing pressure among employed technologists to perform R&D. If the corporation is large, these forces are difficult for corporate management to eliminate. On the other hand, different features of corporate development are to a varying extent a consequence of R&D. Some cases of R&D-based diversifications are described in more detail in Section 3.2.3.

There have been shifts in or significant additions to the dominant technology of almost all corporations. For instance, a progression of generation shifts from carbide engineers to polymer technologists at KemaNobel; a progression of generation shifts in electrical engineering from vacuum tubes to transistors to integrated circuits to microcomputers at Philips; chemistry, biology, electronics and systems engineering have been integrated in mechanical engineering at Alfa-Laval; material scientists have been promoted at SKF; metallurgists and chemists have been added to 'the mining people' at Boliden; biologists and mechanical engineers have been promoted at Iggesund; a transition from chemistry to biology has taken place at Astra; and mechanical engineers have been supplemented at Volvo. These changes in the portfolio of technological competences depend on external technological development and internal conditions such as the rise of advocates or resistance among management and technologists (see Section 9.2.).

Different kinds of diversification of R&D operations may be discerned. First, there is a diversification of competencies pertaining to the core technologies of a corporation, for instance, the differentiation of polymer technology or tribology. This is an 'ordinary' specialization within a technology of decisive importance to the corporation. Second, there is a diversification pertaining to adjacent technologies. These adjacent technologies may concern the supporting technologies such as automation technology in production, surface chemistry for lubrication in a part of a product or materials technology. Corporate R&D often diversifies into adjacent technologies through an initial stage of perception of product problems followed by attempts to solve them by extending internal knowledge, often amateurishly, or hiring external R&D services. Third, there is substitution among different technologies, such as the transition from chemistry to biology in pharmaceutical research. Fourth, a new technology is 'picked up' because of its potential benefit to the corporation or because it will create new businesses (e.g., KemaNobel acquired polymer technology and Astra went into antibiotics).

The diversification into a new technology for new kinds of businesses is quite often evolutionary, with a progression over adjacent or substituting technologies. For instance, the need to preserve milk has led Alfa-Laval into heating and cooling, in turn leading to heat exchangers, microwaves, the preservation of other types of food and finally to a new packaging technology. (At present Alfa-Laval has decided not to go into packaging.) The concept of evolutionary chains is too simplified though; rather, technologies advance along some lines, may then rest until combined with some other technologies, and may then advance a bit further.

Any typology of the diversification of R&D is vague, since conceptions of a technology are diffuse and changing. Confluences and combinations occur. Strictly speaking, diversification of R&D should be considered to decrease if a combination of two technologies gains coherence and recognition. Many corporations encountered different environmental problems in the 1970s and developed counter measures in the form of corrective technologies. New competences had to be acquired, and perceptions of which technologies were adjacent and relevant changed rapidly. Thus the kind of diversification of R&D bred by environmentalism is hard to classify. It may not be considered a diversification at all since environmental technology has become recognized.

3.2.3 Cases of R&D and diversification

Case 3.1 SKF

Soon after SKF was founded in 1907, material and quality problems led to the start of a materials laboratory. Some years later SKF integrated backward into steel production in order to secure the development and supply of raw materials of high and even quality. Developments in industry in general and especially in the car industry favoured SKF in its early years. A good, basic design at an early stage, a high degree of externally financed expansion (higher than the German bearing industry, for example), comprehensive management abilities — plus what may be called a portion of luck in connection with World War I — explain the first decade of successful corporate development.

One of the 'pet ideas' of the founder was to develop bearings of universal applicability. The important and growing railway market required other design concepts with rollers instead of balls due to the high and intermittent loads involved. In the years 1918–1921, a temporary R&D-effort was made for the development of roller bearings. A young engineer was given extensive power to treat the problem. A special R&D organization was set up which represented a new orientation within industrial R&D from individual inventors to R&D teams and organizations, at least in the Swedish engineering industry. (Probably the earliest example of this is Alfred Nobel's truly multinational R&D organization in the 1880s.) In 1921 the R&D effort involved 135 people.

The theoretical basis was weak, and much of the work had to be achieved through carefully designed experiments (cut-and-try), exploring a multitude of parallel possibilities. The specified goals of the project were finally achieved with self-alignment as an additionally achieved feature of the design. (Self-alignment was the basic, global improvement in the original ball bearing design of SKF, giving the corporation its special competitive strength.)

In 1921–22 the R&D organization was dissolved. The new product was transferred to the manufacturing organization, and the R&D people went back to their earlier duties. It was argued that it took about ten years to achieve a truly rational production of a new product type and the design department therefore had to work fluctuatingly. (SKF also experienced a depression in the early 1920s.) The diversification project then had taken three-and-a-half years to complete, of which eighteen months were spent on design, twelve months on tests of tools and machinery, and twelve months on experiments with mass production.

The new roller bearings gave SKF several new markets, especially railways and tramways. Sales in these markets, however, developed slowly since the customers had to perform tests for long periods of time before the costly and radical transition to the new type of bearings could be made.

This R&D project is a milestone in corporate development and could be characterized as the most concentrated and successful R&D effort so far in corporate history. It meant a diversification within the bearing product area of enduring profitability. Achievements in co-ordinating and advancing production technology in the whole corporation were made in the late 1920s. In the 1920s and 1930s a marketing organization with application engineers was developed, and much R&D concerned new applications. After World War II growth and profitability were good and R&D was not of primary interest. ('One doesn't sit and think about development of new products if one can't deliver.')

In the 1960s corporate co-ordination and diversification became the strategic aims. A multinational corporate R&D-laboratory located in Holland was inaugurated in the early 1970s as well as a small semi-autonomous innovation company on the corporate level. The corporate organization was strengthened and worldwide production restructured for increased co-ordination. Diversification has since then been sought through both R&D and acquisitions.

Case 3.2 Astra

Just as Astra had been favoured by World War I, so it was also favoured by World War II; sales trebled, amounting to nearly $5 million in 1945. An important source of profits then was sweeteners. R&D was strengthened, and a new corporate laboratory was inaugurated in 1943. The same year a highly significant event occurred when Astra acquired a newly discovered local anaesthetic offered by two university researchers. After four years of industrial R&D, the new pharmaceutical was introduced and caused a breakthrough with the rapid internationalization of Astra. During World War II Astra also engaged in the production of antibiotics, which soon became of worldwide pharmaceutical importance, because of new methods of production.

In the 1940s diversification outside pharmaceuticals was encouraged because of the perceived risk at that time of nationalization of the pharmaceutical industry. In the 1950s internationalizaton and diversification within pharmaceuticals was also decided on in order to utilize marketing synergies. This was to be achieved through internal R&D at decentralized subsidiaries located close to medical universities and allowed to compete internally. At the subsidiary Astra-Hässle an R&D organization was built up in the late 1950s, and external co-operation with university researchers was initiated. In the early 1960s two different research lines had been established, beta-blockers and analgetics, since Astra-Hässle wanted diversification in R&D in order to spread risks and also to stimulate R&D personnel. The choice of these lines depended very much on external contacts and the sequence in which these were taken rather than on a strategic choice of areas and a controlled selection procedure. This kind of random element was also present during the watershed years when beta-blockers were chosen for continued R&D in the mid 1960s. By this time a third area of R&D was established within ulcus diseases as a result of successful sales and a subsequent decision to engage in R&D in this area.

In 1967 a new pharmaceutical, based on beta-receptor-blocking effects, was registered and introduced on the market. Although a slow starter on the market, it represented a breakthrough into a new product area. It also meant a kind of breakthrough internally in that the R&D at Astra-Hässle, which earlier had been regarded with suspicion and distrust among some corporate R&D authorities, now had proven successful. After this event the need for R&D expertise grew rapidly at Astra-Hässle; 'research breeds research', and there was a conviction that fundamental knowledge was required for the development of subsequent products. R&D volume grew in relation to turnover; this growth caused a certain resistance at the corporate level, since Astra had traditionally budgeted R&D within a narrow percentage range of the turnover.

In the late 1960s Astra-Hässle found unexpectedly that beta-blockers had an effect on hypertension, and because of this a new and important disease area was entered. (It is, however, said to be something of a rule in pharmaceutical research that when a compound is found to have an effect within one area of indication, one has to see whether it has effects in other areas as well. An example is the local anaesthetic from 1943; in 1950 it was found to have effects on disturbances of the heart rhythm. This disease area was incidentally the initial target for R&D on beta-blockers at Astra-Hässle.) A second generation of beta-blockers with effects on hypertension was registered and introduced on the market in 1975. A fourth research line around the central nervous system was also established at Astra-Hässle in the 1960s but was transferred to the parent company, Astra, about 1970.

In summary, four research lines have grown up at Astra-Hässle since R&D was initiated in the late 1950s. Of these four, one has proven extremely successful and raised sales in the cardio-vascular area from $481 000 to $35 million (13 to 67 per cent of the total turnover) in the period of 1960–1975. A second research line was transferred to another corporation, a third was transferred internally, and the fourth (ulcus research) was temporarily halted in 1975, with three compounds having failed at an R&D cost of $5 million and a fourth still being tested.

As far as Astra as a whole is concerned, the strategy with decentralized R&D in subsidiaries close to medical universities was successful in some other cases as well. As a result of growth and diversification of R&D in different parts of the corporation, voices were raised in favour of corporate co-ordination in opposition to the policy of internal competition. The situation with respect to projects and licences had run somewhat wild, and in the mid 1960s a research management committee at the corporate level was created. In the late 1960s R&D was profiled in the corporation, resulting in the internal transfer of a research line at Astra-Hässle. In the 1970s R&D was still concentrated and consolidated within different pharmaceutical areas. Risks have to be taken on a subsidiary level and distributed on divisional and corporate levels. The corporate strategy from the 1950s of internationalization and diversification within pharmaceuticals through R&D has been successful, not the least because of external co-operation with universities and other corporations in R&D and marketing.

The strategy of diversification outside pharmaceuticals has, on the other hand, partially failed. Diversification into chemical–technical and nutritional products has been attempted, and the means in the latter case was R&D rather than company acquisitions. Lack of synergy with competence in pharmaceuticals and inappropriate markets for R&D-based products are among the expressed explanations for the failure of diversification into nutritional products.

Case 3.3 Volvo

At the beginning Volvo had its own internal design, assembly and marketing of cars and relied upon the collective knowledge of the Swedish engineering industry for components. Over the years R&D and production of central components such as engines and gear boxes have been internalized. During World War II a certain diversification took place and among other things the subsidiary Volvo Flygmotor, which produces aircraft engines, was acquired. World War II also resulted in increased skill in solving a variety of problems. A new car was designed 'in peace and quiet' during the war and post-war production could be prepared. This new car became a success, and the design lasted for over twenty years. In the 1950s Volvo went into the United States market and then into European markets. Ideas about diversification came in the early 1960s from the

United States. In the 1960s Volvo grew further and internationalized profitably, and 1969 was a very profitable year. Diversification was then decided on and an acquisition of stock in the ventilation business was first made and later on sold, and then acquisitions were made in sports and recreational articles. This diversification into a low-technology business was not successful, and Volvo 'cooled off' on diversification and concentrated on transportation in the mid 1970s. During the good years around 1970 large investments in R&D facilities were made, and a new factory with a new production technology was built.

At Volvo Flygmotor, which has traditionally been rather autonomous within Volvo, thoughts on diversification existed as early as in the 1940s since the defence market then dominated. An attempt was made with printing presses in the late 1940s, which for certain reasons failed. New generations of jet engines for combat aircraft were developed with the aid of licensed United States technology during the 1950s and 1960s. By 1969 the situation was such that one dominating product went to one dominating customer (within the Swedish defence). R&D on two lines for diversification had started in the early 1960s. One was turbo-compressors for diesel engines. This project was stopped in the late 1960s on the basis of unfavourable market investigations. Hereby R&D resources could be transferred to the other line, which was a hydraulic pump. A first attempt along this line, based on an idea from another company, had failed in the early 1960s. Then an external inventor came with an idea and a development contract was signed (in which, incidentally, a start of production had to be guaranteed by Volvo Flygmotor). Development work built partially on technological competence from military R&D but involved lower performance and cost requirements. (In turning from military to civilian products there is a risk of technological over-achievement.) In 1970 a strategic decision was taken to scale up expansion significantly into hydraulic machines (pumps and motors). Sales in 1977 amounted to $11.5 million. Although a break-even was not reached by 1977, this diversification into new markets with a new technology was considered successful. Two other less significant lines of diversification had grown out of the knowledge of combustion in the 1970s, but two new product areas were still being sought. The experience from diversification into hydraulics through R&D then had created preferences for joint ventures or acquisitions.

Table 3.3 gives a summary of the statistics for Case 3.1, Case 3.2 and Case 3.3.

3.2.4 Situation in the 1970s

3.2.4.1 Corporate growth and diversification

Because of confidentiality and limits of space it is not possible to be very specific about the situation in 1975 with regard to R&D, growth and diversification and the corresponding strategies or policies (see Chapter 5 for further treatment). A summary is shown in Table 3.4. Aggregate corporate strategies (or policies) all emphasize profitability and growth with some variation in relative strength. Internationalization is emphasized in most corporations, especially in KemaNobel, Boliden and Astra. Diversification has been de-emphasized in KemaNobel, Astra and Volvo, while SKF, Iggesund and Boliden place great emphasis on in-

R&D, corporate growth and diversification

Table 3.3 Examples of statistics on product R&D

Product	Corporation	Calendar time	R&D time[*] (years)	R&D cost[*] (million)
Roller bearings	SKF	1918–21	3.5	4.15
Local anaestheticum	Astra	1943–48	4	[†]
New generation of passenger cars	Volvo	1953–56	3	12.05[‡]
Hydraulic machines (pump/motor)	Volvo Flygmotor	1962–67	5	2.41[§]
Jet engine	Volvo Flygmotor	1962–68	6	[¶]
First generations of beta-blockers	Astra-Hässle	1960–67	7	1.69–1.93
Second generation of beta-blockers	Astra-Hässle	1966–75	9	7.28

[*] Beginnings and ends of R&D are diffuse. The figures apply to the period of a recognized industrial R&D project until serial production starts (for pharmaceuticals until marketable product). Sources are internal interviews and documents.

[†] The decisive discovery was made in 1943 by university researchers after several years of work. Sales still growing in 1977.

[‡] The development of a new generation of passenger cars for the 1980s was estimated in 1977 by Volvo to cost around $240 million just using known technologies.

[§] Sales amounted to 48 million in 1977, 83 per cent of which was for foreign markets. Still the break-even point had not been reached in 1977.

[¶] 4 million man-hours were required. The development work was based on a technology licensed from Pratt and Whitney. The figures apply to contract R&D for the Swedish Air Board. The complete development of a new jet engine generation for the future was estimated in 1977 by Volvo Flygmotor to cost around $723 million.

creased diversification, which has to be synergetic. Finally R&D is emphasized at all the corporations, although less so at Iggesund. A short period of stagnation in R&D in the early 1970s occurred at KemaNobel, Alfa-Laval and Volvo. Research remains mostly domestic, while development is increasingly internationalized in some corporations (see Chapter 4). There is also a trend toward concentrating R&D to certain product areas.

The reasons expressed for sustained growth are rather predictable, including references to rising labour costs, technological change, rising costs for R&D and marketing, growth as a necessary condition for enduring profitability, and the vicious circles related to stagnating growth. The reasons expressed for diversification are more varied and more product oriented but still rather conventional, including references to inadequate growth and profitability in existing product areas, the need to distribute political and economic risks, increased insensitivity to business cycles, utilization of excess resources, securing input or output markets or other advantages of vertical integration, achieving synergies in R&D, production, or marketing, filling gaps in or supplementing existing knowledge or

Table 3.4 Aggregate figures of the situation of the corporation studied in 1975

Variable*	KemaNobel	Philips	Alfa-Laval	SKF	Boliden	Iggesund	Astra	Volvo	Correlation† with R&D/sales
1 Size of sales 1975‡	378.7	11 105	853	1650	572	260	307	3298	0.10
2 Sales 1975/ sales 1970		1.80	2.31	1.44	1.85	1.72	2.01	2.57	0.18
3 Sales/employee 1975‡	65.70	28	47	27	55	51	48	52	−0.07
4 (Sales/emp. 1975)/ (sales/empl. 1970)	2.05	1.63	1.95	1.58	1.32	1.73	1.64	1.58	−0.11
5 Cum. profit/cum. sales 1971–75 (per cent)§	8.9	8.3	7.5	10.1	9.5	11.0	7.9	7.3	−0.11
6 Diversification 1975¶	0.79	0.83	0.53	0.21	0.64	0.74	0.25	0.45	−0.28
7 Internationali- zation 1975**	0.18	0.77	0.63	0.79	0.07	0.0	0.51	0.27	0.48
8 R&D/sales 1975 (rank)	6	2 (7.5 per cent)	4 (3.5 per cent)	5	7	8	1 (10.4 per cent)	3	1.0

* Because of confidentiality ranks are shown here for variable 8. Open figures are shown below.
† All correlations are calculated on metric data, not on ranks.
‡ Thousands of US dollars.
§ Trading profit after depreciation but before taxes.
¶ Sales outside largest product area/total sales.
** Number of employees abroad/total number of employees.
Note: Results are influenced by the marked profitable growth in raw material based industries around 1974. Sales increased 1973–74 in KemaNobel, Boliden, and Iggesund 44 per cent, 47 per cent and 52 per cent respectively.

product lines, engaging in promising fields, and finding profitable opportunities. When companies make acquisitions, an unwanted diversification may sometimes occur as a result. There has also been restructuring of industry, mainly on the owner level above the corporate level, which has resulted in diversification. A majority of the corporations do not emphasize diversification, at least not on the level of new sectors or product areas. There is a wide-spread orientation toward the continued existence of traditional products such as steel, bearings, separators, forestry products, and passenger cars and toward the fact that these should constitute the backbone in corporate futures as well. Some of the more spectacular technological threats, which were conceived of previously, have not materialized as substitutions as rapidly as had been expected. Besides, many examples of diversification failures have emerged. Synergies, profit opportunities and the like have been overestimated, and the consequences of lack of knowledge in a new area and division of management attention have been underestimated. In the cases where diversification is sought, a basic effort is to preserve the natural unity of the corporation, and diversification must be related to the present state at least to a certain extent. There is then a strong orientation toward existing knowledge associated with existing productive resources. Although there have been periods of perceived high risks for radical material substitutions (for example, plastics for wood), it is almost inconceivable for corporations such as Iggesund and Boliden to sell raw material assets and buy their way into some area of quite different materials with quite different knowledge needs.

Many corporations want to view themselves as selling market-oriented systems of some kind, but the orientation toward existing technologies and components is strong. Astra, for instance, sometimes claims that it sells systems for medical treatment in different disease areas. Although there is an increased emphasis on providing physicians and hospitals with know how, the pharmaceutical product and its associated knowledge are the basic component. Other technologies such as electronics, surgery and artificial organs are not actual targets for diversification. They may be relevant but are considered too distant from present technologies or too exotic. Similar statements may be made about the other corporations. Admittedly, some are modest in their claims about systems orientation, but the implications for diversification of a systems-oriented strategy or business idea are, as a rule, inadequately explored and judged.

3.2.4.2 Growth and diversification of R&D

The situation of growth and diversification of R&D in the 1970s is to a large extent a consequence of corporate profitability, growth, diversification and internationalization. Historically, there are several instances of growing R&D due to good years and declining R&D due to bad years. An increased readiness to let R&D be less affected by business declines may be noticed in some corporations. For several reasons it is tempting to manipulate R&D resources temporarily, and it is a large step from a general readiness to invest in R&D to making annual budget decisions in times of increased scarcity of resources. Corporate growth is also often a pre-requisite to changing the relative proportions in resource allocations.

Budgeting determines growth and diversification of corporate R&D in a narrow sense. R&D budgeting practices always involve political processes. In some cases R&D budgets are built up project by project, usually when a small number of large projects are involved. Comparisons with the corporate past, competitors and sector averages, often based on R&D as a percentage of sales, are influential factors. Thus there is a direct coupling of R&D growth to corporate growth, which is strong in some corporations, especially in Astra.

R&D is, to a varying extent, being given some new roles in corporate development. This does not necessarily mean a growth in R&D, but sometimes it does occur. Internal R&D, recruitment, co-operative R&D, acquisitions of patents and licences, acquisitions of companies, and purchase of hardware have been the ways in which the corporations have in varying proportions been supplied with technological knowledge. Factors such as increased international competition and advancement of science and technology in general might make it more difficult to secure such a supply without internal R&D. Internal R&D may then be a means of attracting R&D people and partners for co-operative R&D as well as giving the corporation access to the science and technology community and a capability of utilizing technological information. The degree of external orientation and co-operation in the performance of R&D in most corporations is increasing for various reasons, including perceived increases of costs and risks in R&D and increases in the range of relevant technologies and in product specialization. An increased external orientation is especially emphasized at the corporate level at KemaNobel, Boliden and Astra.

Other factors that stimulate growth of internal R&D are dependence on labour, which stimulates changes to more technology-intensive production, more advanced customer technologies, societal pressures for safer products and processes, and the use of R&D as a means of competition. Alfa-Laval dominates some of its markets and has for a long time skilfully acquired patents. These conditions might decrease the need to be technologically offensive, but Alfa-Laval still experiences intermittent technological leads and lags in relation to competitors; thus the corresponding temporary demands on R&D arise. It is sometimes said that a corporation has to develop technology rather incrementally with a few radical advances now and then. A common pattern in electronics and engineering is to develop new generations of products with a batch of advances and to make product improvements in between, often on the component level. Again a temporary growth of corporate R&D might result. Technologically advanced products do, however, require resources, which puts pressures on prices in order to keep profits up. In order to keep high prices, a high level of technology is often needed, at least on competitive industrial markets. Thus, in addition to budgeting principles, there are several other elements of mutual reinforcement between corporate growth and the growth of R&D.

Another category of factors behind growth of corporate R&D has to do with factors inherent in technological change and R&D, which are in that sense self-reinforcing factors. (Research breeds research). Roughly these concern the nature of R&D people on the one hand and the nature of R&D and technological change on the other. The ambitions of R&D people usually favour R&D growth. Such ambitions may also favour diversificaiton of R&D because R&D people tend to distribute their resources among different problems and ideas in order to weaken competition and achieve recognition.

The question to what extent there are self-reinforcing factors in the nature of

R&D and technological change is a complicated one. There are many interesting processes of growth and diversification in different fields of science and technology in general, in the involvement of corporate R&D in certain fields, in the course of a project, and among R&D teams and individuals. The conceptualizations of different fields are also fluid. The stock of discovered problems that can be researched tends to increase with an increased knowledge about the possibilities of combining knowledge. The necessary scale of an industrial R&D project may grow merely by combining known technologies. (Compare the rising R&D costs for subsequent generations of passenger cars, see Table 3.3 in Section 3.2.3.)

There is an ageing process in individual researchers as well as research teams. A research field may also age in the sense that there are diminishing returns on additional research. Some of the technologies of the engineering corporations are referred to as mature technologies, meaning that R&D no longer pays off as well, at least not product R&D. On the other hand, it is hard to find a technology that is nearly perfect and without conceivable breakthroughs. It may be that R&D people in the particular field have stagnated or become emotionally attached to certain solutions and that breakthroughs in the field are more likely to emanate from R&D in another field. However, there is certainly an element of self-fulfillment in saying that a technology is mature and little will happen so that R&D may be kept low in the corresponding product area. Some corporations are influenced by theories about the product life cycle and the maturing of products and markets. The use of a 'milking strategy' with little R&D for a product with a low market growth and a high market share clearly lowers the probability of changes in the product technology.

3.2.4.3 Size of R&D

Closely related to the question of self-reinforcing factors in the growth of R&D and technological change is the question of the effects of size. A distinction must be made here between the cumulative size of R&D efforts in a certain field, and the size of R&D teams, departments, laboratories, and total R&D in a corporation or sector of industry. There is much to be said on this subject, and it is a common topic of discussion among R&D managers and others. There are widespread notions about critical or threshold sizes of an R&D effort, barriers to growth and diversification of R&D organizations, optimal size of an R&D team or an R&D laboratory, and so on. The actual situation, however, gives little support for estimations and generalizations of these notions. The research laboratories at the corporate level in Philips in the early 1970s employed 2250, 580, 440, 400, 330, 175 and forty-five people respectively. Although the work of these laboratories is diversified, they are to some extent involved in similar science and technology fields. The variations in R&D between different corporations in largely the same sector of industry are also large, at least in some sectors. Companies in the forestry, pulp and paper industries fall into roughly three groups; one group of companies with internal R&D, one group with largely collective R&D, and one group that performs almost no R&D. The steel unit of SKF spends little on R&D in comparison with sector averages. The explanations given for this are a relatively concentrated product programme and early R&D success, but also the fact that the vertical integration has led to some stagnation after the initial upheaval. The variations in R&D averages in different sectors of industry are well known. References to the differing nature of different technologies are common, but many other factors accrue and this problem constitutes a research problem in itself. One illustration is that the size distribution of the co-operative (or collective) research institutes in different sectors of Swedish industry ranged in 1976 from around half a dozen people to around 300.

Moreover, size is hard to assess because many external employees may be involved only temporarily. An extreme case is the R&D organization behind the Swedish combat aircraft Viggen; at one point in the 1960s it consumed about 10 per cent of all Swedish R&D funds and as a total R&D effort was comparable in relative size to the Apollo project in the United States. The large Viggen project was organized into a central co-ordination department with a series of contractors, among others Volvo Flygmotor. What, then is the significant measure of size of an R&D organization?

Many factors account for these size variations. One is the variation in views on size effects. It is not uncommon for an R&D manager to view his department as being close to a critical size, while corporate management views it as having a suitable size. The standards of evaluation may differ, and it is also possible but unlikely that both are true, using the same standard. The critical size may also depend on technological change. In electronics the relationships with materials science, physics, chemistry, optics and medicine are becoming closer, increasing the critical size of a research laboratory at Philips. Involvement in systems technology is similarly said to require large and growing R&D efforts. It is possible to use subcontractors, a traditional strategy of Volvo, but the growing complexity of pre-production favours internal R&D.

There is a certain consensus on the existence of optimal size of an R&D laboratory in a corporation. If a distribution of laboratory sizes gives no indication of such an optimum, it is possible that as an R&D laboratory grows, an optimum will be passed, unless the optimum size is very large or is growing faster than the laboratory size does. However, in no case are there indications of such a passage. The R&D manager of Astra-Hässle planned in 1964 to reach an optimal R&D unit of 150 people in 1975. Since then diversification into new and unexpected areas occurred, and the size in 1975 was 175 employees and growth to 250 employees was planned. In the mid-1970s R&D and corporate management estimated the critical size of an R&D unit in pharmaceutical research to be in the range of 100–150 people, and the optimal size to be in the range of 150–300. Problems were anticipated, since there are always internal forces that stimulate growth and diversification in the different R&D units of a corporation. A conceived course of action was to concentrate within each R&D unit, increasing risk-taking on the subsidiary level, and possibly establish new units, which increases demands for co-ordination on corporate R&D management. Besides, there is a fluctuating pattern in R&D costs when R&D projects reach the final expensive stages, and there is a fluctuating pattern in R&D output due to the ageing of R&D teams and R&D fields. Thus, there are R&D growth fluctuations on several levels, affecting an optimal size.

There is actually not very much to say about limits on R&D size on the basis of observations. Sometimes there is a policy of undermanning and compressing time schedules in R&D, but in the absence of such policies there is always an inexhaustible stock of problems, which never constitute a limit to size. Another conception of limit to size is based on diminishing returns. Certainly the flexibility of R&D resources is low, and possibilities to make substitutions are limited. Two mediocre researchers do not equal one top researcher. Adding people to an R&D team may even be counter-productive. These are all intuitive notions used in specific situations, but they seldom give a basis for estimating any limits to size.

There is a consensus that drastic changes upward or downward in the size of an R&D unit are detrimental. Volvo and Alfa-Laval re-organized R&D in connection with divisionalization. Central R&D units were reduced, and the decline was reinforced by a lowered morale and loss of employees. Astra-Hässle, on the other hand, was experiencing some limits to growth. Bio-analysis was planned to be expanded, pharmacology to be doubled within an unspecified time, and medicine to be doubled in five years. The rate of expansion, however, was determined by recruitment possibilities and the speed at which newcomers could be assimilated in the organization without damaging it.

Limits to changes in size obviously limit the use of temporary R&D efforts, like the one in SKF after World War I. Many factors are influential: economic, technological, organizational, social and psychological. Recruitment and transfer possibilities are important and differ among different fields. The mobility of R&D people also changes with age. A most effective limit to growth, finally, is the limits on individual learning.

More pluralistic and temporary forms of organizing and managing R&D are being employed. There is an increasing use of satellite organizations with semi-external employees such as inventors, consultants and university researchers; increased degree of external orientation in general with co-operation, licensing and know-how exchanges; increased use of semi-autonomous innovation companies and increased use of project organizations and R&D units on corporate, divisional and regional levels. Phrases such as task forces, venture teams and *ad hoc* groups as well as the basic idea behind a project organization indicate that temporary organizations are being used. Thus, the organizational ways of conducting industrial R&D have also diversified.

3.3 DISCUSSION

3.3.1 Empirical summary

A great degree of continuity in corporate development was found at both the sector and the product area levels with regard to diversification. The corporations used different mixed strategies for diversification, and internal R&D with external co-operation proved successful in several cases. R&D for diversification into new product areas proved not to be strictly a post-World War II phenomenon.

On the R&D level there has been an important kind of grass-roots R&D, whose results are not as easily recognized and assessed as indisputable innovations. Four kinds of diversification of R&D are discerned: differentiation of a core technology, expansion into adjacent technologies, substitution of technologies, and involvement in a new and so far unrelated technology, which may, however, occur through an evolutionary process.

Ratios of R&D to sales are positively correlated with internationalization (0.48) and size of sales (0.42) in 1975 while weakly negatively correlated with diversification (− 0.28), as approximated quantitatively. Corporate strategies also emphasize growth, internationalization, and R&D, while diversification is de-emphasized in half of the corporations.

R&D grows and diversifies for several reasons. There is an increased degree of external orientation and co-operation in performing R&D, and internal R&D is assuming the additional role of creating access to and possibilities for the utilization of external R&D. The effects of and limits to size and growth of R&D units are often discussed, but the empirical observations provide few guidelines. The concept of size of an R&D unit and the effects of size and growth appear to be a matter of organization and management more than a matter of economic scale. More pluralistic and temporary forms of organizing and managing R&D are being employed.

3.3.2 Relationships between R&D and corporate growth

At the corporate level the different patterns of corporate growth and development cannot be aggregated into a general progression of stages without significant simplification. The invention-based corporations initially developed around a single product or product line and then rapidly internationalized, while corporations based on raw materials or foreign technology initially diversified rapidly into at least two product lines. Diversified raw material sources, by-products in production, costs of transportation, and competition abroad favoured early diversification, while a global advance in a product technology and a small domestic market favoured early internationalization. Thus the origin of the corporation is important to consider as well as the size of the domestic market. Some models for corporate development are based on studies of corporations in the United States that have had uniquely large domestic markets. This fact limits the possibility of generalizing with the help of these models. Especially, they do not consider the interplay between diversification and internationalization in corporate development.

The many means for, and factors behind, corporate development make it difficult to assess the impact both of and on, a certain factor such as R&D. When long periods of time and aggregate patterns are involved, causality is hard to identify. There is a widespread belief that R&D fosters profitable growth. When resources are created by profitable growth caused by several factors, it is likely that R&D will be fostered thereby. This proposition is supported here in two ways. First, one may see how periods of significant change in corporate R&D budgets are preceded by periods of change in profitability and growth. R&D budgets or budget increases tend to be cut when profits decline even if the corporation continues to grow. Similarly, many investments in R&D facilities and projects have been made during good years. (Diversification efforts in both SKF, and Volvo were increased during some good years in the 1960s.) Thus, business cycles or

R&D, corporate growth and diversification 41

fluctuations in general have a marked impact on R&D. Expectations may, however, displace the pattern somewhat.

Second, one may correlate time series of R&D and sales and estimate leads and lags. However, very few quantitative data are available on R&D, since corporate R&D statistics are of recent date and often confidential.

Correlations between the time series for sales, $\{S_t\}$ and the time series for R&D displaced λ years, $\{R_{t+\lambda}\}$ for Alfa-Laval and Astra are shown in Figure 3.1. The calculations are made on raw data, unadjusted for trends and inflation, in order to indicate regions of high correlation, for example for $\lambda = 0$ and $\lambda = 1$. Calculations are not made for fewer than five observations, which does not allow

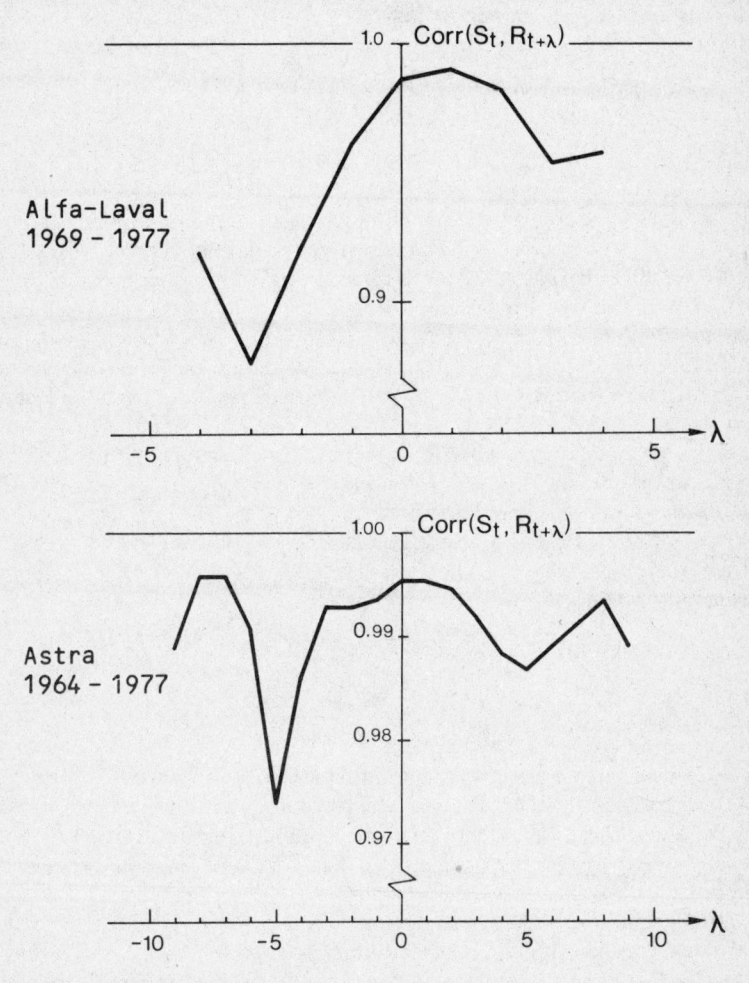

Note: Different scales.

Figure 3.1 Correlations between displaced time series for sales and R&D

one to see other peak regions for Alfa-Laval due to a lack of data. For Astra correlations are also high for $\lambda = \pm 8$. Although the correlations for Astra are generally high, the correlograms suggest both a contemporaneous causal coupling and a delayed one between R&D and sales. That sales lag behind R&D is naturally to be expected. The extent of the time lag depends on the kind of R&D undertaken but also on how fast a new product is marketed and adopted and how fast sales increase. The lag for Astra is estimated, on the basis of the correlogramme, to seven to eight years, which may be compared with an R&D period of seven to nine years for pharmaceutical R&D in the 1960s, as shown in Table 3.3 in Section 3.2.3.

Assuming a linear stochastic model for the process of R&D based growth of sales and the R&D budgeting process gives

$$S_{t+1} = \sum_{i \geq 0} r_{t-i} \cdot R_{t-i} + \sum_{i \geq 0} u_{t-i} \tag{3.1}$$

$$R_{t+1} = s_t S_t + v_t \tag{3.2}$$

Here u_t, v_t are lump variables with stochastic elements and the summation is appropriately extended for non-negative i. Under current practices of budgeting R&D, it is reasonable to assume that R&D is budgeted just one year ahead and partly based on present sales as reflected by s_t. s_t may fluctuate over time and even in the case of Astra, which budgets R&D very much on the basis of present sales, s_t is not a constant plus noise. For Astra s_t has slowly drifted from more than 8 per cent to more than 10 per cent over the last fifteen years.

Equation 3.2 may be modified by including estimations of next year's sales, just as Equation 3.1 may be further simplified by the rough assumption that all $r_{t-i} = 0$ except some $r_{t-\lambda}$, meaning that R&D in year $t - \lambda$ generates sales only in year $t + 1$. The point here, however, is just to show how the two processes reinforce each other.

Substitution gives

$$S_{t+1} = \sum_{i \geq 0} r_{t-i} \cdot s_{t-i-1} \cdot S_{t-i-1} + \delta \tag{3.3}$$

$$R_{t+1} = \sum_{i \geq 0} r_{t-i-1} \cdot s_t \cdot R_{t-i-1} + \epsilon \tag{3.4}$$

Here δ and ϵ are new lump variables independent of $\{S_t\}$ and $\{R_t\}$. Thus, sales and R&D are self-reinforcing through the budgeting process, and if s_t is approximately time-invariant and r_t changes slowly, the rate of reinforcement is roughly the same. Adding to this the assumption that R&D in year $t - \lambda$ generates sales only in year $t + 1$ implies that reinforcement is compounded each $(\lambda + 2)$ years at approximately the same rate. Assumptions that a pulse in R&D yields a delayed pulse in sales, for example, may explain the slight peak in the correlogramme of Astra for $\lambda = 8$. (An underlying assumption is that other necessary investments are done as well. It is not uncommon, for example, for investments in marketing to be roughly of the same size as investments in R&D.)

The statement that growth fosters R&D is supported by Schmookler (1966) at the macro level. Schmookler also shows how inventive activities tend to lag behind investments in capital goods. This lag is also supported by this study, if only on the strength of a few examples on micro level, especially in process industries. In the steel unit of SKF, investments are made with the next fifteen to twenty years in mind, while developing a process to marketable license takes four to eight years and developing a product may take less than five years. Materialized investment decisions largely determine subsequent R&D. At Iggesund a heavy investment was made in the early 1960s in facilities for cardboard production, which meant an integration forward. As a result of this integration, a new R&D department for product development was started in the late 1960s. A decision to acquire a supplier's product technology through capital investments, rather than through internal R&D, increases sales in the supplying sector of industry, which through the budgeting decisions in that industry causes the corresponding product R&D to grow and lag behind capital investments at the aggregate level.

Schmookler further argues in favour of a demand-oriented, rather than a supply-oriented, theory behind growth of technology. On a microlevel, this seems to be a justified view in the early stages of corporate diversification through R&D; in later stages the situation becomes more supply-oriented, at least for a period. Often initial periods in which technology is developed are followed by periods in which the areas of application for developed products and knowledge are extended. For instance, both Alfa-Laval and SKF in the inter-war years widened their areas of application. Much product development work had been done before. The separators of Alfa-Laval were universal process elements, and the rolling bearings of SKF were universal machine elements. Thus, these corporations came into contact at an early stage with a wide variety of applications and customer problems, which stimulated development of a wide range of product variants in their specific product area. Sometimes the range of application of a new product is underestimated, as was the case with the original invention at SKF. At other times an entirely different application is accidentally found, as was the case in Astra when a pharmaceutical product for rhythm disturbances in the heart was found to have effects on high blood pressure. Furthermore, an internal demand may lead to the acquisition or development of a product that is later marketed to other customers as well, as was the case with SKF, which integrated backward to steel and now markets steel products to external customers, who may be competitors. At Astra-Hässle R&D was initially oriented toward large need areas within medical care, but as internal competences were built up, R&D became more oriented around the existing competences. The systems orientation in Alfa-Laval was fostered by demand conditions in the dairy industry in the early 1960s, but the knowledge of how to handle combinations of machines has since been applied and adapted to other sectors of industry. Thus a pattern of 'first pull, then push' occurs over time with respect to products and markets of a corporation.

3.3.3 Relationships between R&D and corporate diversification

R&D has resulted in several marked diversifications. If the conditions pertaining to these diversifications are examined, one finds that in several cases of innovations leading to marked diversifications, there has been some direct external influence (e.g., an offering of an idea from an external inventor—hydraulic machines, Volvo Flygmotor—or ideas and advice from external researchers—several product lines in Astra). In other cases, primary sources of influence have been internal, for example, from top management and R&D people (roller bearings, SKF; trucks, Volvo) or just from R&D people (heat exchangers, Alfa-Laval). Naturally, external market and technological conditions are influential in all the cases, but the positions of persons who exercise direct influence are considered here.

Findings of this kind suggest that marked diversifications based on R&D are influenced by the existence of both internal and external sources of ideas and impulses for diversification together with a kind of permeability in the organization. The permeability in the organization pertains both to the susceptibility of an organization to external ideas and impulses and to the elasticity of an organization in the event that internal ideas and impulses lead to areas outside existing operations (two-way permeability). This permeability, in turn, is influenced by policy decisions, top management attitudes, 'not-invented-here' effects among R&D people, and delineation of organization rules and responsibilities. Such policy decisions may be to stay within certain business areas (not to go into the packaging business, Alfa-Laval) to be restrictive with spin-offs (Astra-Hässle), to limit production (Boliden), to develop adjacent technologies but stay within the original one (KemaNobel), to diversify synergetically into present technologies (SKF) and to strive toward further refinement (Iggesund).

The permeability may differ with respect to internal or external ideas and impulses. A policy decision to concentrate on certain areas or to stay out of certain areas may limit internal initiatives, while external sources of influences may still be active. Bureaucratic procedures for evaluation may kill off external ideas, while improvements of existing products may take place internally without very much notice. There are several examples of how evolutionary steps starting from existing operations lead to new products and markets (see also Salveson, 1959). This process encounters many internal barriers that decrease the permeability and tend to confine the evolutionary process.

3.4 CONCLUSIONS

Different patterns of corporate development could not be aggregated into a general progression of stages. Invention-based corporations initially developed around a single product or product line and then rapidly internationalized, while corporations based on raw materials or foreign technology initially diversified rapidly into at least two different product lines. A great degree of continuity in corporate development was found on both sector and product area levels as regards diversification. On the R&D level there has also been an important kind of 'grass-roots R&D', the results of which are not as easily recognized and assessed as indisputable innovations.

A general conclusion is that a mutual interplay and a give-and-take relationship exist between corporate development and R&D. As the corporations grow, diversify and internationalize, R&D operations also tend to grow, diversify and internationalize. More pluralistic and temporary forms of organizing and managing R&D are being employed and internal R&D is getting additional roles of creating access to and possibilities for the utilization of external R&D. The connections between R&D and corporate growth are shown to consist of both a time lag between R&D and sales and a contemporaneous coupling through budgeting. In some raw-material-based corporations R&D was also lagging behind investments. There is a long, increasing and technology-dependent time lag between R&D work and growth in sales. The time lag between R&D work and a significant degree of diversification is still longer in a large corporation, since R&D-generated sales in a new product area also have to grow relative to sales in other product areas.

Contradictory cases of diversification based on innovations originating internally as well as externally suggest a concept of organizational permeability, pertaining both to the susceptibility of an organization to external ideas and impulses and to the elasticity of an organization in the event that internal ideas and impulses lead to product areas outside the present ones. This means that in considering the antecedents of innovations, radical or incremental, to a corporation, not only the internal or external loci of sources and their inherent characteristics have to be considered but also the permeability of organizational boundaries. The latter may very well constitute a barrier to internal ideas for radical innovation to a larger extent than external ideas for radical innovation or internal ideas for incremental innovation. This in turn, distorts the relative proportions by which internal and external sources of ideas result in different kinds of innovation.

The supply versus demand oriented theories behind the growth of technology are discussed briefly and seem to be reconcilable into a dynamic pull and push pattern when seen over an extended period of time. A process of 'first pull, then push' was found in several cases, which means that a period in which a technology is developed as a response to an originally perceived demand is followed by a period in which the areas of application for the developed products and knowledge are extended beyond the demand initially aimed at.

Chapter 4
R&D AND CORPORATE INTERNATIONALIZATION

4.1 INTRODUCTION

This chapter explores the relationship of R&D operations in a corporation and the process of internationalization of a corporation. The term 'internationalization' is taken to mean the expansion of certain operations to other nations, while 'diversification' refers to the expansion of the variety of products. Corporate internationalization, then, refers to corporate operations and internationalization of R&D refers to the R&D operations of a corporation. Moreover, internationalization may refer to both the process of expansion and a state in this process at a specific point in time. In the latter case a degree of internationalization may be assessed. By a multinational corporation (MNC) we mean a corporation that has acquired a certain degree of internationalization. There are several ways to assess the degree of internationalization or the degree of multinationality. The process of internationalization of an industry, a corporation, or a unit or function in a corporation and the states in this process, may be described by many variables. These variables are often correlated. Thus, if one uses MNCs as a category of corporations, analyses and conclusions will be dependent on the choice of variables used in defining this category.

In this study it has been considered more relevant to use degrees of internationalization than to specify a concept of multinationality. Certainly all corporations in the sample have a nationality, and all of them have a substantial character of multinationality with respect to foreign location of production or sales. Half of them also have multinational R&D in the sense that R&D operations are located in three or more nations (see Chapter 8). The relative measure of internationalization commonly used here will be the ratio of the number of non-domestic employees to the total number of employees. Sometimes simple counts of nations and nationalities will also be used. Such simple measures cannot by themselves capture the many facets of internationalization, and therefore the presentation will largely be made in qualitative terms.

4.2 EMPIRICAL FINDINGS

4.2.1 History of R&D and corporate internationalization

Figure 4.1 illustrates the nationwide expansion of operations. There are two main factors which are important in the early process of corporate internationalization, namely product inventions and raw materials. These factors interact with other factors, primarily initial attitudes towards internationalization, the small size of the domestic market and the need for heavy investments in ex-

R&D and corporate internationalization

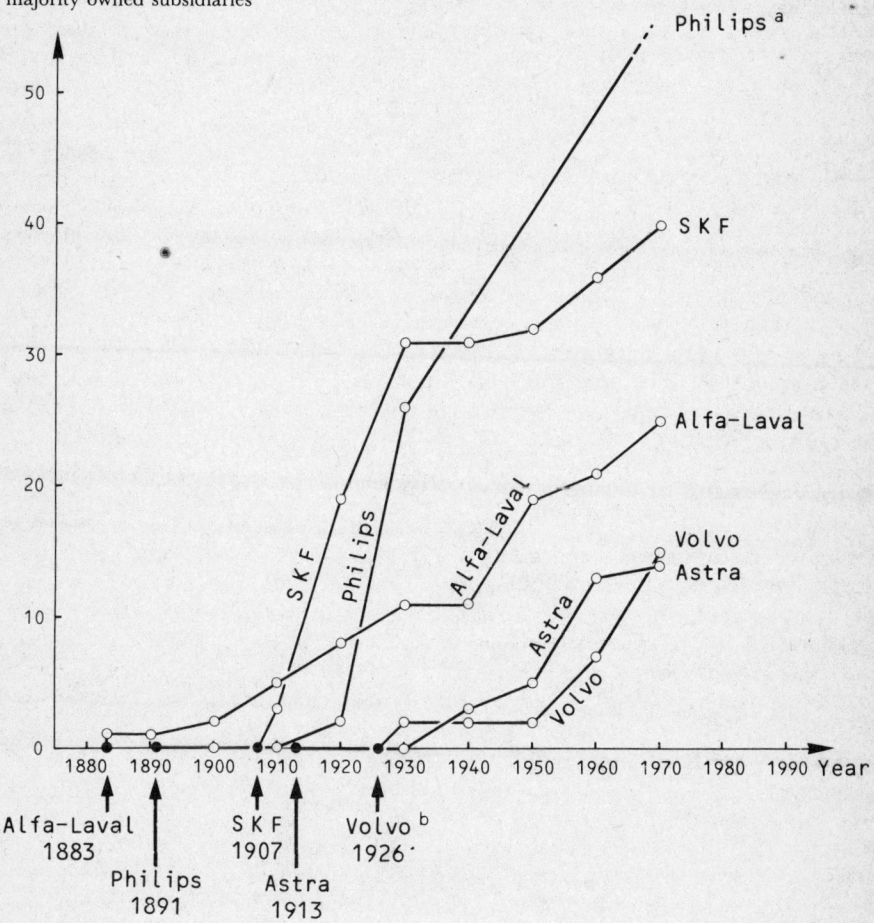

Number of foreign nations
in which a corporation has
majority owned subsidiaries

Note:
a) 64 foreign nations in 1978.
b) Legally, Volvo was founded in 1915. However, operations were initiated in 1926.

Sources: Corporate documents, SOU 1975

Figure 4.1 Historical patterns of corporate internationalization

ploiting raw materials. It is hardly possible to assess the relative importance of different factors. The history of corporate and R&D internationalization will be treated below for two groups of corporations according to the main factors product inventions and raw materials. It should be noted that this is but a rough grouping (see Chapter 2).

The corporations in the sample that are primarily product-invention-based are Philips, Alfa-Laval, SKF and Astra. For these corporations, R&D in the form of a product invention with a world-wide sales potential was obviously decisive in their initial internationalization. All four corporations had small domestic markets, and in the cases of Alfa-Laval and SKF there was a conscious striving from the beginning by the inventor to 'capture the world market'. These corporations also made early foreign investments directly in both marketing and production. The high level of product technology motivated the use of their own subsidiaries rather than agents in international marketing in order to get in close contact with customers and users. The large and growing advanced markets in industrialized nations like England, Germany, and the United States were primary targets. Also, the Russian market was penetrated early, but the Russian Revolution resulted in a loss of a large market for many Swedish corporations. Production operations were located in some of these nations at an early stage as well. This was partly because of the desire to overcome protective trade barriers (e.g., British law required all patented articles to be made in the United Kingdom within four years for the patent to be valid).

The internationalization of the R&D function in terms of foreign location was mainly a feature during and after World War II. While the establishment of sales subsidiaries and production plants abroad, and—to some extent—also foreign acquisitions, resulted from rather conscious strategies, the same does not hold for R&D. Two factors seem to have been of primary importance in the initial internationalization of R&D, namely local ambitions in subsidiaries and acquisitions 'containing' R&D. (Philips provides a special case in that R&D personnel went to foreign subsidiaries to escape the Nazis.)

World War II brought about a breakdown of corporate control of foreign operations, and international co-ordination of R&D was not a primary issue immediately after World War II. Due to ambitions among technicians and management in subsidiaries with production facilities, some R&D developed. One may also note how some subsidiaries in Philips and SKF have started R&D in connection with contract work for the local national defence. Here, national secrecy is useful for local management in gaining more independence vis-à-vis corporate headquarters. The same goes for the anti-trust laws of the United States, which together with interests of local management, have to some extent impeded co-ordination with subsidiaries in that country. Traditionally, the United States subsidiaries have gained a high degree of independence.

Of course, there are many more intervening factors, for example, the need to adapt products to local markets and to have local quality control and technical services, but often local management and engineers have been a primary source of influence in initiating R&D work abroad. Although a local objective, it has not initially been a part of corporate strategy. Moreover, acquisitions of foreign companies 'containing' some R&D have, in general, been made for other reasons

R&D and corporate internationalization

than to internationalize R&D. Thus, one may conclude that R&D has not initially been internationalized due to a conscious corporate strategy.

As far as subsequent internationalization of R&D is concerned, there is a component of gradual behaviour — as in the case of total corporate internationalization — but there are also examples of strategic decisions. SKF, which internationalized early, had diversification and multinational co-ordination as emerging strategic issues in the 1960s. Multinational R&D co-ordination was part of these issues, and it was thought (rightly) that a substantial investment in a central R&D laboratory would promote co-ordination of R&D among the subsidiaries. The laboratory was located in Holland in the early 1970s. The reasons behind the location of this laboratory abroad were, of course, complex, but an obvious one was that a non-domestic, geographically 'neutral', and central location in Europe would facilitate communication and co-ordination. The laboratory was also intended to be truly multinational in the sense of having a mixture of nationalities among the regular personnel in contrast to some other internationalized R&D organizations consisting of several national R&D laboratories. It might also be noted that the chosen foreign location of the central R&D laboratory was neither close to corporate headquarters, nor to local production or marketing facilities.

This example of a foreign location of an R&D laboratory was not the only one in Swedish engineering industry in the first half of the 1970s. R&D personnel economy, specialized fields of knowledge, recruitment problems, and closeness to sources of knowledge and markets were (and are) influencing R&D managers to consider foreign R&D locations. So far, however, there has not been a 'wave' of R&D locations abroad, and most corporations want to have a large part of their R&D 'at home', at least as far as the more advanced parts of R&D are concerned.

The second group of corporations consists of those which are primarily raw-material based and clearly includes Boliden and Iggesund and somewhat less clearly, KemaNobel. These corporations have been oriented around domestic resources and capital investments to exploit these resources, and they formerly perceived no specific incentive to internationalize. It was not until the 1960s that integration forwards, diversification and foreign supply of raw materials emerged as strategic issues. There were also internally developed unwritten policies or management attitudes that limited internationalization.

Without going too far into reasons behind the late start of an internationalization process of this group of corporations, one may just add the influence of production and transportation economies on management concern in these industries. Marketing has traditionally had a smaller 'share of mind'.

4.2.2 The situation in the 1970s

4.2.2.1 Corporate internationalization

Figure 4.2 shows the corporate development from 1965 to 1975 with respect to the state variables of diversification and internationalization. The spread is apparent, but a common trend towards a higher degree of corporate internationalization may be observed. Although data are largely missing, degrees of internationalization with respect to product divisions and different functions could be similarly assessed as ratios between employees abroad and total number of

Figure 4.2 Patterns of corporate internationalization and diversification 1965–1975

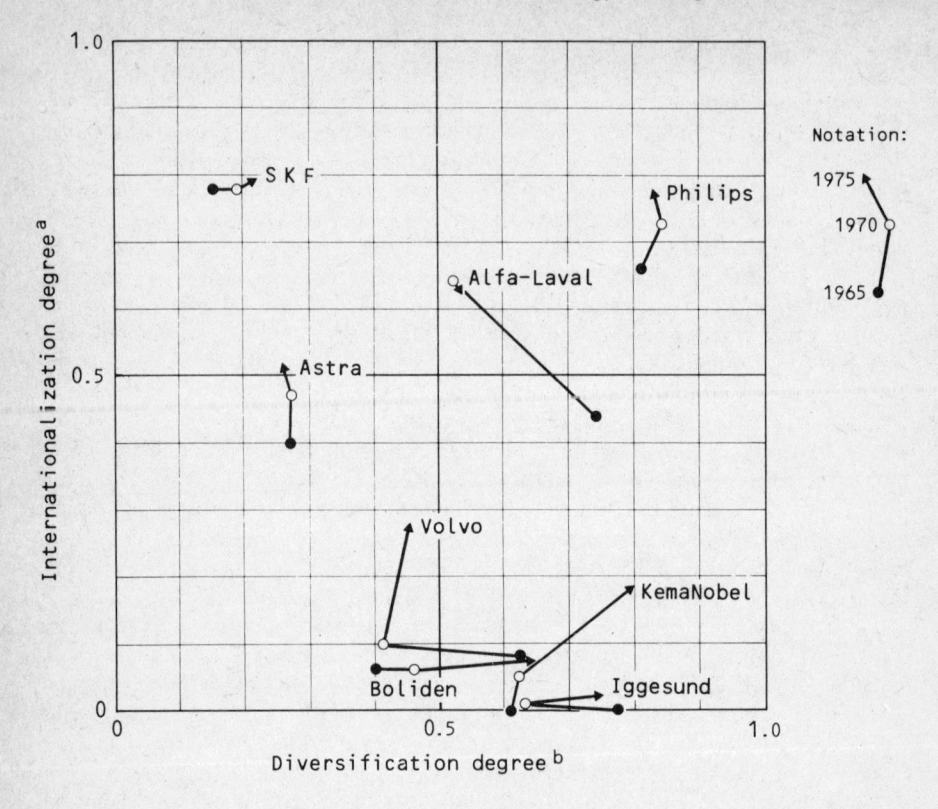

Note:
a) Employees abroad/total numbers of employees.
b) Sales outside largest product area/total sales.

employees in the corresponding division or function. In general, marketing is more internationalized than production, which is more internationalized than R&D for each corporation. For Astra the degrees of internationalization for marketing, production, and R&D were in 1975, 0.72, 0.48 and 0.17, respectively. For Alfa-Laval R&D is internationalized to a degree of roughly 0.2. Thus, in both cases R&D is internationalized to roughly one-third of the degree of corporate internationalization.

The corporations which have a high degree of internationalization also have a high ratio of foreign sales to total sales but the reverse does not hold. The raw-material-based corporations are particularly export intensive, and together with the early internationalized corporations they stayed fairly stable in the 1970s with respect to both internationalization degree and foreign sales intensity. The group of corporations which were in a transitionary stage in the 1970s in this respect were KemaNobel, Astra and Volvo. Of these, only Volvo had a higher pace of change in internationalization degree than in foreign sales intensity. It must, however, also be noted that the early internationalizers (Alfa-Laval, Philips and SKF) are in a transitionary stage in the sense that co-ordination of multinational operations has been increasing. For example, this gives an increase in cross-national deliveries and world trade, which also may give an increase in export intensity (i.e., exports from many nations to many nations rather than from one nation to many nations).

A strategy of further internationalization is encountered in almost all the corporations studied (see Chapter 5). The ways to achieve internationalization are many, but for late internationalizers (such as KemaNobel, Boliden, Iggesund and also Volvo) acquisitions or co-operation are the most common. The corporations with a developed network of sales subsidiaries naturally also want to use it for the marketing of new products on an international scale. A repellant effect may then occur if the subsidiaries are oriented around a traditional product. This has happened to Astra, Alfa-Laval and SKF. The effect is similar to the one encountered in development work, where traditions tend to dominate over new development work. Instead of trying to push the new product through the existing marketing organization, responses may be to build a new marketing organization, to license the product, or to market it on a joint-venture basis, possibly giving the existing marketing organization a 'first refusal right'.

A tendency to utilize existing marketing resources by no means excludes the use of acquisitions, joint ventures, or the development of new marketing resources abroad. In fact, there is a wide variety of options employed within and between the corporations. While, formerly, there was a concordance between corporate and product level regarding internationalization, there is now in a full-blown, diversified MNC—a diversity of international operations that makes it hard to extract simple patterns.

One common and important feature, especially of Philips, SKF and Alfa-Laval, is the striving for multinational co-ordination. Because of World War II, in these cases internationalization went through a stage that was not concomitant with co-ordination. Local ambitions among managers and engineers, adaption to local conditions, nationalism, local opportunities, protectionism, barriers to communication, etc. were all contributing factors. Corporate control, mainly by financial indicators such as growth, profitability and market shares, has given independence to successful subsidiaries. Tight corporate policies, guidelines and standards have often been absent, sometimes consciously so since, on the corporate level, it was sometimes thought that it was necessary to be cautious about centralization in multinational operations. Without going very deeply into the actual way these corporations co-ordinate, a few features may be pointed out.

First, a matrix organization of product divisions and foreign subsidiaries is common. The matrix may be more or less full blown with respect to horizontal and vertical degrees of coverage, and many variations of a matrix organization exist (compare Figure 8.1).

Second, it is common to use the centre concept as an integrating device. Such centres are profit centres, strategy centres, development centres, production centres, or supply centres. The formation of centres sometimes coincides with or is contained within divisional boundaries or national borders, but development, production and marketing responsibilities of foreign subsidiaries may be relocated. This is a kind of centrally co-ordinated internationalization of subsidiaries, which represents a new stage in the internationalization process of the product-invention-based corporations. In the sample here it is only SKF, Philips and — somewhat later — Alfa-Laval that definitely have reached this stage.

The formation and location of centres of different kinds are sometimes complex, at least as far as development and production centres are concerned. Local management ambitions are clearly important, and one encounters conscious strategies on the subsidiary level such as striving for:

- suitable structure of the subsidiary without conglomerate growth;
- products with advanced technology, low labour intensity, and markets with advanced industrial customers. Systems development is preferable in this respect over development of components;
- product concentration, for instance limited engagement in the product divisions of the parent corporation;
- production with accompanying development.

The infrastructure of different nations is also important, and industrial nations with advanced technology and advanced customers are attractive for development work but often not for non-advanced mass production due to high wages. Development and production responsibilities may then be transferred among subsidiaries according to how products and markets develop, although such transfers may involve a great deal of discord.

Third, co-ordination requires information and communication along with power for implementation. A structure of committees, boards, temporary working groups, consultants, agents, co-ordination units, liaison people and international commuters is present with various degrees of 'richness' in the corporations. This is not only a matter of large staff organizations for intrafirm co-ordination but also a matter of scanning the environment and finding opportunities for external cooperation as well. Case 4.1 gives an example of the co-ordination of multinational R&D.

Case 4.1 SKF. During the 1960s SKF sold ball bushings under licence. In 1971 corporate management decided that SKF should develop ball bushings of its own, since the prospects of continued licensing agreements were uncertain. At the corporate level the small innovation company started the development work, but the Germany subsidiary was dissatisfied with the results and started development work along alternative routes. The first evaluation of the two internal R&D competitors was made in April 1974 at a corporate management meeting, which approved of continued development both in Sweden and Germany. In early 1975 a thorough review was made of the nine alternatives developed so far. Through a sequence of meetings at the project level, at the central R&D-laboratory, in the product R&D management committee at the corporate level and finally in corporate management, a corporate R&D project based on an alternative emanating from Germany, was approved. The work on this project was done in the central R&D laboratory in Holland. A new review in late 1975 assessed substantial technical problems. At the same time the pressure for rapid market introduction of a bushing of their own increased due to the licensing situation. Development work based on another alternative, emanating from the innovation company, was therefore decided upon by the product R&D management committee in early 1976, and a new corporate R&D project with a new project leader was approved. Essentially, this alternative involved known manufacturing techniques, and with an energetic project leader the project resulted in market introduction of a new bushing in August 1976. However, work continues on the project, which is classified as a project of corporate interest aiming at a product new to SKF within non-conventional bearings, which is an identified diversification class apart from conventional rolling bearings and a class within which growth has been found particularly desirable and natural. [End of Case 4.1]

Some important features of Case 4.1 are:

— initiation of self-development sparked by an uncertain licensing situation;
— fruitful internal R&D competition and subsequent evaluation and direction of work made possible by a system for R&D co-ordination;
— the many 'turns' of the development work with respect to project objectives, location of work, origins of alternatives, market aspects, project leadership and status;
— the long time from initiation to market introduction in spite of the fact that similar products have long been on the market and the experience of SKF in related technical fields.

In relation to the multinational context in this case of product development, one may observe that it does not conform to the 'ordered' patterns of innovation within and diffusion between nations.

4.2.2.2 Internationalization of R&D

In general, so far there has been a more or less expressed policy and established behaviour to 'keep' R&D domestic in Boliden, Iggesund, KemaNobel and Volvo. These corporations are late internationalizers, and so far it has been considered rather natural to have R&D together with other domestic production and marketing operations, especially since process R&D is a large part of R&D in these corporations. Foreign R&D has only marginally been existing and then in the form of co-operative R&D and as a by-product of acquisitions.

In the highly internationalized corporations (SKF, Alfa-Laval, Philips and Astra) there is a tendency to keep the more basic and far-reaching R&D domestic and/or close to corporate headquarters. (A parallel holds for production in several cases in the total sample in that advanced production is preferably done domestically and assembly and supporting production may be located abroad.) The geographical location is, however, not necessarily decisive, and the central laboratory of SKF, which is located in Holland, is organizationally 'closer' to headquarters than, for instance, the domestic subsidiary laboratories of Astra are to the headquarters of Astra.

Reasons for the tendency towards domestic research and advanced development in the highly internationalized corporations are complex, and one should note that all these corporations, with the possible exception of Alfa-Laval depending upon the definition of research, actually perform some non-domestic research. Some reasons for the tendency are top management's idea of the need to have vital R&D close to its supervision, the need to have access to the R&D potential in Sweden (e.g., in pharmaceutical and metallurgical research) and also tradition, nationalism and cautiousness.

Decentralization of those parts of R&D that are more tied to products and markets is considered to be natural and in some cases a deliberate policy. Clearly such decentralization tends to result in internationalization of parts of R&D in already internationalized corporations. But, also, the more genuine new product development is internationalized in SKF and Philips through the establishment of different development centers among the foreign subsidiaries. A deliberate policy change from local development for local markets to mobile local development for global markets is taking place in these corporations. This is, however, difficult to accomplish not only because of uncertainty and market differences, but also because new products and variants develop in subsidiaries influenced by local conditions. Much R&D is duplicated, and corporate co-ordination may come in late, especially if technology moves fast but is internationally homogeneously or if international market differentiation is high.

4.3 DISCUSSION

4.3.1 Empirical summary

Historically, two groups of corporations can be distinguished, the raw-material based ones and the product-invention based ones. However, the grouping is rough and Volvo, for example, does not fit in. Also a progression of stages in corporate development is not always clear. Initially, the product-invention based corporations internationalized rapidly, based on the product invention. After a subsequent stage of gradually continued internationalization, a new stage has emerged with multinational co-ordination as a main feature. However, this stage is more diverse and unordered in the options employed. At this stage corporations are also large and diversified, and patterns of internationalization are differentiated at the divisional, subsidiary and product level. Generally, there is a trend towards a break-up of traditional patterns of internationalization and increased emphasis on international flow of technological and managerial knowledge.

Formerly, internationalization of the R&D function has followed the internationalization of production, and acquisitions and local ambitions among managers and engineers have often been strongly influential. Initial internationalization of R&D was hardly part of a corporate strategy. At present there is a tendency to keep research and advanced development domestic and/or organizationally close to corporate headquarters and decentralize and internationalize development work. Permanent location of R&D operations has decreased in importance, and temporary organizations and flows of knowledge are gaining emphasis. The link between R&D and internationalization appears to grow stronger.

The raw-material based group of corporations has begun to strive for internationalization in the 1970s and generally tries to accomplish this by joint ventures and acquisitions rather than by internal R&D. Also, these corporations have started to exploit foreign raw material sources and market their technology internationally. So far R&D in this group is mainly kept domestic.

4.3.2 Corporate internationalization

First, concerning general patterns of corporate internationalization it is hard to be conclusive on the limited basis of this study. There is, in this sample of corporations—all of which have small domestic markets—a correspondence between rapid internationalization and product inventions based on global technological advances. Internationalization of production has further been stimulated by national trade barriers.

That the pattern of corporate internationalization in general is characterized by a gradual component, has been emphasized by Johansson and Wiedersheim-Paul (1975) and Carlsson (1979). It is naturally hard to agree on distinctions between the gradual and the non-gradual. The pace of internationalization may be assessed in absolute or relative terms, qualitative as well as quantitative ones. A simple count of nations in which a corporation has subsidiaries does not give more than a first approximation of expansion patterns.

Normally there are shifts over time in the pace of internationalization, although not necessarily giving rise to distinct stages. The pace of global industrialization, wars and periods of protectionism are influential as well as the advent of inventions. It is also conceivable that corporate internationalization interplays in a periodic fashion with other dimensions of corporate development, such as diversification or consolidation. At least in the early phases of corporate development, this interplay may be observed in that no corporation initially internationalized in parallel with substantial diversification.

Second, concerning internationalization of different functions, Johansson and Wiedersheim-Paul (1975) in their study of internationalization of four Swedish corporations propose the concept of the establishment chain as a specific sequence of functional types of operations a given corporation is likely to follow in locating operations in a given nation over time. They conclude:

> The establishment chain—no regular export, independent representative (an agent), sales subsidiary, manufacturing—seems to be a correct description of the order of the development of operations of the firms in individual countries. (Johansson and Wiedersheim-Paul, 1975, p. 321)

This pattern also finds support in this study. In fact, the establishment chain may be extended in the sense that manufacturing operations are likely to be followed by R&D or at least 'D' operations. Such an extension also finds support elsewhere:

> Once some technical capability has been established, domestic scientists and engineers are certain to see additional opportunities for improvement. There is an almost irresistible creepage from production engineering upstream into design and development. (Steele, 1975, p. 212)

Ronstadt (1977) found in his study of foreign R&D investments made by seven United States multinationals that more than 90 per cent of these investments were related to foreign manufacturing investment and mostly created by managers in foreign manufacturing subsidiaries to aid in the transfer of technology provided by the United States parent.

On the other hand, an extension of the establishment chain is not valid in all respects. Progression through the sequence may be rapid, partial or disrupted. This is particularly so if separate products are also considered and the corporation has multinational co-ordination of its different functions. There are several examples in this study, as well as in Ronstadt (1977), of R&D units being located in a foreign nation without any connection to local manufacturing subsidiaries.

4.3.3 Internationalization of R&D

Concerning internationalization of R&D and decisions to locate R&D facilities abroad, several factors have been found in this study to be influential, such as:

- local ambitions among management and engineers;
- acquisitions 'containing' R&D;
- scale advantages, both small-scale and large-scale advantages;
- integration with production and/or marketing functions;
- differentiation with respect to national market conditions, for example need for market adaption, local product testing and quality control;
- cost/benefit ratio for scientists and engineers;
- access to national R&D potentials and infrastructure;
- communication costs and difficulties to transfer technology;
- recruitment considerations;
- subsidiaries are psychologically encouraged by having R&D;
- creating good will locally;
- tradition and attitudinal preferences for different nations.

Usually internationalization of R&D has followed the pattern of corporate internationalization and has not been strongly connected to a corporate strategy. It may also be noted that tax advantages in locating R&D abroad in this sample do not appear to have been influential although there is a growing awareness of these, not only regarding R&D costs but also because of tax benefits through patenting in low-tax nations.

Concerning multinational co-ordination of R&D for corporations in that stage of internationalization it is difficult to assess advantages of scale, synergy and multinationality, which may be achieved (see Mansfield, Teece and Romeo, 1979, for one of the few studies of this). Certainly multinational co-ordination presents difficulties, which may outweigh co-ordination benefits. Essentially, Steele (1975) adopts this standpoint regarding R&D. Several factors are important in an assessment, such as communication possibilities, the extent to which the corporation has a long-standing experience as an MNC, corporate history and culture, and type of technologies and markets. The highly internationalized corporations generally operate in oligopolies, and both markets and technologies often have low international differentiation.

The speed of development in technology, as for instance in electronic components, may require R&D flexibility and responsiveness at the expense of immediate co-ordination with other technologies and functions. There is also the problem of secrecy in co-ordination by communication. In the case of Eastman Kodak the international homogeneity of its technologies makes, among other things, co-ordination between different R&D laboratories worthwhile (Hanson, 1971). On the other hand, economic and technological differences among nations call for regionalized and loosely co-ordinated agricultural R&D in Farbenfabriken Bayer of West Germany (van Rumker, 1971).

A situation similar to that of Eastman Kodak is reported by Papo (1971) for IBM with a uniform and compatible product line and R&D performed in multinational laboratories. These are, however, reported to be multinationally located, not multinationally composed to any large degree. This is also essentially true for the multinational research organization of Philips with a dominating domestic laboratory. IBM, Philips and SKF share the feature of continental R&D co-ordination with looser co-ordination between the United States and Europe. The one-day return travelling distance actually seems to supersede market and/or technology homogeneities.

Concerning the relationship between R&D and internationalization at the corporate level, there are a variety of connections. R&D initiated internationalization in invention-based corporations. In fact, there are almost no examples of successful internationalization in which a technological advantage has not played a crucial role. It is also important to realize that the product inventions behind initial internationalization of the corporations in this sample were based on R&D and not on a flash of genius out of nowhere. In the cases of Alfa-Laval, SKF, Philips and Astra the inventors were well-educated men performing development work, albeit on an experimental rather than a theoretical basis. Moreover, there was a second important product invention made or acquired within about fifteen years after the first one was made in all these corporations. It might also be added that the international product life cycle theory applies to hardly any of these inventions, or at least the initial progression through the stages in the theory was very rapid in that the products were developed for world markets and also production was soon located abroad (see Vernon, 1966; Leroy, 1976).

The coupling between R&D and international operations has been mutually strengthening. Although looked upon as a means in an internationalization process, the causality is intertwined in MNCs. Without R&D they would mostly be unable to stay on international markets, and without large markets they could hardly pay for their R&D. This is especially true in pharmaceuticals, electronics and advanced engineering. Simple quantitative correlations give additional reasons to believe in a coupling between R&D, size and multinationality, rather than in a coupling between R&D, synergy and diversification (see Table 3.4). Moreover, growth is correlated with an increase in internationalization rather than with an increase in diversification. The correlation between sales in 1975 divided by sales in 1965 and the change in degree of internationalization from 1965 to 1975 is 0.66 while the correlation between sales in 1975 divided by sales in 1965 and the change in degree of diversification from 1965 to 1975 is 0.14. This, then, speaks in favour of specialization and internationalization as a growth strategy, which, however, requires R&D. Needless to say, the sample in this study is small and inconclusive.

Technological knowledge is, however, exploited in more ways than just through direct pay-off in sales of products (see Chapter 5 for different strategies for technology procurement and exploitation). There are a growing number of examples of how such knowledge may be licensed, cross-licensed, exchanged for raw materials, utilized in sales of systems, or as a means to cope with national requirements or attract foreign partners for co-operation (see also Baranson, 1980, for similar findings). There is an increased frequency of temporary international business relations in which knowledge of management and technology plays a vital part. Thus the concept of multinationality based on a more permanent location of operations is becoming somewhat diffuse, and the global information processing capacity of a multinational corporation is gaining increased importance.

The state of a technology tends to be internationally more homogeneous the more effective the cross-national flow of knowledge is. The increasing cost of industrial R&D in certain technologies stimulates both supply of and demand for technology. Often most R&D of relevance to a corporation is also performed outside the corporation, and scanning, access, co-operative and absorption capabilities have to be developed inside the corporation. External technological developments may mean an opportunity as well as a threat, which further enhances the incentives to keep abreast or become attractive for co-operation.

Technological leads may diffuse rapidly, which SKF and some other Swedish corporations have experienced, and technological lags may be hard to catch up, which Philips has experienced in the field of general-purpose computers. Sometimes the necessity at least to keep abreast has to supersede internal co-ordination when technology moves fast as for Philips. The situation is similar in Alfa-Laval and SKF, which operate in mature industries with a 'differential cost/benefit warfare' that may require timely responses also to small advances in a conglomerate of technologies.

4.4. CONCLUSIONS

Regarding R&D and corporate internationalization, two groups of corporations may be distinguished, those based on product inventions allowing an early and rapid internationalization, and those based on raw materials, tying their locations to domestic supply markets until recently, albeit with high export intensity.

There is a common trend towards increased internationalization. Late internationalizers have a preference for acquisitions and joint ventures. The pace of internationalization has historically been influenced by shifting external conditions in interplay with the internal dynamics of corporate development. A lead in product technology in combination with internationally oriented entrepreneurship has been a crucial factor in internationalization, while advanced process technology has been associated with domestication.

Corporations also internationalize their R&D, although there is a tendency to domesticate the 'R' part. The establishment chain model may thus be extended to R&D in some respects. Initial internationalization of R&D was not, in general,

R&D and corporate internationalization

part of corporate strategy but often resulted from acquisitions and local ambitions.

The evidence points in favour of R&D-based specialization and internationalization as a growth strategy. The highly internationalized product-invention based corporations have entered a stage of multinational co-ordination, which reinforces a strong coupling between R&D, size and multinationality. Small domestic markets, a high degree of internationalization, multinational co-ordination and increasing emphasis on technological and managerial knowledge give a limited relevance to models of orderly patterns of internationalization, innovation and diffusion.

Chapter 5
R&D AND CORPORATE POLICY MAKING

5.1 INTRODUCTION

This chapter presents and analyses policies and policy making with reference to R&D in the corporations studied. The presentation will be descriptive rather than normative in order to provide empirical insight. There is a gap between empirical observations and normative literature on policy making in general. At present, it seems more meaningful to try to narrow this gap mainly from the descriptive, inductive side than from the normative, deductive side. There is also a gap between R&D and corporate policies (or strategy), and it is of primary concern to discuss policy making in the light of this lack of integration.

The concept of policy will be used broadly and will not in any important way be distinguished from strategy and similar terms where empirical material is concerned. An important distinction is made between pursuing a policy (or a strategy) and mere behaviour. A policy, as the term is used here, has to include some degree of conscious determination of future action. Of course, it then becomes difficult to apply this distinction in retrospect. Analytically, several distinctions are relevant and a variety of terms are in use.

Etymologically the term 'policy' has the same origin as 'police'. A common dictionary description of 'policy' refers to a course of action adopted and pursued by a government, ruler, political party, etc. (Note how 'strategy', on the other hand, has been associated with military courses of action.)

It is not difficult to find, in the literature, different conceptual positions, sometimes involving inconsistencies, tautologies or mere vagueness. In trying to synthesize, some common underlying conceptions may be identified, as shown in Figure 5.1. These ideas give rise to overall value statements about desirable future states for a distinct whole and corresponding guidelines or outlines for possible future courses of action or behaviour for different parts of the whole.

Often policies are used for decision making in repetitive situations or as general guidelines. Strategy, on the other hand, is sometimes used for decision making in competitive situations but often also as an overall concept at the highest level of importance for the whole. Different wholes may be considered (e.g., a corporation, a division, a department or an individual) and strategy may correspondingly be used as a relative concept. The same goes for policy and objective.

A conceptual review reveals a variety of views on what could be meant by a policy. Is it not important, then, to make a choice between the possible distinctions? The standpoint taken here is that it is more important to be inclusive and make the necessary distinctions, when called for, in an analysis.

What actually produces policies of different kinds in different situations with different impacts is not well understood. This is especially true of R&D and technological innovation in general, since uncertainty is high and repetitiveness low.

R&D and corporate policy making

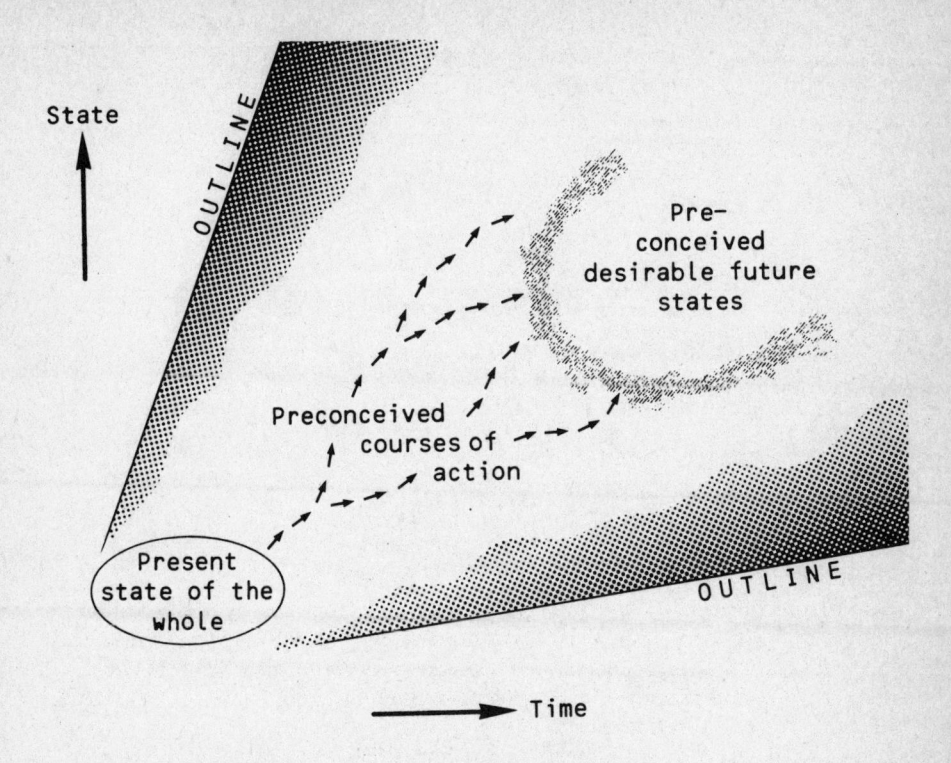

Figure 5.1 Elements of concept formation in policy making

The affluence of the 1960s and the crises of the 1970s seem to have stimulated a demand for improvements in policies and policy making, both public and corporate. Science and technology have been focused on, both as a promise for industrial prosperity and as an evil 'force' that has to be harnessed by better policies, if it is possible to harness at all. The limitations of different ways of making policies and the design of proper ones have gained increased attention as the insufficiencies of traditional rational–deductive approaches become evident. At present a central problem is maybe not so much under what circumstances a specific policy is good in some sense and what policy to use in a specific situation, but how to create insight into the process of policy making.

5.2 EMPIRICAL FINDINGS

5.2.1 Corporate policies

Table 5.1 gives an overall picture of the policy situation with respect to some basic dimensions of corporate development. The information in this table is ex-

Table 5.1 Emphasis in corporate policies 1975

Corporation	Profit	Growth	Diversification*	Internationalization†	R&D
KemaNobel	↗	↗	↘	↗	⌒
Philips-Sweden‡	↗	↗	↘	↗	↗
Alfa-Laval	↗	↗	→	↗	⌒
SKF	↗	↗	↗	→	↗
Boliden	↗	↗	↗	↗	↗
Iggesund	↗	↗	↗	→	→
Astra	↗	↗	↘	↗	↗
Volvo	↗	↗	↘	↗	⌒

*Diversification refers to product areas. Different types of diversification are not distinguished here, but strong synergetic diversification is preferred.
†Internationalization may be carried out in several ways with respect to location of operations and markets, but no such distinctions are made here.
‡No accurate data available for Philips as a whole.
Notation:
  ↗ Emphasized elements in corporate development.
  → No special emphasis.
  ↘ De-emphasized element in corporate development.
  ⌒ Changes in emphasis during the 1960s and first half of the 1970s.

tracted from documents and interviews and reflects an aggregated, qualitative judgement based on several sources of information. As will be discussed later, a policy situation is heterogeneous in several respects, and the arrows in the table are only rough indications of explicit stands taken in policy matters as expressed in documents and interviews.

First, Table 5.1 shows that profit, growth, internationalization and R&D have at least some emphasis in corporate policies, while diversification is de-emphasized in half of the corporations. However, there are several ways of emphasizing diversification, internationalization and R&D. While Philips-Sweden and Volvo are trying to concentrate their range in general, they are at the same time trying to weaken their dependence on military markets through diversification. That KemaNobel and Volvo de-emphasize diversification in general is due to bad experience from previous efforts to diversify. Astra has only partially failed in diversification outside pharmaceuticals but de-emphasizes diversification due to successes in the pharmaceutical area. The return on investments is higher in this area, and the perceived need to spread business risks as a response to a nationalization threat has decreased. Some corporations, especially Alfa-Laval, try to develop an increased capability to market product systems, but they also make disinvestments and concentrations in their product portfolio. Similar comments may be made about internationalization. The table also shows that R&D is in general emphasized. This is so in terms of both resources and top management attitudes and attention. The distribution of emphasis on different kinds of R&D naturally varies among the corporations.

Secondly, changes in policy emphasis have occurred to different extents depending upon how the corporation has developed in relation to expectations and standards for comparisons. Policies for diversification and R&D have, however, been the least stable in this respect and, with some exceptions the changes emanate from distorted expectations on behalf of top management.

R&D and corporate policy making

Thirdly, two groups of corporations may be distinguished on the basis of similarities in policy emphasis. One group includes KemaNobel, Philips, Alfa-Laval, Astra and Volvo, and the other SKF, Boliden and Iggesund. The emphasis on diversification is the main discriminating variable; SKF, Boliden and Iggesund are typically vertically integrated. In addition, they are at least partially based on raw materials such as ore and timber. (KemaNobel has changed its raw material base, see Chapter 2). Thus, in this sample, policy emphasis on diversification is correlated with degree of vertical integration and raw-material dependence. Table 5.2 illustrates corporate goals and strategies as formulated in KemaNobel.

The rationales behind statements about goals and strategies are inter-related in complex patterns. The strategies are generally thought of as a means of reaching the financially oriented ends, but enduring profitability, for instance, is both a means of survival in the economic system and a means of increasing the competence of corporate personnel or increasing R&D efforts. The latter two

Table 5.2 Written corporate goals and strategies in KemaNobel 1975

Corporate goals	Corporate strategies
The overall goal for KemaNobel is good enduring profitability.	The competence of corporate personel is to be increased.
Corporate return on equity is within the planning period to be increased to 20 per cent before tax.	Environmental and safety issues are to be given great and increasing attention.
Corporate debt-equity ratio is within the planning period not to fall below 30 per cent and preferably be closer to 40 per cent.	Corporate development is primarily to be based on advanced knowledge about production, marketing and use of chemical products.
Corporate liquidity is to be held at high level.	The corporation is to be developed towards increased internationalization.
The average return on net operating assets for operative units is within the planning period to be increased to 13–15 percent.	The corporation is to be developed towards a maintained or increased degree of distribution of risk and independence of business cycles.
(*Note:* Increased rates of inflation forced later revisions of certain figures.)	Sectors that do not fit into the corporation and/or which cannot be developed with reasonable effort, are to be separated from the corporation.
	Knowledge-intensive projects are to be given priority.
	The R&D efforts are to be increased in intensity and efficiency.
	The corporate information systems are to be developed — as well as the ability to utilize them.

strategies are thought of as a means of operating with knowledge-intensive products. Such products are thought of as a means of reducing risks and smoothing out results over business cycles. A depression might, however, force KemaNobel to cut down R&D efforts even at the expense of long-term profitability according to the Corporate Managing Director.

These features of goal (policy, strategy) inter-relatedness apply to all corporations. Moreover, different key individuals and groups of people inside and outside the corporation have different ideas about the corresponding causal relations, and they place different values on the perceived structure of means and ends (or causes and effects). Thus, there are neither simple hierarchies of means and ends nor any deep, wide, or stable consensus about a specific means/ends structure as reflected in written policies. The inter-relatedness of policy matters, however, makes it possible to some degree to reconcile different ambitions in a corporation. In Astra, for example, profitability, internationalization and R&D have been correlated, and it has been possible to reconcile business-oriented ambitions with R&D-oriented ambitions.

5.2.2 R&D policies

The R&D policy situation in the corporations was heterogeneous with respect to:

— specificity of policies on different organizational levels such as corporate, divisional, departmental, product, programme, and project level;
— form (written/unwritten, explicit/implicit);
— degree of secrecy (internal/external restrictions on distribution);
— area of application such as research, development, patents, licensing, relations to production and marketing, external cooperation and bodies of management;
— consensus and acceptance in the corporation;
— stability of policies over time;
— sources of influence in policy matters;
— motives behind a policy, for example, to guide decision making, motivate selective behaviour, co-ordinate, direct attention, support a manager, or create an image for internal or external use;
— content with respect to sciences, technologies, products, processes, markets and applications;
— relations between R&D policies and other policies, for example, the coupling between corporate policies and R&D policies.

With respect to the content in statements about policies, goals, strategies, etc., for R&D, it is possible to discern common R&D policy elements or classes of R&D statements. These policy elements concern:

(a) role of R&D in corporate development;
(b) resource allocation;
(c) area priorities;
(d) relations to competitors and customers;
(e) acquisition and utilization of technology;
(f) organization of R&D;

(g) R&D management philosophy;
(h) meta-policies.

Naturally, all policy elements are not found in all corporations but rather than describing each corporation in this respect, each policy element will be described:

(a) *Role of R&D in corporate development.* Several natural roles may be discerned with respect to profitability, growth, diversification, internationalization and other features of corporate development, for example, good will. The roles also vary within the corporations with respect to different product areas. At SKF, for example, R&D has a defensive role as far as bearings are concerned ('the R&D goal is to protect us from surprises'), while it has an offensive role along some lines of diversification.

(b) *Resource allocation.* This is a natural and explicit element in policies concerning R&D. Budget proportions and profiles with respect to total R&D resources and different kinds of R&D resources are used with different degrees of rigidity among the corporations. Astra, for instance, has rigidly adhered to allocating a certain percentage of the turnover to R&D, while others dismiss such a policy as unsuitable. (Note that pharmaceuticals are not sensitive to business cycles.) KemaNobel, Alfa-Laval and SKF stress some ratios between development of old and new products respectively. Similarly, policy statements may concern other subdivisions of R&D work and resources (for instance, product versus process development or research versus product development). Astra allocates a certain percentage to what is called explorative research, while within KemaNobel 'no basic research or R&D with the sole objective of making discoveries should be done'.

(c) *Area priorities.* Areas or fields of science, technology and application are distinguished, and levels of ambition or priorities are formulated. Sometimes this is done in a negative way, as for example, when a corporation declares that it should not develop in-house competence within biology or medicine or that it should not go into the packaging business. Such negative delimitations may be of much guidance to R&D and sometimes act as a deterrent on R&D ambitions or serve the purpose of slowly killing a project. Mostly, however, area policies are formulated in terms of existing areas to concentrate on and which areas to develop into. The latter areas are almost always adjacent, in some sense, to existing areas of competence. Since much R&D is connected to products ('Our R&D is mostly a consequence of our products'), R&D policies are often tied to product areas and differentiated with respect to the corresponding product and market features. The conceptualizations of areas differ, however, in specificity and focus, and it is not always clear what distinguishes, for example, a product area, an area of application, or a technological area (compare 'refrigerator area', 'food preservation area' and 'cooling technology').

(d) *Relations to competitors and customers.* Policies that focus on competitor and customer relations are mostly formulated on levels where groups of competitors and customers may be relatively well identified. Policies may thus concern leadership or followership with respect to product quality and performance, product price and time of introduction. Policies may also be formulated in terms of unique or advanced competence in certain areas. Sometimes policies regarding leadership and advanced technology are formulated for public consumption, both internally and externally. Invention-based corporations such as Alfa-Laval and SKF have developed traditions and reputations of superior product performance, technological leadership, and universality of applications (a kind of 'first and best everywhere' policy). Standards of judgement have become ends in themselves and the relation has weakened between R&D operations on the one hand and corporate economy, customer economy and competitor capability on the other.

(e) *Procurement and exploitation of technology*. To an increasing extent R&D policies are connected with more general policies or strategies regarding the procurement and exploitation of technology. The following is an inventory of such policies/strategies.

Table 5.3 Inventory of policies/strategies for the procurement and exploitation of technology.

Technology procurement policies/strategies:	Technology exploitation policies/strategies:
Internal R&D	Internal exploitation for production and/or sales of products
Purchasing of licenses, patents, or know how (monetary or by barter)	Licensing out (monetary or by barter)
Acquisition of companies Acquisition of personnel	Offering R&D or Engineering services
Support of external R&D Joint ventures	Joint ventures Divestment
Absorption of externally disclosed information	
Collection of information from closed sources	

Naturally these policies may be used in combination. It is important to note the many policy options besides the traditional ones of internal R&D and internal exploitation by the production and marketing of hardware. The policies also have different impact on corporate development in terms of profitability, growth, diversification and internationalization. For example, licensing out may be more profitable than internal exploitation but may result in less growth.

(f) *Organization of R&D*. Often R&D policies focus on the organization and location of R&D operations, responsibilities and objectives of R&D units, R&D management positions, and procedures for co-ordination and communication etc.

(g) *R&D management philosophy*. Almost every manager has some idea about the nature of R&D and R&D personnel and how R&D should be managed. Managers with influence in these matters may give a policy standing to some of their management principles or philosophies. Examples range from what may be called proverbial management ('Never change a winning team', 'Necessity is the mother of invention', 'Control kills innovation') to more elaborate philosophies, attitudes and views. Resulting R&D policies may, for example, concern scale effects in R&D work, handling of ideas and innovative people, organizational climate, and degree of management control.

(h) *Policies about policy making*. Sometimes policy statements concern the form rather than the content of R&D policies (i.e., what kind of language to use, how specified policies should be, and what ideals to strive for in policy making). This may be the case, for instance, when corporate policies outline how policies should be made on lower levels. In a sub-study of Alfa-Laval about people's views on what an R&D policy should look like in general, 20 per cent of the key words used referred to spatial conceptualizations such as area, direction and position.

5.2.3 Policy making

As already mentioned, the policy situations in the corporations studied here are heterogeneous, especially with respect to R&D. Such activities have in some cases been initiated in connection with divisionalization, while in other cases they have been initiated after the reorganization into divisions, when decentralization has been considered too far-reaching or otherwise improper by top management. The development of corporate, strategic or long-range planning and policy making has been focused initially on financial and marketing planning, while the consideration of R&D aspects has been superficially done, postponed, or relegated to lower levels in the organization. The situation in 1975 with respect to strategic planning at the corporate and R&D level is summarized in Table 5.4.

To introduce strategic planning at the corporate and/or divisional level is just one way of articulating goals, policies and strategies, and a study of policy making has to go deeper into the organization and its history to reveal features of the policy-making process. Thus the schemes, responsibilities and procedure for how strategic plans, policies and resource allocation are formally accomplished through breakdowns, 'rounds', planning cycles, etc. will not be presented here. Instead, three examples will be given in order to illustrate some approaches to policy making and determinants in the policy-making process.

Case 5.1 SKF

SKF is an example of an early internationalized corporation. World War II caused, among other things, a deterioration in co-ordination and central control, which became permanent in the 1950s. For several reasons, multinational co-ordination gained the attention of top management as a strategic issue of the 1960s, from which R&D co-ordination derived as a strategic R&D-issue. Heavy investment in a central R&D laboratory located in another country was made around 1970, partly as a means of achieving co-ordination of R&D operations in

Table 5.4 Status of strategic planning/policy making at corporate and R&D level 1975

KemaNobel	A new corporate managing director initated strategic planning in the early 1970s. Emphasis on developing financial targets and general strategies at the corporate level. R&D planning mainly at the divisional level. Corporate R&D planning and policy making have been postponed. Work on product strategies influenced by product-cycle and learning-curve models.
Philips	Strategic planning on the corporate and divisional levels has been established with the main part being carried out by the product divisions. Heterogeneous state of R&D planning with respect to different divisions.
Alfa-Laval	Partial failure of too ambitious an effort to start strategic planning around 1970. A second effort with strong support from the corporate managing director has resulted in the initial establishment of strategic planning in all divisions around 1975. Corporate R&D planning and policy making have been initiated but have developed somewhat in the shadow of corporate planning.
SKF	Partial failure of too ambitious an effort to plan strategically around 1970. Strategic planning has later on been reintroduced. Corporate R&D planning has been established with a 'bottom-up' approach, and corporate R&D policies are underway. R&D policy making activities have so far been only weakly connected to corporate and market (business) planning.
Boliden	Corporate policy making has been established. Strategic and market-planning activities on the corporate level are being developed. Corporate R&D planning has been initiated.
Iggesund	Small efforts have been made to plan strategically and then with emphasis on market planning. No explicit corporate policy making in general or with respect to R&D.
Astra	Strategic planning on the corporate and divisional levels has been established, with initial emphasis on the corporate level on finance and budgeting. R&D planning and policy making have also been established but mainly on the divisional and subsidiary level.
Volvo	Strategic planning on the corporate and divisional level has been established. No substantial R&D planning and policy making on the corporate level but in some divisions and subsidiaries.

foreign subsidiaries. R&D policy making has been approached in a 'bottom-up' way so that R&D resources have been initially 'taken up' by suitable projects without any specific policies being defined for the portfolio. Earlier efforts had been made to formulate long-range plans and use management by objectives, but these efforts had largely failed, and in 1975 it was considered to be wrong to use R&D policies or objectives of the kind: 'By 1980 we shall have $X million in R&D, of which Y per cent shall be put into research, and we shall put $Z million into the area of powder metallurgy'. Successively, however, work on corporate policies, business plans and R&D policies is being carried out. So far at the time

R&D and corporate policy making   69

of writing (1975), the coupling between R&D and corporate strategy and between R&D and marketing is weak. Many factors contribute to this situation, one of which is that top management more or less avoids making commitments through policy statements. The role of R&D in diversification, which is a clear element of current corporate strategy, has also been differently emphasized. The chairman of the board, who was the former corporate managing director, has a personal interest in product development and has been advocating a general policy in favour of in-house R&D. The central R&D laboratory and a small innovation company came into existence very much through his efforts. The present corporate managing director, on the other hand, favours acquisition of companies as a means of growth and diversification. ('It is probably not feasible to diversify through inventive work'.) Around 1975 there was a wait-and-see situation among subordinates, a situation in which the pattern of influence generally worked in favor of the Corporate Managing Director in a somewhat concealed way. [End of Case 5.1]

Case 5.2 Astra

In the 1950s Astra debated how to grow profitably and how to weaken the dependence of the pharmaceutical industry upon Swedish markets and Swedish politics. Internationalization through in-house R&D within pharmaceuticals became a corporate policy, and by the end 1950s the new corporate managing director began to implement these policies. There were two main ideas (or supplementing policies) about R&D, namely that R&D should be located close to medical universities and research centres and that R&D should be managed through decentralized subsidiaries. Astra-Hässle developed accordingly and established some research areas in the early 1960s, partly through external cooperation. The areas of research could just as well have been other ones within pharmaceutical research if the pattern of initial contacts and advice had been different. Concerning the content of the research, corporate policies were more or less unspecified, although reorientation from chemistry to biology, pharmacology, and pharmacy was encouraged by top management. During the 1960s, conflicts arose with respect to the relation between Astra-Hässle and central R&D authorities. R&D policy discussions became heated. There were several sources of conflict, but on the whole the conflicts pertained to corporate controls versus ambitions and need for autonomy within Astra-Hässle, chemical orientation versus biological and medical orientation in pharmaceutical research, and research standards versus commercial values. A power struggle took place, which in the early 1970s resulted in R&D policies emphasizing high standards of quality in research and marketing, based on a biological orientation, and medical ethics and values have been reconciled with commercial values. Leadership and contributions to pharmaco-therapy have been preferred instead of some kind of followership. (One admits though that the advances often are marginal). Market aspects are considered on a macro level of broad disease areas, but on a micro level R&D is mainly managed according to pharmacological mechanisms rather than according to immediate identifications of markets.

This period of policy conflicts at Astra, mainly during the late 1960s resulted in

shifts of power among key individuals in which the corporate managing director was acting behind the scenes. Also, shifts in the balance of power among various professional groups took place but these occurred during the whole decade. The corporate–subsidiary relation with respect to control was in 1975 still a controversial issue with latent conflicts. Astra-Hässle wanted to develop a third generation of products in one of the established research areas (beta blockers), but the central R&D authorities (which now included a former professor of medicine) were pressing in other directions.
[End of Case 5.2]

Naturally, there are more nuances of the policy-making process at Astra than can be accounted for here. An important circumstance is that Astra and Astra-Hässle have been successful. This has created possibilities for reconciliation. Successful policies and behaviour have been internally strengthened and have also influenced policy making in other corporations. It may be added that the policy of diversifying outside pharmaceuticals has partially failed. Some efforts to diversify into chemical products have been successful as business ventures but in relation to sales of pharmaceutical products they have not led to an increased degree of diversification. On the whole, internal R&D rather than acquisitions has been a preferred means of diversification.

Case 5.3 Volvo
A policy or a business idea that has been practised right from the original foundation of Volvo is the performing of internal design and assembly functions in car production and utilizing external production and R&D capabilities of a system of suppliers. Over the years, production and R&D operations concerning vital components, such as engines, have been internalized and R&D, including design, has become an integrated element of work.

Volvo has successfully grown and has internationalized since the 1950s, much on the basis of product quality. In the early 1970s a new corporate managing director carried through a second step of divisionalization, in which technological competence and power and R&D resources were dispersed to some extent. Questions then arose as to whether R&D was properly organized and managed, and a large management conference was held in 1973 on Bermuda with invited experts of world-wide reputation within science and technology and management. After this conference a corporate R&D policy was made, which largely confirmed the present organizational situation and did not signal any significant policy changes. The corporate R&D policy also outlined how different units were to formulate plans and policies—for example, how they should identify different levels of ambition with respect to different areas. This policy has not been applied throughout the corporation, and perhaps the most significant result of the conference was that yearly internal R&D management conferences on the corporate level were initiated. These conferences have mostly been informative and have had a marginal influence on R&D and policy making.

The outcome of the conference in Bermuda with respect to R&D policy making has been interpreted in different ways. Top management has felt that the existing way of organizing and managing R&D was justified. Others have interpreted the outcome as meagre and have requested further policy making efforts. [End of Case 5.3]

These cases point to some common features of policy making processes with respect to R&D, such as:

— policy evasive behaviour on the part of top management;
— policy seeking behaviour in the organization;
— evolutionary formation of policies with periods of confirmation of past behaviour and periods of transition;
— policy conflicts.

The role and behaviour of top managers in policy making is important but not necessarily in the sense that the group of top managers coincides with the group of individuals exercizing key influences in each policy matter. A common situation is that people in the organization want guidance through policies, while top managers are evasive, especially with respect to R&D policies. Various reasons for this evasive behaviour are indicated in the interviews.

One reason is the attitude towards specificity of control through policies. Some top managers simply look upon R&D as something which should not be very much guided from the top or at least should not be guided through specified policies. 'The policy is to have no policy' was an aphoristic utterance by a top manager in a subsidiary of Iggesund, in which R&D related to new products had just been initiated. The attitude towards specificity varies among top managers with respect to different policy matters and different kinds of R&D. A top manager may, for instance, strongly advocate a form of organization for R&D or an R&D management philosophy, while he does not take any specific stand with respect to areas or technological content of R&D.

Another reason for the evasive behaviour in policy making of top managers is the stage of maturation in a policy matter. There are periods in which processes of intellectual and emotional maturation with respect to a policy matter occur in the organization. Leading actors 'go around thinking' and involve themselves selectively in policy discussions. Policies evolve in the heads of people, and 'some policies are in more heads and others are in fewer heads'. Different actors apply different amounts of pressure in different directions. ('There is never just one man who applies pressure in policy matters in a large corporation'.) A dominant policy may be crystallized and then adopted. (The adoption of a policy has similarities with the process of adoption of new products by customers with some leaders and some laggards and a majority in-between.) Sometimes, then, top managers are not prepared to adopt a policy, or they do not feel that the time is ripe for implementation. Both cases seem to evoke evasive behaviour.

A third reason is the attitude that is taken towards risks, especially political risks. In conflicting policy matters top managers may act politically 'safe' and try to avoid any commitments through policy statements. The uncertainty in R&D and technological change, together with a varying understanding of R&D may cause top managers to refrain from being active in policy making. It may be a question of being cautious without appearing to be an indecisive manager or of delaying a matter and 'letting time work' or of handling radical policy proposals without disavowing sub-ordinates or of not creating or engaging in a power struggle. Some top managers also view policy conflicts among R&D people as desirable to some extent and the resolution of policy conflicts through direct involvement from the top as improper. ('Sooner or later the unsuitable people will disappear from the scene, if necessary, with top management acting behind the scenes'.)

A fourth reason for evasive behaviour is selective and sequential management attention. Different issues attract the selective attention of top managers in different periods. Issues relating to R&D, 'technological gaps', etc. are given attention intermittently. Shake ups and re-orientations occur, R&D policy concern decreases and primary attention is given to something else. Suppression and ignorance are extreme behaviours in this respect. R&D and technology are primarily portrayed by top managers as important to the corporation and something they are interested in. Such statements may serve the purpose of creating motivation and good will, but at the same time an evasiveness in more specific policy matters tends to prevail during periods when R&D policies are not of primary concern.

These are some general reasons that have appeared relevant to the evasive policy making behaviour on the part of top managers with respect to R&D. But if such behaviour is common, how then do R&D policies evolve? A very accurate answer cannot be given, but some patterns in the evolution of a policy were found over time and in the organization. With respect to evolution over time, R&D policies tend to evolve continuously rather than being the direct result of strategic decisions, at least this is true for the technological content. (Indirectly, however, a strategic decision—for example, to invest in a new production facility or to acquire a company—may activate discussion about R&D policy changes.) Periods of intensified effort regarding evaluation and policy making do occur, but generally do not result in revolutionary changes. This process of policy evolution over time may, to varying degrees, adapt to environmental changes and put pressure in new directions, or simply confirm the past behaviour of the corporation.

With respect to evolution in the organization, R&D policies tend to evolve loosely coupled to corporate policy making processes. The stockholders, the board of directors and the employees exercise marginal influences on R&D policies in general. Top managers, on the other hand, may be very influential depending on their experience, preferences and power. In case of top management evasiveness in policy making, sub-ordinates in and around R&D naturally become influential. In some cases, sub-ordinates were 'upwardly' active and, for instance, watched the behaviour of the corporate managing director and tried to recognize policies implicit in his behaviour.

The submission of proposals could be helpful in this learning process. In other cases, subordinates were more passive in policy matters and at most complained of the inability of top management to formulate policies. In still other cases, subordinates were actively making policies in their part of the organization but more or less isolated from other parts of the organization. Many variants of such

R&D and corporate policy making 73

policy making behaviour could be found, but most of them seem to have in common a preservative effect upon policies and behaviour in the corporation.

5.3 DISCUSSION

5.3.1 Empirical summary

Policies and policy making concerning R&D in a number of corporations have been presented from a descriptive rather than normative point of view. Differences in emphasis on profit, growth, diversification, internationalization and R&D in corporate policies were found between corporations and over time with respect to, especially, diversification and R&D. To some extent, a strong emphasis on diversification as well as a weak emphasis on R&D was associated with vertical integration and a raw materials basis. On a more detailed level, there was a complex inter-relatedness between matters and people in policy making. There were no simple hierarchies of means and ends; nor did a deep, wide, or stable consensus about a specific means/end-structure exist.

R&D policies were, in general, vague and loosely connected to corporate policies. Eight classes of R&D policy statements were discerned. These classes concerned the role of R&D in corporate development, resource allocations, area priorities, relations to competitors and customers, procurement and exploitation of technology, organization of R&D, R&D management philosophy and policies about policy making.

With respect to policy making, the corporations differed substantially. A common feature was, however, an evasiveness in R&D policy making on the part of top management, and some reasons for this behaviour were identified. Also, some differences were found in connection with policy evolution over time and in the organization.

5.3.2 Corporate goals and policies

Goals, objectives, strategies, policies and similar purpose-oriented concepts essentially aim at focusing attitudes and behaviour. It is tempting to formulate a set of fundamental goals, a basic mission, or similar as a common point of departure in policy making. Several corporations do this, emphasizing such factors as survival, profitability and satisfaction of customer needs. As a complement to such traditional goals, quantified or not, there are sometimes conceptualizations of a basic business idea or a *raison d'être*. In this vein of thought Levitt (1960), in a well-known article, argues the need to define what kind of business a corporation is in, citing the standard example of the American railroad industry, which failed to consider itself as being in the transportation business. In doing so, Levitt claims, management of the railroad industry was not intellectually prepared to take advantage of opportunities in the development of alternate means of transportation, and through a narrowly defined scope of business, management became defensive and threat oriented. Levitt then pointed out that the oil industry would end up in a similar situation unless this industry defined itself as being in the energy business.

Levitt's ideas became influential and also created misinterpretations and abuse such as superficial phrases, too wide and too demanding definitions, or nominal rather than real policy declarations. Thus, one finds examples among the corporations studied of attempts to define themselves as being in the business of 'friction elimination', 'preventing exhaustion', or 'medical care systems'. Such conceptual exercises may challenge traditional implicit policies as being in the mining industry and 'stop' at the refined metal. The importance of Levitt's ideas is, however, that they focus on two common phenomena. One is technological substitution and the other is 'innovation by invasion'; for instance, the source of radical technological substitution in an industry is more likely found outside the industry than inside. The weakness of Levitt's idea is that it invites us to think in terms of the unique existence of a proper conceptualization, which is fundamental and static in character. As such, the conceptualization chosen may be too narrow, which could develop defensive attitudes and cause too many changes in technologies and markets to be identified as threats rather than opportunities, or it may be too wide, which would scatter attention and resources if implemented, or it may simply misdirect attention by its singularity. Should a manufacturer of pneumatic machinery consider himself as being in the business of pressure energy and consequently engage in hydraulics, or, if he already has done that, should he consider pressure energy to be the most important common denominator in his operations? Similarly, a manufacturer of sports cars may ask whether he is in automotive transportation, private transportation, surface transportation, or just transportation, or if he is in leisure vehicles or leisure articles. Obviously, functional relations between technologies and markets are not easily conceptualized and are more complex than hierarchic.

Viewed in a dynamic perspective, the weaknesses of singular conceptualizations are even more obvious. Consider, for instance, the process of evolutionary entry into new businesses, as described in Chapter 3. In such a branching into new technologies and businesses, which is mainly internally generated, a conceptualization in Levitt's terms would have to be wide or else it would act more or less as a policy straitjacket, unless reconceptualizations were continually made. For example, Alfa-Laval — in efforts to preserve milk — developed a competence in heating and cooling and later on in microwaves. Heat exchangers as well as separators, the latter originally used for the separation of milk, have found applications in several industries over the years. The application of microwaves in the preservation of different foods required, on the other hand, the development of a new packaging material. In this case, what would a conceptualization of the business of Alfa-Laval have looked like, how would it have influenced corporate development, and how would it have been influenced by corporate development? What boundaries of the corporation should from a normative point of view have been established in terms of milk separation, general separation, centrifugal separation, food handling, etc.?

Consider the process that complements an internally generated entry into new businesses, that is engagement in new businesses initiated mainly from the outside of the corporation. This process is often less evolutionary, as for example, when an offer to make an acquisition suddenly arises. Sudden discoveries or ideas in internal R&D leading directly to revolutionary changes are conceivable but rare. In this case a rigid conceptualization may lead to a premature decision to turn down the offer. Also a search for new ideas in the corporate environment may be hampered by a rigidly or narrowly conceptualized policy.

Thus, there are several weaknesses inherent in formulations of basic business ideas. From the point of view of implementation, simplicity in formulation and stability over time are normally perceived as desirable features of a policy. Weak and singular conceptualizations are tempting and frequently occur but tend not to consider the dynamic complexity in technological substitution and the sources of innovation.

5.3.3 Policy making

There is a rationalistic normative vein of literature on the making of goals, policies, strategies, etc., as well as one with opposing views, centred around concepts such as 'muddling' and incrementalism. When it comes to policy making with respect to R&D and innovation, similar veins may be found in the literature, but on the whole R&D and innovation are mostly superficially dealt with in literature about policy making at the corporate level. This is also paralleled by the loose coupling between R&D policies and corporate policies, as described in Section 5.2. There are different notions about how to make such a coupling more effective. The view adopted here is that it is through the process of policy making, rather than through requirements on the outcome of this process, that a coupling may be achieved. Such a normative view must take into account the descriptive findings in this and other studies. We will focus on the role of top management below.

The situation in which people in the organization want guidance through policies while top management is evasive in policy matters has been observed by others, notably Wrapp (1967) and Quinn (1977):

> But as the organization clamors for statements of objectives, these are samples of what they get back from him (the manager): 'Our company aims to be number one in its industry', 'Our objective is growth with profit'. . . .
> (Wrapp, 1967, p. 94)

Now the combination of policy-seeking behaviour in the organization and policy-evasive behaviour of top management may lead to a kind of stalemate, which makes it important to understand both kinds of behaviour.

That some R&D people and R&D managers want guidance by clearer goals, policies, etc. may seem surprising and that they want this guidance from the top even more so. Similarly, policy-evasive behaviour at the top may appear to be surprising. Simplified, this is a situation with the demand for guidance exceeding the supply of it. Conventional wisdom about R&D management suggests that it is rather problems with the opposite situation that require attention.

There are naturally many specific aspects of a situation where R&D policies are lacking, and some different patterns of behaviour were described in Section 5.2. Generally speaking, a policy reduces uncertainty but also involves a risk, and there has to be a distribution of personal risks in policy making. Policy-seeking behaviour among R&D people is not a search for control but rather an effort to reduce uncertainty and anxiety by their knowing what is expected of them, how they will be evaluated, how they may argue about resources, about concentration, about co-operation, about room for action on an operational level, etc. They may feel that there is enough uncertainty in R&D work anyway and that being creative requires an amount of certainty about organizational matters. Besides, common organizational behaviour such as hierarchical thinking, pressing for articulated support of one's own preferred work, fear of failure, and striving for 'law and order' applies to a certain degree to all members of an organization, inclusive of R&D people and managers.

Similarly, policy-evasive behaviour among top managers may have different causes. In Section 5.2 four reasons were identified as having to do with the attitude towards specificity of control through policies, the stage of maturation in a policy matter, attitude towards political risks, and selective and sequential management attention. Wrapp and Quinn point at similar factors in top management behaviour in policy making. Concerning specificity, Wrapp speaks about 'the art of imprecision' and how a successful manager satisfies the organization with a sense of direction without actually getting himself committed publicly to a specific set of objectives.

Concerning the stage of maturation, Wrapp discusses the value of sense of timing in policy making, and Quinn describes the managing of the stages in the incremental process of policy making. Risk taking in a political context is an important factor in policy making. Quinn outlines different reasons why top managers do not announce goals, one reason being security. External security reasons for the corporation may make top management reluctant to announce goals, but internal security reasons seem just as powerful. An important factor to consider is how successful the corporation presently is, that is to say that there is an influence of business cycles. When growth and profitability are good, it may be easier to stick to the conventional ideas of strategic planning, while in recessions the political game becomes intensified. In the former case secrecy reasons may not be of primary concern, while in the latter case internal secrecy may be a prime factor behind the reluctance of a corporate managing director to formulate goals and plans, which, for example, would reveal how cuts are to be made in the organization.

Concerning the fourth factor, finally, selective and sequential management attention, Quinn writes:

> At any given moment, an executive can push only a few specific new goals, giving them the attention and force they need to take hold. . . . In fact, the essence of strategy is to identify this small number of truly essential thrusts or concepts and to consciously marshall the organization's resources and capabilities toward them. Then—to capture the organization's attention—the executive must consistently reinforce these strategic goals through his statements, his decision patterns, and his personnel assignments. (Quinn, 1977, p. 28.)

In looking at corporate histories one finds that there is also a very limited number of strategic achievements which can be attributed to a corporate manag-

R&D and corporate policy making

ing director (see also Section 7.2). Naturally, the question may be raised about how a top manager should behave in relation to strategic or policy issues he does not get involved in himself. According to Wrapp, a good manager makes sure he is well-informed on these issues, but he 'trains his subordinates not to bring the matters to him for a decision'.

This points to the need for an adaptive role differentiation between parties in policy making and mutual understanding of policy-seeking versus policy-evasive behaviour as a managerial implication. Often R&D and innovation are not included in the small set of policy issues of real top management concern. There are many complementary roles of R&D management and top management can play in the making of R&D policies and corporate policies. The role of R&D differs with respect to different corporate strategies such as growth, diversification, internationalization and profitability and the type and degree of coupling between R&D and corporate strategies is different in different technologies and markets.

Much specialized, as well as generalized, knowledge has to be combined in policy making. In order to reinforce a process coupling of R&D to corporate strategies, top management may choose to:

- initiate policy-making processes involving internal as well as external competencies;
- supply new angles of analysis, for example, reviewing the product portfolios with respect to technological substitution;
- dive into the specifics of some policy issue;
- require reconceptualizations;
- create parallel policy study groups;
- provide both broad policies such as pre-eminence of decentralization, which may promote cohesion and motivation, and specific policies such as 20 per cent growth rate and X per cent of turnover to R&D, which may challenge and promote focus;
- build up dialectic rhetoric to support transitions;
- promote action-oriented rather than planning-oriented uncertainty resolution;
- have concentrated policy reviews after a period of consistent action;
- promote policy changes by moving people and committing resources rather than through policy decisions;
- train subordinates to develop policy alternatives.

There is hardly any way to make such a process coupling orderly or to eliminate the political game features of policy making. However, paying attention to the need for a coupling between R&D and corporate strategy may reduce the stagnation effects on R&D from policy seeking at the R&D level, combined with policy evasion at the top management level.

5.4 CONCLUSIONS

Differences in emphasis in corporate policies on profit, growth, diversification, internationalization and R&D were found, especially with respect to diversification and R&D. To some extent, a strong emphasis on diversification as well as a weak emphasis on R&D was associated with vertical integration and a raw material basis. A complex inter-relatedness between matters and people in policy making was found which is far from the picture of a stable consensus about a specific hierarchical means/end-structure. A tendency to conceptualize a fundamental objective or a basic business idea could be observed. Evolutionary expansion of corporate technologies into adjacent areas, considered as 'naturally' connected to existing ones, was commonly emphasized.

R&D policies were generally vague and loosely connected to corporate policies, as were considerations of patterns of technological development and sources of innovation in corporate policy making. Common reasons for this situation were limitations of rationalistic procedures and conceptualizations, inexperience in policy making, and limitations due to behaviours in policy making. To varying extents, policies confirmed historical corporate development, and to varying extents they resulted from action and reaction at different levels in the corporations. A combination of policy-evasive behaviour at the top management level and policy-seeking behaviour at lower organizational levels was found in several cases regarding R&D and innovation. Four reasons for policy-evasive behaviour were indicated, namely attitude towards specificity of control through policies, stage of maturation in a policy matter, attitude towards especially political risks, and selective and sequential management attention. Strong support, on similar grounds, for a policy-evasive behaviour in general management was found by Wrapp (1967) and Quinn (1977). As a general conclusion, a need was found for a closer coupling between corporate and R&D policies through interaction in the policy-making process.

Chapter 6
R&D AND STRATEGIC DECISION MAKING

6.1 INTRODUCTION

Strategic decisions concerning R&D in the corporations are examined in this chapter. A strategic decision is often associated with a 'big' decision in some sense. Bigness may then refer to the size of a concentrated decision-making effort as well as to the size of a change resulting from the decision. Braybrooke and Lindblom (1963) discuss the concept of size of change in connection with decision making. They come close to suggesting that the 'distinction between a "small" and "large" change is the difference between structural changes and changes within a given structure' (Braybrooke and Lindblom, 1963, p. 63), but they emphasize the continuum between incremental and non-incremental change. The concept of importance is sometimes used for distinguishing strategic decisions. Mintzberg, Raisinghani and Theoret (1976, p. 246) define a decision as 'a specific commitment to action (usually a commitment of resources) and . . . strategic simply means important, in terms of the actions taken, the resources committed or the precedents set'. Ansoff (1968), on the other hand, discards the notion of importance in defining a strategic decision and uses 'the term strategic to mean pertaining to the relation between the firm and its environment . . . . Depending on its position, the firm may find operating decisions to be more important than strategic ones'. (Ansoff, 1968, p. 18).

Ansoff also defines by specification three principal decision categories in the firm: strategic, administrative and operating decisions. This subdivision is common and may be thought of as a general subdivision on a continuum of importance. The term tactical is then often used for the intermediate category.

Here a strategic decision means a decision at the highest level of importance for the whole. This is presumably in accordance with common ideas, although it may be difficult to sort out strategic decisions on a continuum of importance. However, a concentrated and substantial decision-making effort will also render to a decision the quality of being strategic, regardless of the size of the resulting change. Finally, importance may here pertain to different wholes and, in particular, to a corporation, on one hand, and to its R&D operations, on the other. Thus, a decision may be strategic on the corporate level but not on the R&D level and vice versa.

One has to be cautious about the misconception that large effects ought to have large causes. In particular, large effects do not necessarily derive from strategic decisions. Conversely, a strategic decision in the form of a great concentrated decision-making effort does not necessarily have to cause large effects. Naturally, the opportunity to observe strategic decisions varies. There is a tendency among interviewees to make attributions to discrete events and decisions, but when a low frequency of strategic decisions is observed, this tendency strengthens the validity of the observation.

Literature on decision making in relation to R&D is rich, especially concerning what possibly could be called operational and tactical R&D decisions, such as project selection, project control, and R&D budgeting (see Clarke, 1974; Winkofsky, Mason and Souder, 1980, for surveys). A common feature is that uncertainty resolution is focused on, while the political dimension of R&D decision making is not. Studies that specifically focus on the processes behind strategic decisions, seem to be missing despite their possible importance by definition.

6.2 EMPIRICAL FINDINGS

6.2.1 Strategic decision making in corporate histories

There are several developments in corporate histories, which appear as possibly resulting from strategic decision making. Examples include:

— the movement into light chemicals in the 1970s by KemaNobel;
— the establishment of local production and R&D at Philips-Sweden;
— the transition from component to systems orientation at Alfa-Laval;
— the establishment of a central R&D laboratory at SKF;
— the opening of a new generation of mines at Boliden;
— the integration forward in the 1960s at Iggesund;
— the acquisition of an external invention by Astra in the 1940s;
— the diversification into hydraulics by Volvo.

In examining these and other parts of corporate histories, the question arises in what sense and to what extent decisions involved in these developments were strategic. Case 6.1 gives a more detailed account.

Case 6.1 Alfa-Laval

After World War II Alfa-Laval experienced rapid growth within an extended range of applications. The scale of production of many of the customers also grew. R&D were split up into machines and plant design. A small revolution occurred in the technical design of one component, but otherwise the 1950s were characterized by continued growth in the technical parameters of the products, for example, in motor power. Alfa-Laval developed equipment for mainly dairy and starch factories and the food industry. The handling of combinations of machines became increasingly important, and knowledge of the customer processes in which the machines operated accumulated.

For Alfa-Laval the 1960s meant a transition from a component orientation to a systems orientation. This transition happened successively, determined by the ways in which markets and internal knowledge of customer processes developed. Studies were made of changes in customer needs in the marine and chemical industries, dairies, farming, etc. all around the world. R&D grew, disinvestments were made of products and companies which did not 'fit in', and at the same time companies were acquired to supplement technological knowledge.

In the second half of the 1960s new technologies became relevant. One reason was an increased systems orientation, which brought Alfa-Laval into contact with a wider range of technologies. Another reason was external technological change in general and still another was problems with products and processes. Thus, mathematics was modernized and computers came into use, automatic process control became increasingly important, and within food processing the use of microwaves was actualized. In the late 1960s top management also initiated an analysis of all products with respect to possible technological substitutions. Attention was paid to the risk involved in basing corporate operations on old principles and technologies, for example, separation by centrifugal forces. R&D were initiated within filters and membrane technology, resulting in new processes.

In the 1970s R&D have grown after some years of stagnation. The base of competence has been enlarged into areas such as biology, protein chemistry, agriculture and electronics. The more complicated customer technologies become, the more R&D in diverse fields are needed. Also, the nature of R&D has changed from trial and error to more scientifically oriented R&D. A special unit for automation technology has been created. Also a corporate R&D laboratory has been built up, where R&D not naturally belonging to a single product division or being of a long-range nature can be performed.
[End of Case 6.1]

In summary, Case 6.1 illustrates:

— the incremental and branching nature of learning about technologies and markets;
— the influence of developments regarding size and complexity in customer technologies and regarding developments of science and technology in general;
— the few strategic decisions, if any, involved.

Naturally, it is hard to assess the nature and frequency of strategic decisions based on accounts like this one. Rather than singling out and classifying decisions on a general basis, some decisions common to the corporations studied will be described below with respect to their possible strategic nature.

The acquisition of a company often appears as a strategic decision. The pre- and post-history of such a decision may, however, vary significantly. The acquisition may be made as a result of sudden offer or of a search for companies to acquire or a perceived threat that a competitor will make the acquisition. Often minor acquisitions are made as a means to obtain experience. The risk involved may be rather low as in the case when KemaNobel, in moving into light chemicals, acquired a company in consumer products. This company could always have been sold if the experiment did not turn out well. Similarly, Volvo acquired—and shortly afterwards also sold—some stock in the ventilation business as part of a diversification strategy. Almost all corporations have made acquisitions of this experimental kind with varying degrees of success. Often the direct economic risk involved has not been extraordinarily high. On the other hand, an acquisition may later on divert management attention, involving another kind of risk, which, however, is indirectly related to the decision to acquire. Major acquisitions certainly may be strategic in the sense that if they did not come off, the corporation would significantly have to change its strategy, as when SKF acquired a tool company. However, R&D aspects seldom play a major role in this kind of acquisition.

The decisions to acquire inventions and licences resemble decisions to acquire companies. The decision-making process may be short, as in the case when Alfa-Laval in 1889 and Astra in 1943 were suddenly offered an external invention, and a deal was made within one day. Both inventions turned out to be of great importance for corporate development. The economic risk involved was minor to the corporations, since the deal was mainly made on a royalty basis. To turn down an offer of a patent, licence, or company may also involve a short decision-making process. The risk involved in a decision not to acquire is difficult to assess in retrospect but sometimes appears to have been underestimated. It should, moreover, be noted that the length of a decision-making process and the degree of risk taking are influenced by the way opportunities arise and become recognized as well as by the preparedness of the decision makers and their attitudes towards risk.

In raw-material based and capital-intensive corporations, investment decisions clearly could be considered as strategic. The relative proportions of sums involved are of quite a different magnitude than in other industries. The long-range nature of investment decisions, the few possibilities to make incremental investments and undifferentiated products with fluctuating prices are features that make the nature of decision making quite different from that in many other industries, in which risk taking may be more connected to product technologies than to process technologies and supply. The decision by Iggesund to integrate forward into the manufacturing of cardboard clearly was a strategic decision that involved high risks (see Chapter 2). However, investment decisions of this kind may be strategic and may also have strategic consequences for internal R&D, but they are not strategic decisions with respect to R&D. In fact, both size and content of R&D operations tend to lag behind this kind of strategic decisions (see Chapter 3).

Iggesund also made a decision to transplant a fast-growing Canadian pine as a response to scarcity of forests. This decision was perceived by top management as a strategic decision involving high risks, while biologists with greater familiarity with the problem considered the decision making as a sequence of 'ordinary' decisions (see Chapter 9). The familiarity with a decision situation is associated with the degree of its recurrency to the decision makers, which in turn affects their perception of degree of risks involved. Thus, it is conceivable that there is a tendency to characterize decisions in connection with diversification as strategic. To the extent that non-divisible resource commitments are made, this seems to be the case, but such decisions may often then be preceded by many other decisions, which sometimes will put the strategic decision makers in a situation of *fait accompli*. If strategic decisions to scale up resource commitments are made on the premise of a clear acceptance of recognized high risks, it is possible that a discontinuation of a diversification project would be facilitated, although many individuals still might have their interests and emotions tied to it. There are many examples of the difficulties involved in stopping diversification projects as well as projects in general. In fact, two such projects, one at KemaNobel in the late 1950s and one at Volvo Flygmotor in the late 1960s, were referred to as requiring a new managing director to be stopped. In the latter case there were two lines of products for achieving diversification, turbo-compressors and hydraulic machines. After the turbo-compressor project was stopped, only the work on hydraulic machines remained as a recognized promise of diversification without having to develop something new. The decision in 1970 to scale up the expansion into hydraulic machines involved risks of a new product technology and entrance into new markets, and the decision may be considered as strategic. On the other hand, there was no viable alternative if diversification was attempted in order to distribute the overall risks. In the light of the urgent need for Volvo Flygmotor to diversify outside the military product area, it is difficult to see how the Board of Volvo Flygmotor could have stopped this project, which already had passed a stage of market introduction of a proven technology.

The decisions involved in establishing and locating new R&D units are as a rule preceded by years of discussions and preparations. These decisions are seldom, if ever, responses to sudden pressures or opportunities arising externally. Also, the resource commitments are often divisible. The location may indeed be crucial. The location of subsidiaries close to medical universities by Astra and the foreign location of the central R&D laboratory in SKF, geographically separated from production and marketing operations, appear as strategic decisions in retrospect. However, R&D resources may be shrunk or transferred and locations may be changed in many cases. Moreover, it is not just the choice of a certain location *per se* that is important, but also subsequent decisions to recruit R&D personnel and develop external relations. Thus, a successful outcome of locating an R&D unit may hardly be traced to a single strategic location decision. On the other hand, there are examples of decisions to locate production operations, which have later given rise to difficulties in recruiting personnel to R&D units, as preferably these should be integrated with production. Thus a partial failure may sometimes be traced to a single strategic location decision.

The acceptance of a large order may result in considerable learning as well as a foothold on the market. A company, acquired by Philips-Sweden, in fact, 'contained' a large order, which provided a means for Philips-Sweden to enter a new market. There are risks in accepting a large order, which requires extensions of corporate technologies and also often requires rapid decisions. These risks may be hedged against by relying on managerial skills in subcontracting or by making agreements of a joint-venture type.

A major reorganization is sometimes regarded as a strategic decision. However, it is also the subsequent commitments to a chosen organizational form that are of significance. Decisions to implement a new organizational form may, at least in principle, be thought of as reversible decisions. However, internal relations may be damaged for some time, and key personnel may leave the organization for good. Also, the process of internalizing and externalizing some operations may be irreversible. The decisions by the product-invention-based corporations to substitute sales agents with sales subsidiaries were hardly reversible and also signified strategic marketing decisions. Similarly, the organizational separation and formation of a new unit may be difficult to reverse. (An example would be a merger between SKF and Volvo, Volvo once being a subsidiary of SKF.)

Manning decisions are often considered to be strategic. Certainly, there are several examples in corporate histories where the change of the corporate managing director has had a profound effect on corporate development. Similarly, the recruitment of a top-ranked researcher or technologist may be highly significant for the technological development of the corporation. In fact, Astra considers such a recruitment as a strategic decision or rather as a strategic decision area. There is a policy in Astra to invest in highly qualified R&D personnel, but this policy has hardly evolved as a result of a strategic decision. In connection with manning decisions, one may also argue that they may be reversed and thus are not necessarily strategic. To a certain extent this is true, and there are possibilities to fire, replace or demote a person. However, certain positions *per se* are equipped with power, and certain individuals are powerful in themselves, and with their instinct and need for power they will change the power relations in the organization. It may then be a difficult task for other decision makers in the organization to reverse the decision to combine a certain position with a certain individual. The possibilities of making manning decisions in a step-wise or incremental manner may be used in recruiting and sometimes also in promotion, but are seldom used for the position as corporate managing director.

The dependence on certain key individuals in R&D and innovation is witnessed in almost all corporations, although the strategic nature of recruitment decisions may vary. Also, decision-making behaviour differs regarding personal orientation or content orientation in managing R&D and innovation (see Chapter 7). For example, in R&D-intensive corporations (such as Philips-Sweden and Astra) cases may be found where certain individuals are supported on the merit of their being competent and expansive rather than certain areas of competence being supported *per se*. This increases the strategic nature of such manning decisions.

Decisions to enter a new area of competence or to specialize or to define a business idea are also sometimes considered as strategic in retrospect. However, they are often conceptual decisions, loosely connected to significant resource commitments. Rather, this is a case of R&D policies evolving without strategic decisions (see Chapter 5).

In general R&D budgeting decisions are seldom considered to be strategic decisions. A principle of budgeting, if applied, is mostly arrived at by learning and bargaining. Naturally, exceptions may be found, such as the commitment to a large R&D project or a sharp cut in R&D budgets. The discontinuation of, as well as a disinvestment in, a large project not only often signifies a strategic decision regarding the termination of certain operations but also creates financial room for new strategic decisions. In fact, there are several cases of R&D operations that have been initiated or strengthened as a result of a marked increase in available resources.

R&D and strategic decision making

As to R&D policies or strategies concerning technological leadership or forms for exploitation of technological knowledge, these also develop in an evolutionary manner. They may be influenced by other strategic decisions, but they hardly derive from strategic decisions made with respect to these policies or strategies. Technological leadership, however, is sometimes achieved in an intermittent fashion by a corporation in certain product areas and markets, and significant R&D efforts may result from a perceived threat or a perceived need to gain a lead. Sometimes, the intermittent behaviour derives from a suddenly raised awareness, but often it is also a conscious strategy. This relates to the formation of product generations, which in certain industries is a common feature. Examples include passenger cars, jet engines, certain pharmaceuticals, computers, certain instruments, and certain separators. The extent to which generations are formed may vary and may be subjected to decision making. Certainly, the development of a new product generation may be considered a strategic decision in some technologies and markets, as well as a decision to skip one generation in a succession of generation shifts. In Philips-Sweden one has experienced several substitutions in product technologies, and in certain areas strategic decisions in this respect have been made, sometimes with 3-4 years in between, during which time ideas arise and market requirements develop.

On the whole then, several types or areas of decisions may be distinguished, and for some of these types or areas strategic decisions are more likely than for others. Strategic decisions made with respect to R&D are, however, in general difficult to find. Rather, R&D decisions are conditioned upon other strategic decisions or appear as strategic only in combination with subsequent decisions.

6.2.2 R&D decision making

If historically there has been a low frequency in general of strategic decisions made with respect to R&D, one may ask how the R&D decision making processes are structured. An illustration is given in Case 6.2.

Case 6.2 SKF

Throughout SKF there is a superimposed organization for R&D management, comprising permanent and temporary bodies for general, technical and R&D management levels of operation. The principal R&D management bodies at corporate level are:

(a) *Product Board*. Principal tasks are strategic decisions and policy making with respect to R&D and corporate development, especially diversification. It supervises a small innovation company at corporate level.
(b) *Technical Executives Board*. Principal tasks are formation of R&D policies and evaluation and control of product R&D projects. It recommends the establishment of development centres and supervises the central R&D laboratory.
(c) *Machinery Board*. Principal tasks are policy making and evaluation and control of process R&D projects.

The essential composition of these bodies is shown in Table 6.1. These R&D management bodies are permanent. Attached to Machinery Board and

Table 6.1 Essential composition of principal R&D management bodies in SKF

	Product Board	Technical Executives Board	Machinery Board
Concern management			
Corporate managing director	c		o
Divisional managers	x		
Director group engineering and research	x	c	x
Director group manufacturing engineering	x	x	c
Operating management			
Manufacturing managers in major subsidiaries			x
R&D managers in major subsidiaries		x	
Management of the innovation company	o		
Management of the central R&D laboratory		x	

Notation:

c = Chairman
x = Regular member
o = Attend non-regularly

Technical Executives Board are, moreover, committees for different areas and temporary multinational working groups. In total, 230 persons were engaged around the world in this R&D management structure in 1976.

The system for R&D project control differs between, on one hand, product R&D as managed by the Product Board and Technical Executives Board, and, on the other, process R&D as managed by the Machinery Board. Process R&D is controlled in a less formal and elaborate way partly because of the in-house nature of the 'market' for process R&D. Corresponding co-ordination is taken care of through overlapping management bodies and project information routines.

All non-process R&D projects will be classified along the following principal dimensions:

— the range of interest among subsidiaries;
— project purpose (e.g., diversification);
— product line;
— technological character;
— responsibility for project management and sponsor.

This main classification of projects determines the different courses of management action in relation to the project. Criteria for evaluation of projects are rather conventional and, for example, concern credibility of technical and commercial success, cost, timing, size and share of potential world market, market growth characteristics, and strategic need. These criteria apply with different

accuracy, depending on project type and stage. Together with qualitative judgements on both portfolio and project level, ratings along these criteria form the basis for project priorities.
[End of Case 6.2]

SKF represents a case with formal and elaborate routines for project establishment and control and structured R&D decision making to a higher extent than in most of the other corporations, although there are several similarities to the other corporations with respect to structure and processes of R&D decision making. The Product Board has strategic decision making as a principal task, but it is doubtful to what extent such a decision-making body will be able to make strategic R&D decisions. Such a decision-making body may be difficult to gather for strategic decisions. Often decisions are made on lower levels, and higher levels may be left with more or less counter-signing roles. This tends to be the case particularly when technology moves fast, as in Philips. Moreover, many strategic R&D decisions, such as manning of key posts or investing in R&D facilities, may be made 'outside the system'. However, it is, in fact, too early to assess the impact of the R&D decision-making system in SKF on the nature and frequency of strategic decisions. It should also be added that a prime purpose of such a system may be to achieve consensus and co-ordination in R&D (see Chapter 4). The making of strategic decisions may not be desirable in itself but rather the collective quality of R&D decisions has to be considered. This is also indicated by the few possible future strategic R&D decisions conceived of in the corporations by the interviewees. The validity of this observation is, however, questionable.

6.3 DISCUSSION

6.3.1 Empirical summary

In general, a low frequency of strategic decisions was indicated, especially strategic decisions made with respect to R&D. R&D decisions were often conditioned upon other strategic decisions, such as large resource commitments. Examples of strategic decisions or decision areas for R&D are manning on key posts, investment and location of R&D facilities, acceptance of a large order, introduction of a new technology in products and processes, and discontinuation of a project. An over-riding impression is, however, the difficulties associated with sorting out strategic decisions from other types of decisions and events. The decision-making pattern, moreover, varies according to industry, technology, and corporation.

6.3.2 Strategizing and R&D decision making

Large decision-making efforts are neither a necessary nor a sufficient condition for large decision-making effects. If a decision is assessed to be strategic on the basis of some threshold values to be exceeded by efforts and effects associated with the decision, the frequency of strategic decisions is naturally dependent upon the choice of these threshold values. Any quantitative assessment will not be penetrated here, but rather the nature of R&D decisions related to the nature of strategic decisions.

First, the size of the effect of a decision could be assessed with respect to duration, number of other decisions affected, and degree to which the conditions of these other decisions are affected. Naturally, effects of decisions become interconnected, and it may be highly difficult to assess the size of the effect of some specific decision. Nevertheless, the inflexibility resulting from a decision is important for assessing its strategic character. Here irreversible resource commitments are typically giving a strategic character to a decision. R&D decisions in capital-intensive industries are largely conditioned upon materialized investment decisions, similar to the way R&D decisions in a laboratory are largely conditioned upon expensive instrumentation. The commitments may be both of an economic and psychological nature.

Manning decisions and decisions to reorganize may to some extent be thought of as revocable, although some relations may deteriorate to an irreparable degree. However, they often have long lasting effects, even if the effects may not always be profound. For example corporate managing directors, (CMDs), technical directors, and R&D managers may be in office for decades. For the corporations in this sample, the CMDs in 1977 were appointed CMD in 1966 on average. CMDs in large corporations in Sweden, as studied by Bolin and Dahlberg (1975), had occupied their posts for seven-and-a-half years on average. These and similar lengths of time for other significant actors may be compared with times from idea stage to innovation and product life times. In this sample of corporations no statistical connection was indicated between turnover of significant actors or frequency of organizational changes and, for example, R&D intensity, although clearly there were cases in which technological changes were associated with such changes in organization and manning. The point is, however, that decisions in connection with these kinds of changes are not necessarily strategic *per se* but only in combination with the way subsequent decision making is conditioned upon these decisions.

Second, the empirical difficulties associated with assessing whether a decision is strategic or not indicate the limited possibilities there are for classifying decisions into strategic, tactical and operative ones. To slice the importance of decisions in this way necessarily involves some arbitrariness. Moreover, it is doubtful if a specification of three general types of decisions captures the interdependence in decision making. Is it a tactical or a strategic decision to re-centralize strategic decision making when decentralization has been perceived by top management as having gone too far in connection with divisionalization? Decisions may naturally be sequentially dependent over time as well as connected to each other in the organization. Inter-organizational decision making is also increasing in importance, due to the cost and complexity of technological innovation (Gerstenfeld, 1977). Thus, the commonly encountered subdivision of decisions by three into strategic, tactical and operative ones may become increasingly inapplicable due to increased interdependence in decision making.

A third question, then, is why decisions concerning R&D are made with a low

R&D and strategic decision making

frequency of concentrated decision-making efforts in the corporations. Keeping in mind the arbitrary element in assessing frequency and the many kinds of R&D decisions, some general features of R&D decision making may be brought forward as explanations. Decisions concerning R&D and innovation are characterized by a high degree of uncertainty, a low degree of repetitiveness and a long time perspective. Also, there are seldom distinct alternatives and expected values of outcomes may be fuzzy over the set of alternatives. The outcomes may, however, differ widely — and a large risk may be involved. In general, there are time pressures involved but not often in the form of clearly recognized deadlines after which the value of decisions drop radically. The distribution of relevant information for making R&D decisions is generally skew among managers and personnel. Moreover, the process by which relevant information is generated and a decision situation is triggered typically involves randomness. Finally, there may be disparities in the values and behaviours of the people involved in R&D and innovation, which is to be distinguished from uncertainty in value assessments and uncertainty in the assessments of behaviour. Several of these general features, which apply to varying extents to different decision situations, appear to smooth out decision-making efforts in decision making concerning R&D and innovation. For example, a lack of deadlines in combination with diffuse alternatives — as in the choice of direction for building up new competence — will not promote a concentration of decision-making efforts. This tendency may be further accentuated by skewly distributed information and a disparity in values.

Often there are parallel projects or lines along which, say, a diversification objective or an R&D objective is attempted. When total resource requirements increase relative to total resource availability, the number of lines may be cut according to some criterion of expected profitability or utility as in capital budgeting in general. The decision to terminate a line could be thought of as a tactical decision, while decisions about the structure of the whole portfolio and the criteria on which to judge projects could be thought of as strategic. However, as empirical observations show, there will be individuals in the organization who successively tie their interests and emotions to current projects. If the number of parallel projects is cut down to a final one, the continuation of this last alternative may be reinforced. Also, people involved in an R&D project will underestimate costs and time involved, even with some regularity with respect to type of situation.

An analytical reason to continue work on an old R&D project, which has caused cost overruns already, is that in the selection of projects in the portfolio, the continuation of an old project may be considered analytically as a new project. If, as is mostly the case, the benefits of the project accrue in its later stages more than proportional to costs of completion, the expected profitability of costs of completion will rise. It is then easy to see how regular underestimation in early stages of an R&D project, combined with arguments in later stages based on expected profitability of costs of completion, will reinforce the tendency of R&D work to continue along the lines once established.

This suggests that the real opportunities for strategic R&D decisions concerning R&D projects are in the early stages of initiation and establishment and in the late stages of termination. The acts of omission to initiate new R&D projects may be of significance collectively but can hardly be considered as a series of strategic decisions. The same holds for the acts of omission to terminate a current R&D project.

An emphasis on the strategic nature of embryonic decisions in R&D, (i.e., decisions in the early stages of initiation and establishment), may be found in Steele (1975) and Gluck and Foster (1975). The attention paid by top management to R&D may also be scarce, especially in the early stages of an R&D decision-making process in which resource commitments have not yet become conspicuous. These circumstances lead to a simplistic conclusion that top management should be engaged in the making of embryonic R&D decisions as described by Gluck and Foster (1975). This conclusion is not shared by Steele (1975), who considers it doubtful whether top management interventionism as a matter of routine would contribute to the quality of R&D decision making (see Section 7.3). On the other hand, a series of interconnected commitments made by embryonic decisions may create a type of unwanted *fait accompli* or inertia in the organization as described above. However, one has to distinguish between the desirability of making a strategic decision and the desirability of involving different individuals in the strategic decision. To design a decision-making process by interspersing large decision-making efforts in the series of decisions may be called strategizing the process; to involve an expanding collection of decision makers in the decision-making process may be referred to as politicizing the process. Simplified, it then appears that certain R&D decision-making processes in a large organization benefit from being strategized early while being politicized late. At least, it may be concluded that early politicizing without strategizing may be hazardous in light of the skew distribution of innovative and entrepreneurial talents in a large organization. Naturally, strategizing and politicizing are matters of degree. Uncertainty resolution and consensus seeking in R&D may benefit from sequential and political decision making to different extents. An extreme case would be a 'one-shot' strategic decision made by a single person. The influence exercised by significant actors, such as entrepreneurs and inventors, may occur, but group decision making is a common feature in R&D and innovation in large organizations, at least in the later stages of innovation. The emphasis in SKF (Case 6.2) on careful preparation and early consensus seeking in the R&D process followed by a determined action is not uncommon and in fact resembles the Japanese way of decision making, the Ringi system (Yoshino, 1976, p. 165), at least in its superficial aspects. (Socialization in a corporate culture as practised in Japan is a 'soft' way of achieving co-ordination and motivation but may present difficulties when implemented in a multinational organization.)

6.4 CONCLUSIONS

By definition a strategic decision has been determined by the size of a concentrated decision-making effort as well as by the size of the effect of a decision. A low frequency of strategic decisions made with respect to R&D was indicated. However, due to increased interdependence in decision making, there was a

R&D and strategic decision making

limited applicability of the subdivision of decisions by three, into strategic, tactical and operative decisions based on notions of importance.

Often R&D decisions were conditioned upon other strategic decisions or appear to be strategic in connection with subsequent decisions and omissions to make decisions. The low frequency of strategic R&D decisions may derive from general features of R&D decision making, such as diffuse alternatives and lack of deadlines.

To design a decision-making process by interspersing large decision making efforts in the series of decisions is called strategizing. To strategize R&D decision making in embryonic stages is found to be important as well as in the later stages of the termination of a project. In a large organization consensus seeking also has to supplement uncertainty resolution at some stage, but it is doubtful that politicizing the decision making about R&D and innovation at an early stage is effective, at least as far as radical innovation is concerned. In particular the effectiveness of the Japanese way of decision making could be questioned in this context.

Chapter 7
R&D AND CORPORATE MANAGEMENT

7.1 INTRODUCTION

The role of management in corporate histories, policy making, strategic decision making, organizations, subcultures, conflicts and barriers to innovation has been discussed in other chapters. The aim of this chapter is to present personal views of top managers and R&D managers concerning their way of handling R&D. Another aim is to point out some important dimensions of the management of R&D based on these views and the information presented in the other chapters and literature.

Since 'management' and related terms have been discussed in Section 1.2, only a few points will be added here. 'Management is what managers do' is one example of a trivial definition, which simply defers the question of definition to the definition of manager. As will be discussed in the following sections, it is far from clear what managers actually do, and it is very important to realize that R&D management is not solely what R&D managers do.

'Management' may refer to a group of managers; to a set of activities, functions, roles and tasks, or to a body of knowledge and skills. Thus, R&D management may refer to activities carried out by top managers concerning R&D or to a group of R&D managers or to the activities carried out by R&D managers. The phrase 'top manager' refers to a member of top management as recognized in the specific corporation. 'General managers' are those with a cross-functional responsibility for a business unit, for instance, a corporation, a division, or a subsidiary. R&D managers may be found on several levels, such as in corporate staffs, R&D departments, laboratories and project teams. The boundaries between R&D management and R&D personnel are often diffuse. Finally, it should be pointed out that 'manager' is used here in a wide sense and may include both 'entrepreneur' and 'administrator'.

It is well known that management has been professionalized and separated from the ownership of capital. Furthermore, the growth, diversification and internationalization of corporations have given rise to differentiation of managerial roles as well as to a kind of general management covering different functions, products and regions.

Another long-term trend is the growth of R&D within industry. R&D management has also been professionalized to some extent and often also separated from providing R&D skills. As industrial R&D grows, diversifies and internationalizes in interplay with corporate development, a need also arises for specialized as well general R&D managers. In large corporations entrepreneurial roles have largely been separated from R&D management, and managerial specialization has caused a fragmentation of managerial responsibilities in the innovation process.

There is often a separation between top management and R&D in the sense that many problems are caused by too little involvement in R&D matters from the top, rather than from too much involvement. The problem studied here is how managers at these two management levels view R&D and their respective roles in managing R&D.

7.2 EMPIRICAL FINDINGS

7.2.1 The board and R&D

In all the corporations studied, managerial influences on R&D seem to be exercised through key individuals rather than through management bodies such as a committee or the board of directors. Moreover, shareholders are not generally considered to have any influence on R&D, and it is interesting to note that the corporate board exercises only a marginal amount of direct influence. The board engages in the investment in a new R&D laboratory and is occasionally informed about other issues concerning R&D, but in general very little of the board's time is devoted to R&D. The start of the production of a new product, the implementation of a new process, or the progress of a large-scale project are other examples of issues which may be brought up to the board, but mostly then it is too late to influence R&D.

Two factors have been presented as the important factors behind the marginal role of the board in R&D management, namely competence and secrecy. R&D issues often appear intricate, and many people are afraid to delve into them. This view on R&D issues is widely accepted and may be used as a reason to avoid bringing them up. In the words of the Chairman of the Board and former Corporate Managing Director of Volvo: 'Both during my time and my predecessor's it was said that the Board will not comprehend this thing about product development'. Traditionally, the competence profile of corporate boards has not included the competence to judge R&D and technological change to any large extent.

The second main argument for not dealing with R&D is secrecy. Corporate boards constitute an information network in industry, but there are definite secrecy barriers in this network concerning R&D and it has been said that 'If you have said something about a new product to the Board, the next day the whole country knows'.

Thus, one may conclude that top management, and especially the corporate managing director, has large possibilities to exercise influence on R&D. One may see this as a delegation of responsibility, but it is a delegation with very little supervision. Moreover, the inter-corporate integrative role in industry played by interlocking corporate boards is negligible concerning R&D.

7.2.2 Top management relations to R&D

7.2.2.1 Top management views on the nature and role of R&D

In interviews with top managers about R&D and its management, some underlying attitudes and basic distinctions recur. These concern the nature of R&D

and R&D people and the role of R&D in the corporation. Starting with top managers' conceptions, in general terms, of the role of R&D in the corporation, a common feature of the answers is the emphasis on the corporation as a whole and the corporate economy. A common theme is the economic contribution of R&D to corporate economy, although this contribution may not be correctly assessed. Importance for the whole, concern about resources, overall priorities, balancing corporate parts and external relations are among issues of primary concern. The corporate managing directors of large corporations sound like pronounced institutionalists in their emphasis on corporate existence, stable development of the corporation and corporate identity. This constitutes a basic context in which industrial R&D is judged. Moreover, there is a prevalent opinion that R&D activities easily drift away from corporate goals. The Corporate Managing Director of Alfa-Laval has said that 'A university is not permitted to be built up within the corporation'.

Naturally, the answers vary. First of all, R&D is considered to play different roles in relation to profit, growth, diversification and internationalization. This is a natural dimension of variation, considering that the corporations represent a diversity of industries, products and technologies. References are also often made to the characteristics of a specific industry. These views have implications for the utilization of R&D personnel in the corporation and for policy making concerning product leadership. The Corporate Managing Director of Astra is a definite advocate of growth through R&D aiming at new products. He considers growth, in turn, to be a necessary condition for existence to be able to cope with cost increases. On the other hand, the Corporate Managing Director of Iggesund does not believe in R&D as a source of new products. Leadership in product R&D is not considered profitable at Volvo, while it is considered as a necessity at Alfa-Laval. Similar examples may be given of top managers' views on the role of R&D in diversification. The Corporate Managing Director of Iggesund does not want internal R&D to aim at inventions but just to keep the company informed about external technological change and to maintain a capacity to assimilate new developments. Volvo and Astra do not aim at diversification any longer and R&D is not supposed to play a role in that respect. Top managers at Volvo and Astra admit that radical inventions within the corporations would create embarrassment. 'It is hard to take care of innovations that crop up at random in a large organization'. On the other hand, diversification is an objective at SKF, but the Corporate Managing Director does not believe in R&D as a means of achieving it and has stated that 'It is probably not possible to invent oneself into diversification. It is like a drop in the ocean.'

The threat orientation varies among top managers. That is, the confidence in a traditional product or technology varies as well as the readiness to respond to signals of technological changes. A majority, however, do not believe in any severe threat to the traditional product of the corporation. A marked exception is the Corporate Managing Director of Alfa-Laval, who has initiated an examination of each product in order to identify possible and probable technological substitutions. An absence of a threat orientation among top managers does not imply, however, a corresponding absence in the organization. One reason is that a threat orientation may be instrumental in R&D work. In other words 'You can't go around and tell people that there is no threat'. Besides, the kind of event that corresponds to a threat or an opportunity is to a large degree a matter of speed of response in relation to present and future competitors.

Other differences of opinion among top managers on the role of R&D concern the role of R&D in relation to marketing and production, the role of product R&D versus process R&D, the role of research versus development, the role of internal R&D versus external R&D and the role of radical versus incremental innovation. Top managers seem to have formed many of these views gradually and were influenced, naturally, by their background, career, successes and failures, etc. They have come to more or less strong beliefs about R&D matters. The provability of these beliefs is low, which tends to reinforce them. Another reinforcing circumstance in the formation of these views is that confirming social constructions of reality are favoured in some corporations and industries. Finally, some of the views are reinforced simply by their self-fulfilling properties. This is especially true when a particular view prevails in a whole industry, for example that the industry is not innovative and that innovative work does not pay.

Concerning views on R&D people, or rather on technologists in general, which is the category most commonly referred to, it is difficult to tell from the answers where experience leaves off and theory begins. An elitist view prevails — a few high achievers are considered responsible for most of the R&D achievements. Examples of the results from fiery spirits and gifted technologists have a great impact on the formation of views on technologists in general. Examples of lack of results from a large number of R&D people point in the same direction, even if questions of resources and organization are also involved.

High achievers are considered different in other respects as well. The eccentric guy in a garage lives on as one stereotype of the inventor, at least when radical invention is considered. Similar stereotypes exist of professional researchers, the latter often being distinguished from inventors. The devotion of technologists to a certain solution or technology is often noted. Not only do technologists fall in love easily with a solution or a technology, especially if it is advanced, but they also remain faithful to it and easily become defensive and possessive. As the Corporate Managing Director of Alfa-Laval stated:

> Since technologists easily identify themselves with an existing technology, it is laborious to initiate R&D aiming at substitutions. One possibility is to engage people, who haven't been too involved in the past work of the corporation. However, it is doubtful if one should use any form of technical auditors as a kind of inspectors . . . .Presumably the primary barrier to R&D aiming at substitutions is not ageing knowledge or stagnating people, but the emotional involvement of R&D people.

Another recurring element in the views on R&D people is the effect of age on performance and behaviour. The correlation between youth and creativity is a commonly held belief, both in theory and practice. Young people are also presumed to be more flexible and to have more drive. In addition, they usually have a more recent university education. The preference for young people in R&D work may, however, have a self-fulfilling effect on the underlying views.

7.2.2.2 Top management roles in relation to R&D

In this subsection the focus will be on the roles of the corporate managing director in relation to R&D as perceived by the corporate managing directors themselves. First of all, it may be observed that not much of the corporate managing director's time is allocated to R&D and that there may be several causes for this (for example, that R&D is considered to be of secondary importance to the corporation, or that the corporate managing director's involvement in R&D issues is considered to be of secondary importance to the corporation, or that the corporate managing director wants to become more involved but feels a lack of competence or seldom finds time due to pressing daily matters). Moreover, R&D may be narrowly defined or R&D may be discussed in terms of technology, technological change, quality and innovation. Also, discussions of this kind may be so integrated with other top management discussions that it is meaningless to identify and quantify a certain proportion of management time allocated specifically to R&D issues. However, the opinion that more management time should be spent on R&D is often presented by top managers. Now, if this is so, what kind of roles would corporate managing directors play in R&D?

According to the general pattern of the interview answers, these roles coincide with ordinary managerial functions such as resource allocation, manning, organizing, planning and decision making. The frequency to which these managerial functions are explicitly referred to is roughly in the order mentioned. However, distinct emphasis is placed on resource allocation and the manning of key R&D posts, and a typical answer would outline the most important tasks of a corporate managing director in relation to R&D as follows:

(a) to determine overall economic dimensions for R&D in the corporation;
(b) to appoint R&D managers and align ambitions of R&D people with corporate goals.

Naturally, the answers are more detailed, varied and circumstantial than indicated above. The corporate managing directors vary in explicit emphasis within the list of ordinary managerial functions as well as with respect to the content they give to a certain role or function. Thus, the Corporate Managing Director of Alfa-Laval points out that the determination and integration of objectives and policies for R&D have to dominate over questions of organization, and the Corporate Managing Director of KemaNobel stresses the initiation of strategic planning with integrated R&D.

Concerning resource allocation, which is most frequently considered an important task of the corporate managing director, there are marked differences in budgeting behaviour. The Corporate Managing Director of Astra has a purely financial outlook. The resource generation process has to be balanced in certain respects and investments in R&D, production, and marketing dimensioned accordingly. In other words 'The equations have to balance'. A certain percentage range of the turnover is used for allocating resources to R&D, and the corporate managing director can be a barrier if anyone wants to go beyond this range. In other respects this corporate managing director does not interfere in the resource allocation process. Usually, in the resource allocation process, a corporate managing director is taking a more active interest also in the content of R&D work. Additional roles may then be to secure a proper balance between R&D of existing and new products (Corporate Managing Director, Alfa-Laval), to secure the choice of suitable areas (Subsidiary Managing Director, Astra-Hässle), to make sure adequate R&D resources exist in the different divisions in the light of the tendency of divisional managers to think in the short term (Corporate Managing Director, KemaNobel), or simply to curb the ambitions of R&D people, since these tend to be self-generating (Corporate Managing Director, Iggesund).

There is a similar variation among corporate managing directors in their active interest in the work of R&D people. Appointing R&D managers is naturally very important, and the tendency of R&D people to have too high or otherwise misdirected ambitions in relation to the corporation as a whole is commonly noted by general managers. Few corporate managing directors, however, emphasize other managerial roles in relation to R&D personnel. One may also think that a financial orientation precludes a people orientation. That this is not necessarily so is illustrated by the following answer by the Corporate Managing Director of Alfa-Laval:

> ... For a managing director, total responsibility and priorities are of primary importance. It is therefore natural that caution and a certain threat-orientation dominate over promises and new developments. . . At the same time the entrepreneurial spirit has to be kept alive, which may be difficult. Moreover, a managing director must articulate certain basic principles, for instance, the need to be market oriented.
>
> One of the most important contributions of top management is the changing of unfavorable attitudes of people. . . Thus navel gazing and Not-invented-here resistance have to be discouraged, and R&D people have to be made aware of the fact that some kind of profitability objective is required. It is undoubtedly difficult for R&D to operate with the overriding objective of a business corporation. Profit must be generated and the resource renewal has to be controlled.

An example of an explicit people orientation is provided by the Subsidiary Managing Director of Astra-Hässle. He points out the importance of the spirit in the company and the fact that the subsidiary managing director 'understands R&D' and has a positive attitude to R&D. He does not, however, influence the content of R&D or give ideas for it: 'A managing director can't invent new pharmaceuticals'. When R&D was established at Astra-Hässle and began to yield business results, new demands were placed on management style, which meant more work on strategies and internationalization. The subsidiary managing director also sees his role as providing resources for the R&D people he has confidence in, especially making provisions for two or three key researchers in the company, and at the same time balancing the criticism against favouritism. Moreover, he has to protect the R&D people from disturbances arising, for example, from resource struggles or from other people impatiently waiting for R&D results. His confidence in the researchers is based on evaluations made by other professionals. The latter is not uncommon for managers who do not feel capable of a direct evaluation or consider a financial evaluation of R&D insufficient.

The emphasis on planning seems to correlate with management experience. Top managers, including divisional and subsidiary managers, tend to emphasize planning *per se* when they are new to the post. As their familiarity with operations in general increases over the years, they tend to be more content oriented. Planning is thus an instrument for providing management with information and also for generating information in the organization. This informational role does not, however, have to be manifested in formal planning. Other less formal ways are for managing directors to ask R&D people perceptive questions, to 'dive' into an R&D project more or less at random, or to initiate analyses with new concepts or new angles of approach. To 'keep informed' actively is also a way for a managing director to encourage the thinking and behaviour of R&D people.

Organization and co-ordination are mentioned as important managerial roles in several cases, although not as often as resource allocation and matters of personnel management. It is common to refer to a past corporate managing director as an entrepreneur, an administrator, a production man, an internationalizer, and so on. The situation of SKF in the 1970s made it natural for the corporate managing director to view himself as a co-ordinator and a diversifier. Moreover, he has to concentrate his efforts on basic matters of corporate development, that is, 'A managing director can hardly get more than two things done'.

Organizational matters of top management concern in R&D include the proper balance between centralization and decentralization, the balance between traditional and new divisions, the handling of new ideas organizationally, and the co-ordination of inter-divisional R&D. The organizational solutions to some of these problems vary among the corporations, as described in Chapter 8. To initiate re-organization is a traditional role of top management, but an additional one is to maintain consistent implementation of a chosen organizational principle for a period of time, with such comments as 'Choose the organizational form and then be consistent.' and 'The organization has to settle'. Thus KemaNobel and Volvo have chosen an almost complete decentralization of R&D to the divisions, and interdivisional co-ordination of R&D is marginal. A future phase of co-ordination is conceived of when different technical solutions have appeared in the present organization: 'Then maybe a new managing director will come and say that it must not be this way'.

Frequently, the traditional part of an organization has gained attention from managers and R&D people more according to its relative size than to its relative potential. To 'lift up' other parts then becomes the natural task of a successor. Besides, traditional parts tend to suppress or drive out deviant activities. The Corporate Managing Director of SKF thus considers it an important task to make sure that an organizational separation is made between work on traditional and non-traditional products. He also wants to stimulate innovativeness and opposes the tendency in traditional activities to focus R&D work on small, 'molecular' refinements.

Decision making as a top management role in R&D is discussed only marginally. Of course, resource allocation involves decision making, but beyond that no special reference is made to decision making. The Subsidiary Managing Director

R&D and corporate management

of Philips-Sweden wants to be involved in decisions about R&D that cannot easily be changed or that involve high risks, but since technological change is fast and R&D decentralized, he is often confronted with proposals with many commitments already made on lower levels. Sometimes top management in such situations is left with a more or less ratifying role in R&D decision making.

7.2.2.3 Competences and sources of information in top management

An important question is whether or not a managing director should have technological competence or, less bluntly stated, to what degree an managing director should involve technological competence in top management and how he should utilize it. It is a commonly accepted principle of general management that a managing director should not involve himself 'too much' in technical matters, and most managing directors express their awareness that it could be risky to do so. It may be detrimental both to the managing director and to the technical work. The role as a generator of technological ideas is considered obsolete for a managing director, at least on the corporate level. Many also express their concern over not directing R&D 'too much' in technological aspects. The behaviour and attitudes, however, vary depending upon the background of the managing director.

Those who have a technical background have special areas of interest, which they may want to follow after they have become a managing director. They see it as an advantage to have this kind of background, making it easier for them to talk with R&D people and understand their problems and also to avoid delays in decision making about R&D due to a lack of competence in top management. They may contribute technically with a broader overview, thus making new combinations of knowledge possible. In some cases, however, the corporate managing director may go far in intervening in technical matters. The Corporate Managing Director of SKF, for instance, made a decision about the design of railway bearings against the opinion of other technologists, as he perceived it: 'Technologists often become defensive. I have to change such attitudes.' A technological background certainly gives a manager the capacity to 'dive' into technical work. The former Corporate Managing Director of Volvo was always concerned with the technical functioning and quality of a product. On the basis of customer complaints he could go right down into the organization and 'make a fuss'. Obviously, 'diving' can be done in several ways, and here it refers to a direct and sudden observation of some part of the operations of an organization, not necessarily followed by intervention. This may be an efficient way for a corporate managing director to keep the necessary contact with operations without having his attention absorbed by them, while at the same time it may be effective in 'moving the organization'.

Non-technologists, such as the Corporate Managing Director of Astra, take an active part in R&D matters in aspects other than purely technological ones, and it is a misconception that a technical background is a necessary or sufficient condition for beneficial involvement of a top manager in R&D matters. The Corporate Managing Director of Alfa-Laval points out that it is more important to have technical competence on the marketing side, for example. However, as a non-technologist, he has a need for popular science, and he has to find good popularizers within and outside the corporation. The need to supplement internal sources of information on R&D and technology with external ones is also pointed out by the Corporate Managing Director of Astra and other general managers. Astra also has a scientific advisory board at the corporate level. The Corporate Managing Director of Alfa-Laval sees the advantages with such an organized connection with external expertise in science and technology but adds that: 'A too multi-disciplinary and general scientific advisory board without a product connection may, however, become a downright drawback'. The majority of attitudes among technologists towards a scientific advisory board are quite negative and summary. For example:

> An advisory board without responsibility has difficulties in functioning. (Corporate Managing Director, KemaNobel)

> Can't see the value of such an advisory board. Maybe some American company needs it. (Former Corporate Managing Director, Volvo)

> A scientific advisory board is of value only the first year. Then the professors have little more to contribute. (Corporate Managing Director, SKF).

The question of a corporate managing director's sources of information concerning R&D and technological change is closely related to the provision of technological competence in top management. In addition to what has been said above, some dimensions of variations in information-seeking behaviour may be pointed out. First, there is the balance between the managing director's reliance upon internal versus external sources of information and to what extent he relies upon his own previous experience and knowledge. Non-technologists here seem to rely to a larger extent on external sources than technologists do.

Secondly, the corporate managing directors vary with respect to their reliance upon formal and regular reporting versus informal, selective, and *ad hoc* oriented sources of information. For internal information some rely mainly on regular meetings, plans and reviews, while others supplement their information by initiating reviews and analyses, by having informal speaking partners or reporters, by following certain R&D projects, or by 'diving' and 'looking more than listening'. In other words 'It is always difficult to get people to spontaneously report when something goes wrong'. For external information, on the other hand, the information sources are mostly *ad hoc* oriented, and 'Information comes at you from all sides'. Obtaining external information relevant to R&D for a diversified corporation is a problem. It was also mentioned that the larger the corporation is, the more *ad hoc* oriented the sources of information are. Travel to foreign subsidiaries and customers may give a corporate managing director a picture of actual situations and an international perspective. Also, work at the board level in industry may give valuable contacts and information about trends, but—as already mentioned—there is much secrecy on this level concerning R&D. The well-developed network of professional organizations and contacts in a nation like Sweden is also considered valuable in providing top management with external information.

Finally, it should be noted that top management seldom consists of just the managing director (although this is the case at KemaNobel). The way in which

R&D and corporate management

working roles in general are differentiated within top management is an elusive subject. Sometimes, corporate long-term successes are attributed to a good top management team with complementary personality characteristics and abilities. With respect to management of R&D and technology, responsibilities may be formally assigned to a technical director as at Philips-Sweden, Alfa-Laval and Boliden or more or less informally assigned to a deputy managing director as at Astra and Volvo or shared by the corporate managing director and his deputy as at Iggesund or formally assigned to corporate staff directors as at KemaNobel and SKF. It is beyond the scope of this book to analyse these different types of solutions. Besides, it is more a matter of personal abilities and interests than formal solutions. It is not at all certain that having a man as technical director is a good way to 'anchor' technological competence and concern for R&D and technological change in top management. Often technical directors are production oriented rather than R&D oriented, and also they often develop a selective technological focus (see Chapter 11).

7.2.3 Working roles of R&D managers

There are many individuals in a corporation who influence R&D. Among these some are formally recognized as managers of R&D and technology on different levels, such as corporate, divisional, subsidiary, department, laboratory and project levels. There are also many ways for a manager to perceive and articulate his working roles. In answering the question about their most important working roles in relation to R&D, some describe their many assignments and formal duties, while others try to go beyond the formally recognized roles. For some, a written description of their responsibilities comes first to mind, for others a developed management philosophy.

In this section the focus will be on more or less full-time R&D managers above the project level and their self-perceived working roles. It is natural that there is a normative content in the answers, and a variety of aspects are due to corporate specifics. An attempt has been made to avoid the character of a management handbook.

References to different working roles, tasks, functions, etc. have been grouped as follows:

— R&D personnel oriented roles;
— R&D content oriented roles;
— relation-oriented roles;
— traditional 'Fayol' roles;
— miscellaneous roles.

This grouping is somewhat unspecific, but although the groups of roles overlap, the classification has been made mutually exclusive to make an aggregated measure of emphasis possible. Thus, the relative frequency of references to roles in the different groups are 41 per cent, 30 per cent, 15 per cent, 13 per cent and 1 per cent, respectively. These are approximate figures, with perhaps just one digit significant, but still they reflect the distribution of emphasis among many individual R&D managers.

7.2.3.1 Management of R&D personnel

Almost every R&D manager perceived recruitment, retention and utilization of R&D personnel as highly important managerial roles. The skill necessary in performing these roles was considered to be more an art than a science. Incidentally, it was pointed out that a personnel department can assist very little in these matters.

The recruitment situation varies among corporations. Some claim they traditionally attract good people (then good people in turn tend to attract good people); others are hampered by prejudices against industrial R&D, inadequate graduate education in a new or narrow field, remote location, difficulties to allow for proper compensation, or internal resistance to recruitment of highly qualified personnel. Counter measures considered were creating co-operative and supporting relationships with universities and young researchers, creating a special professorship, internalizing education, externalizing R&D work, internationalizing, or otherwise relocating and making acquisitions—or investing, when possible—in over-qualified personnel for future use. Mostly, these are long-term arrangements, which depend upon corporate strategy concerning activity areas, technological leadership, alternatives to R&D etc. The problem of recruiting wisely is also complicated by the fact that R&D performance is unevenly distributed among individuals and that the elite in this respect is often deviant in other respects as well. Individualistic elitism, for instance, is often not desired in industrial R&D, and in the words of an R&D manager from Astra-Hässle:

> An advantage of research in the pharmaceutical industry compared to academic research is that the research atmosphere of a company makes people develop more by forcing them to cooperate. Academic researchers and institutions compete more about being first with publications and receiving appointments. At Astra-Hässle the individual effort means less if it cannot be combined with the efforts of others since teamwork is essential in developing a new pharmaceutical. Pharmacologists, physiologists, chemists, biochemists, and medical people have to cooperate with each other.

That 'the academic world develops egoists' is one dimension of the difficulties in performing multidisciplinary R&D and cross-functional co-operation in industry. Another is the difference in value systems between the academic world and industry. Some R&D people accept the business culture when employed in industry, sometimes even in an exaggerated way to distinguish themselves from academic colleagues, while others keep to the science and technology culture in such a way that co-operation with production and marketing people becomes difficult.

The academic world is, however, not the only source of recruitment, and one sometimes gets the impression that corporations are somewhat prejudiced in exploring different sources of recruitment of R&D personnel and also often 'go for the best' according to academic standards. Admittedly, some corporations do not look for top R&D people very eagerly, and for some it might be natural to downgrade academic education depending upon the kind of R&D work involved.

There are several requirements and desirable characteristics of an R&D individual which limit the basis of recruitment. To be able to co-operate with, and assimilate in, an industrial R&D organization and to be able to work within a business context are important factors in addition to the ability to do R&D work. Moreover, the ability to learn and re-learn is possibly more important than pure knowledge in certain fields: 'In our field the half-time of graduate knowledge is roughly two years'. Also, certain general personal characteristics are mentioned as highly desirable such as imagination, generosity and the ability to combine insight with perspective.

A further complication in the recruitment of R&D personnel is the balance between different categories of personnel, or what is in other contexts called portfolio aspects. The following general dimensions of mixing and balancing competences among R&D personnel have been mentioned as examples:

— inventive versus researching abilities;
— technological versus administrative abilities;
— practitioners versus theorists;
— competences in new versus old technologies;
— young versus old people;
— competences in different interdependent technologies.

It may seem as if the problems of recruitment are somewhat overstated. The difficulties are dependent upon how large the R&D organization is and in what aspect it is to grow. In some R&D organizations the recruitment of R&D personnel is not thought of as a problem at all; in some it is considered a minor problem to recruit a new man now and then and maybe extend the competence into an adjacent field, while for some R&D organizations this is a major problem.

The concern about retention and utilization of R&D personnel is generally great. A circumstance often mentioned is that qualified people may be retained only through qualified work. Although this is perhaps a necessary rather than a sufficient condition, it points out the fact that qualified R&D work has two parallel aims. Similar lines of thought are behind the support of an R&D project apart from the mainstream or the support of an inventive individual in order to motivate and establish productive relations. In this respect, an R&D manager may function in the role as a supervisor of professional quality and provider of tasks, being both productive to the corporation and attractive to the professional.

The value differences between the organization and its professionals have already been mentioned. Here the R&D manager may function as a kind of value adapter and motivator. This is not just a matter of making R&D professionals more market oriented. More profound questions about the ethics of science and technology and business arise, but R&D professionals show different amounts of sensitivity to questions of, for example, side effects, environmental issues, global problems and a materialistic culture. The professional may, in this respect, care little about the corporation as an institution.

Management's role in relation to deviant behaviour is often mentioned as being important. This is natural since R&D performance is recognized as being dependent upon an elite. There are, however, some variations on this theme. First, there are R&D managers who emphasize the suppression of the negative effects of elitism and say such things as 'these researchers should not become prima donnas', 'the department must. . . avoid becoming an ivory tower and above all avoid becoming a snob unit', '. . . avoid the emergence of "strong men" and territorial behavior'. One R&D manager projects the latter on himself and tries not to become a know-it-all. Domineering R&D managers are otherwise not uncommon. Secondly, there are R&D managers who emphasize the protection and support of not only high achievers but individuals who, in general, are perceived as deviant. This protection and support may concern a self-taught inventor as well as a reputable scientist, a 'weak' project leader as well as a domineering one. The point that the deviant behaviour of high achievers must not result in isolated individualism but has to be integrated in the organization has already been mentioned.

7.2.3.2 Management of ideas, information and projects

The second largest category of perceived R&D management roles is associated with the content of R&D work rather than the R&D workers themselves.

In relation to ideas and projects, two roles may be discerned from the answers: the role of generator of ideas and projects and that of evaluator of these for purposes of selection. Often an R&D manager, at least on the higher R&D management levels, is evaluative and selective rather than generative, while the situation is often reversed on lower levels of an R&D organization. The relations between age, creativity, experience and promotional habits contribute to this circumstance. As the Technical Director of Boliden said 'People are more creative when they are young. . . . When you get older, you develop the ability to evaluate creativity.'

Higher R&D managers generally do not perceive themselves as direct generators of ideas. Their role is more indirect in stimulating the generation and transmittal of ideas and creation of suitable conditions for creativity and communication. Of course, exceptions occur as for example at SKF, where the corporate R&D manager sees as one of his roles to create projects in new areas and asks 'How will people who are engaged in traditional R&D work be able to do this?' It should be noted though that ideas do not emerge distinctly and remain unchanged in large organizations. The evaluation and selection of ideas constitute complicated processes in a large organization, and there is never only one man involved and never only one point of decision. An R&D manager, as well as many other individuals, may be influential in idea work in many ways and it may be hard to separate all the pieces of information that go into R&D work. For instance a manager, with his overview and access to information, may act as a combiner of ideas, information and people.

Thus, R&D managers vary in attitudes and behaviour within the generative–selective dimension. The variations have to do with seniority and level in the organization and with the situation of the corporation with respect to supply and demand for ideas and the resources to work on them. Yet there are variations that seem to be attributable to the personality of the R&D manager. There are R&D managers who strongly pursue their own ideas or forcefully stop projects as well as R&D managers who more timidly 'sell' their ideas or convince people of the desirability to go on with a project. A good way to sell ideas and 'anchor' deci-

R&D and corporate management

sions is to get other people to take the credit, a behaviour which, when effective, distorts the picture of the sources of ideas. An R&D manager at Alfa-Laval expressed this as follows:

> You have to be generous and daring with your own ideas and those of others in R&D work and create a spirit against 'not invented here'. You should be happy when someone proposes as their own idea, what you yourself once have proposed. Don't kill the creation of ideas by self-sufficiency.

Another role often mentioned is that of a scanner and disseminator. Again, this may be done on several levels but to scan more broadly and try to judge the professional competence of the subordinates in relation to different lines of development is a natural thing to do for a manager. Some R&D managers are very active as information workers, picking information here and there, keeping channels open, establishing contacts, attending meetings, scanning journals, visiting customers, etc. and much may be said about different behaviour and 'tricks' in relation to this. It is, however, enough here to point out that their orientation inwards–outwards and upwards–downwards varies.

7.2.3.3 Management of critical relations

The third category of important roles concerns different critical relations, such as between R&D and marketing, external relations, or between central R&D and divisional R&D. Communication and co-ordination are thought of as the means to make these relations become productive. Some R&D organizations have been afflicted with many conflicts, and it may be the most natural for the R&D manager to restore good working relations. He may even have been appointed in his capacity of being uncontroversial, easy to handle, or talented in building relations. The different histories of the central R&D laboratory of Volvo and Alfa-Laval must be viewed against the different abilities in these respects of their R&D managers.

In a large organization much more effort has to be put into the 'internal marketing' of ideas and R&D results than in a small one, where perhaps the resources for external marketing, however, are more limited. The R&D manager has an important role here as an internal marketer both upwards and to the sides. This task is often described as time-consuming drudgery, requiring internal political skills.

With respect to relations to marketing, many R&D managers emphasize that R&D people have to be more market oriented and that the R&D manager has to work for a better coupling between R&D and marketing where product R&D is concerned. An important point is that no one explicitly views it as their role to take care of the whole process from R&D to the market if something should go wrong. This is in contrast to the traditional entrepreneurial role. Also, there are some variations in the way the coupling between R&D and marketing should be made. Essentially, these variations concern how early in R&D work marketing aspects should 'come in' and how strongly connected to customer needs different phases of R&D should be. Some R&D managers are in favour of a strong and early coupling (for example, at KemaNobel with negative experience from a reverse situation in earlier chemical R&D), while others favour a more gradual connection (for example, at Astra with experience of the unpredictability of useful pharmacological discoveries and their market impact). The kind of R&D and markets is, however, not decisive in this respect. Personal experience from successes and failures, fashionable trends and personal relations also are highly influential.

Perceived success in innovative work is to a surprising extent attributed to good co-operation in combination with talented people. Internal co-operation concerns relations among R&D people, between R&D and other functions and between R&D and corporate management. The basic solidarity within a corporation is often marked with a typical comment being 'There has been a feeling of closeness within SKF on the technical side, despite the problems of co-ordination which have existed and still do exist'.

References to external co-operation are not frequent but are noticeable at KemaNobel and Astra. Some corporations are also more externally oriented, while others are more internally oriented, not the least in connection with their R&D departments. Among technical people there is a tendency to develop a degree of introversion. A few R&D managers counteract this tendency, by trying to open up the R&D organization and making R&D more externally oriented. It does not have to be a question of a perceived need for change, however. Some managers just seem to be externally oriented as a feature of their personality and style of management. They build external relations for communication as mentioned above, look for people to recruit, look for licensing agreements or joint ventures, etc. They may manage a kind of fluid satellite organization of individuals and ventures, which for several reasons are not suitable for or cannot possibly be internalized into the ordinary R&D organization, at least not for the moment (see Chapter 11).

R&D managers (as well as top managers) may work effectively in an indirect way in securing productive internal and external relations. Partly this is a question of creating an atmosphere in which it is understood that formally established relations are secondary and personnel relations and competence are of primary importance, for example:

> R&D co-operation has to be based on personal acquaintance. (Boliden)
>
> There have been good contacts between top management, marketing people, R&D and production. The formal organization is in this respect a secondary question. (KemaNobel)
>
> Build up the organization around persons and competences. (Boliden)

Partly, it is also a question of forcing people into communicative situations. Many professionals are very pressed for time, which keeps them from making more than the necessary contacts. In Philips-Sweden, top management has chosen to create projects across organizational boundaries, send people to courses, etc., and above all concentrate locations instead of creating formal bodies for communication and coordination.

7.2.3.4 'Fayol' managerial roles

References by R&D managers to the traditional managerial roles, that is to say, to planning, co-ordination, resource allocation, administration, etc., comprise the fourth and smallest group of perceived working roles. This does not mean that R&D managers do not believe they play these roles, only that references to such roles might be of less interest from descriptive and normative points of view. Besides, some of the Fayol roles have a ring of bureaucracy, which is usually a 'dirty' word among managers. Concerning the degree of control in R&D, there are some variations in attitudes. It is commonly understood that the degree of control increases as an R&D project proceeds, the scale is increased, and more people and functions become involved. The balance between managerial control and 'freedom' or individual autonomy is often a matter of discussion, and the standpoints vary. At KemaNobel it is said that 'we don't believe very much in the free creation of ideas' and similar opinions are presented by SKF. At Astra-Hässle 'explorative, uncontrolled research has to exist', and a certain budget percentage is reserved for that. (This is not an uncommon intention, but its implementation often fails.) One R&D manager 'detests formalities in the range of $10,000 – $20,000, but then formalities have to come thick and fast'. Another admits that:

> we are strict now in R&D control; maybe we have gone too far. Four or five years ago we were rather flexible. Then American consultants came with proposals about strict control of R&D.

Naturally, it is hard to assess what kind and degree of control is applied, and individual standpoints in this matter are hard to compare. The control versus autonomy discussion is of long standing in R&D management and policy making and the subject may be much more elaborated on. Variations in behaviour and attitudes among corporations and managers are certainly attributable to such variables as phase and scale of work, kind of technology, economic situation, corporate strategy, and past personal and organizational experiences with different forms of R&D control. Management interests and ambitions must also be considered. An R&D manager may want to get insight through planning and co-ordination if he is new on the post, or he simply wants to reinforce his power over certain sheltered activities. Reversely, he may feel that his informal influence would be threatened by formal procedures. Similarly, a technical director, with a lukewarm attitude to R&D, may for several reasons find it convenient to advocate a policy of 'not too strict control' applied to 'small, efficient R&D groups'.

7.2.3.5 Miscellaneous

In this category only one point will be discussed, namely to what extent R&D management may be separated from R&D operations. It is natural that proportions between R&D and managerial work vary among different levels and positions in the organization. Past experience with R&D and R&D people is a natural ingredient in the background of an R&D manager. Few R&D managers, however, make reference to any necessity for them to perform R&D in order to manage R&D. Many R&D managers on higher levels also do not consider themselves capable of performing R&D. As a manager at Astra-Hässle said: 'To perform R&D is too difficult for an R&D manager who acts as an administrator'. The dividing line between performing and managing R&D is admittedly diffuse, however, but it is a basis for role differentiation. Some individuals refrain from administrative tasks in their R&D work, while others may find relief in using administration as an excuse. It is also a common conception that the ability to perform R&D decreases with age, while managerial abilities may increase. It is considered natural that promotion changes the proportion between performing and managing duties in favour of the latter, although dual ladders of promotion sometimes exist. Moreover, it is believed difficult and perhaps unattractive to return to the research frontier once a retreat has been made. Besides, active R&D work in some areas could disfavour other areas and managerial work in general. (This is analogous to the argument that a general manager should refrain from operative work.) The seldom-questioned conclusion of these arguments and conceptions is that an R&D manager does not have a role as a performer of R&D.

7.3 DISCUSSION

7.3.1 Empirical summary

7.3.1.1 Top management

The boards of the corporations studied play virtually no direct role in R&D, the main reasons being the lack of competence and need for secrecy. This leaves room for top management to exercise influence on R&D. On the average, however, top managers pay little attention to R&D and if they do, the attention is not infrequently misplaced. Generalized and opinionated views on the nature and role of R&D and R&D people are common, although many variations in views are observed. Also, corporate managing directors of large corporations appear to be pronounced institutionalists in their emphasis on corporate existence and stable development.

The most important tasks for top management in relation to R&D are said to be resource allocation, the appointment of R&D managers, and the alignment of ambitions in R&D with corporate goals. Top managers also differ with respect to their orientation within the behavioural, financial and technological dimensions.

Several pros and cons are presented about technologists as corporate managing directors. The important question, however, concerns the provision and utilization of technological competence in top management. Corporate managing directors are found to differ on internal versus external sources of information and in their reliance on formal and regular reporting versus informal, selective, and *ad hoc* oriented sources of information. Thus, there are differences in the use of such things as scientific advisory boards, selected popularizers, external consultants, 'diving' as an information-seeking behaviour, or formal planning as a tool for generating and processing information.

7.3.1.2 R&D management

Many individuals influence, directly or indirectly, R&D in a large corporation. Also, there is a diffuse distinction between managing and performing R&D and

R&D and corporate management

Table 7.1 Summary of working roles of R&D managers in large corporations*

I	Roles in management of R&D personnel (41 per cent)
	Recruiter/keeper
	Team composer
	Value adapter
	Motivator
	Handler of deviant behaviour
	Creator of atmosphere and environment
II	Roles in management of ideas, information and projects (30 per cent)
	Generator
	Evaluator/selector
	Scanner/disseminator
III	Roles in management of critical relations (15 per cent)
	Handler of conflicts
	Internal marketer of ideas and R&D results
	Builder/maintainer of productive relations around R&D
IV	Fayol managerial roles (13 per cent)
	Planner, co-ordinator, budgeter, administrator etc.
V	Miscellaneous roles (1 per cent)

*Perceived by R&D managers above project level. The classification has been based on their references in answers and percentages denote relative frequencies of references. Classes of roles and their labels have been post-constructed and percentages are approximative.

between R&D managers and R&D personnel. Managerial influences, functions, roles, tasks, activities and so on differ among, for example corporations, organizational levels, projects and phases of projects. The focus here has been on the most important managerial roles in relation to R&D, as perceived by R&D managers above project level. Table 7.1 summarizes these findings.

7.3.2 Top management relations to R&D

7.3.2.1 Role of the board

Although the role of the board of a corporation in relation to R&D is not, and has not been, of primary concern in this study, some comments are called for. The existence of secrecy and competence barriers between the board and R&D in a corporation together with traditional notions about the role of a corporate board probably to a great extent explains the lack of involvement in R&D. The situation may, however, change due to increased professionalization of corporate boards and increased concern about technological change from community and employee representatives. Besides, there are strong arguments for board involvement in R&D, which are based on examples of innovation by invasion, increasing R&D costs calling for intercorporate co-operation, and a tendency by top management to focus on present business and urgent problems. It may not be so much a question of increasing technological competence among members of the board as increasing their competence to put pressure on top management to analyse the R&D situation properly. In this respect it appears instrumental to increase the frequency of board connections between top management in different but related industries as well as board connections to external technologists, both in industry and at universities.

7.3.2.2 Role of top management

There are strong arguments for top management to pay increased attention to R&D. The top management level has the prime capability of processing information and exercising power. As is well recognized, divisionalization with a profit-centre approach, rather than a strategy-centre approach, tends to produce short-term considerations among divisional managers. Strategic considerations are supposed to be left to corporate managers, and top management is supposed to withdraw from operations and concentrate on policy making and strategic decision making. R&D is then likely to receive limited and/or misdirected attention, especially because of the tendency towards policy-evasive behaviour described in Chapter 5 and the importance of embryonic decision making in R&D, as described in Chapter 6. It is also tempting for a general manager to become absorbed in urgent non-R&D problems and to limit himself to providing general guidance of R&D on request.

Naturally, there are many factors to consider in the time allocation of top managers, for example, the increased need for external orientation and negotiating. Several means are available for increasing top management attention to R&D. A succession of top managers, especially corporate managing directors with different orientations, offers a long-range possibility to balance the attention at the top. Examples of wilful use of this possibility may also be found in corporate histories, when 'a production man' is succeeded by 'a marketing man' as corporate managing director, for example. A balanced succession of managers is a long-range alternative to a balanced or truly general manager, who may be good at many things but not particularly good at anything.

A continuously working complementary alternative is to compose a well-balanced top management team: A straightforward measure would be to have an R&D director on the corporate level together with a production director and a marketing director. It may also be argued that the traditional idea of a technical director is inadequate, since such a person will be absorbed by present problems and also is likely to be biased in favour of production technology rather than product technology. The composition does not, however, necessarily have to be in terms of formally assigned duties as, for instance, at Philips with dual technical and commercial managers on low as well as high levels. Instead, it may be a question of informally complementing each other with respect to sources of information, competence, risks, attitudes and other personality features and intangible assets.

A means of increasing top management attention to R&D, in addition to general means such as succession and composition, is to use top managers as 'divers' in the corporation in as far as R&D is concerned. Their role as a diver has also been recognized by some corporate managing directors, as described in Section 7.2. Diving has the double aim of informing top management about R&D

operations and motivating and 'moving' the R&D organization. There are many possible permanent items in reports on R&D—for example, from the staff R&D director giving budgetary information, project statistics and typologies, forecasts of technologies and new applications, information on large projects or projects of corporate interest or deviant projects or high-risk projects, information on resource utilization and R&D investments, on personnel, on R&D in subsidiaries, on new internal or external discoveries, on the future competitive situation, on technical service and quality control, on the R&D situation in different divisions, on interdivisional R&D co-operation, on support to universities and external R&D co-operation, on patents and licensing, on spin-off companies, on R&D policies and principles for R&D management, etc. Diving may be a complement to this. The awareness that top management may want to have a direct look at any project right on the spot at short notice is also likely to create motivation at all levels in the R&D organization. In the light of the prevalence of conflicts and barriers to innovation in large organizations (as described in Chapters 10 and 11) diving would give a top manager, whose intuition may be obsolete, feelings and information about R&D and the way it is handled that are not transmittable to the top in an ordinary fashion.

7.3.3 Working roles of R&D managers

It is natural to start with Fayol (1949), whose administrative principles and elements are still deeply rooted in literature as well as in practice. Fayol articulated five basic managerial functions—planning, organizing, commanding, co-ordinating and controlling—and his writings are to a large degree still valid on a general level. Fayol has, however, been criticized, especially by Mintzberg (1973).

At a high level of aggregation, the Fayol typology may be recognized in this study. Planning, co-ordinating etc. are in different proportions important activities of any manager. One weakness of these activities is that they are not easily empirically separable, as Mintzberg (1973) and Carlson (1951) point out in their studies of general managers. This weakness has special relevance to managing R&D, which cannot be clearly separated from the performance of R&D. Admittedly, the personnel-oriented and content-oriented roles in managing R&D are also not easily separated in practice. Often R&D people constitute substitutable or additive resources only to a very limited degree. Moreover, ideas are difficult to separate from their carriers, and performance in R&D is skewly distributed among R&D people. On the other hand, the distinction between R&D personnel and R&D content is a recurrent theme and does provide a valuable dimension for thinking about R&D management orientations.

Thus, it may be argued that the weak separability in the Fayol typology is not critical. However, another characteristic of the Fayol typology is that it is general and does not adequately emphasize crucial roles in R&D management as well as in other specialized areas of management. Considering the differentiation of the management profession since the days of Fayol, this is not surprising. The generality of the Fayol typology may be considered as both a strength and a weakness, but it should be complemented, not substituted by another typology with claims of general applicability to all types and areas of management. As mentioned above, there are elements in R&D management which correspond to elements in general management, but there are also specific elements, which may be swept away by claiming generality to an exaggerated extent, resulting in colourless management principles or elements.

7.3.3.1 The R&D manager as the corporate entrepreneur

At a less aggregated level of comparison of management typologies, one managerial role in particular will be discussed in the following, that is the entrepreneurial role in management. As already mentioned in Section 7.1, the title 'manager' is here used in a wide sense, including the entrepreneurial role. In one way, there has been a parallel between the notion of innovator and entrepreneur, on one hand, and the notion of technologist and manager, on the other, in the sense that individuals with technical knowledge and skills have been distinguished from individuals with management skills. Simply expressed, the traditional difference between innovator/entrepreneur and technologist/manager is that the latter pair of roles has to do with running operations, while the former has to do with change.

What motivates a discussion of the role of an entrepreneur in the context of R&D management is partly the current interest in entrepreneurs on the whole and partly the problems surrounding R&D in large corporations. It is well known that as corporations grow, they tend to lose some of the entrepreneurial spirit which prevailed in the early stages of corporate life. A current theme, then, is that large corporations may combine large-scale advantages with advantages of small and young organizations through internal entrepreneurship, small venture companies etc. The growth of industrial R&D and the internalization of R&D in large corporations certainly give rise to a host of special problems with barriers to innovation, and it may be argued that these problems have not been sufficiently recognized in the narrow conception of recruitment, education, and career progression of R&D managers, which is common in large corporations.

As seen from the empirical section, R&D managers did not emphasize the entrepreneurial role, although some of their roles in managing critical relations may be interpreted as having entrepreneurial elements. Mintzberg (1973), on the other hand, recognizes the role of the entrepreneur in his group of decisional roles. Now, provided that there is a need 'to make R&D managers more entrepreneurial', what concept of an entrepreneur is applicable to R&D management?

A common idea is that an entrepreneur is a doer, a mover, an activist, who can cut through a difficult bureaucracy and who has a sense of comprehensive responsibility. In this respect, the concept has appeal to management in most organizations. Steele (1975) dwells on the role in innovation of the corporate entrepreneur as distinguished from the autonomous entrepreneur and connects his concept of entrepreneur to risk taking. A corporate entrepreneur has to face other types of risks and rewards than an autonomous entrepreneur, who typically risks large amounts of his personal assets. Naturally, there are intrinsic differences between large and small organizations in such respects as the risk/reward structure and the power/autonomy structure, and people are differently attracted by pros-

R&D and corporate management

pects of being a corporate entrepreneur or an autonomous entrepreneur. Steele's main argument is that the large corporation has opportunities to exploit in corporate entrepreneurship, since this type of entrepreneurship has advantages as well as disadvantages compared to autonomous entrepreneurship.

There are several studies of the characteristics of an entrepreneur. The concept of need for achievement, as originally explored in McClelland, Atkinson, Clark and Lowell (1953), is one important factor. Studies of barriers to entrepreneurship in large organizations are not as common. The interviews in this study, as well as the literature (see Birney, Burdick and Teevan, 1969), indicate that fear of failure also exists in large corporations (see also Chapter 11). It may very well be, therefore, that the need for achievement has more explanatory power in relation to autonomous entrepreneurship and fear of failure in relation to lacking corporate entrepreneurship. A large corporation certainly offers opportunities to diffuse blame, but 'for the corporate entrepreneur, the specific consequences of failure are largely beyond his control' (Steele, 1975, p. 24). A large corporation also has many watchers and potential blamers. Because of the many barriers to and conflicts in innovation, an R&D manager may have difficulties in arranging for co-operation with contractual bindings as well as avoiding concealed counter action.

Risk taking is connected with basic attitudes but also with perceptions and the way expectations are formed. Steele distinguishes between intrinsic risk (which is actually the probability of whether a venture will succeed or fail), personal financial risk and ego risk, the latter connected to what impact a failure will have on the individual himself. He then goes on:

> Perhaps most important is that corporate management has the opportunity to influence the way in which ego risk will be perceived. . . Decisions on personal commitment are basically made on subjective appraisal of the balance of risk and reward, and if the penalties for failure are regarded as too high, the commitment will never be made. The organization unhappy with the extent to which risk taking is assumed would do well to reexamine its equation of risk, penalty and reward. (Steele, 1975, p. 24)

Top management may thus have an important role in relation to R&D in stimulating corporate entrepreneurship, by creating a climate more benevolent to failure. There are, however, other problems as well.

The recruitment basis of R&D managers is usually narrow, and in combination with a specialist's education their experience of the whole innovation process is restricted or at least heavily biased. Their mobility in the organization is limited, and they may be afraid of temporary assignments because of worries about re-entry. Moreover, the career paths are long in a large corporation, and preference for youth in internal recruitment to higher posts decrease the merit of achievements in R&D, which are difficult to evaluate, except possibly over the long term.

It is doubtful on what levels of R&D management corporate entrepreneurship should be stimulated. The role of idea generator is becoming obsolete for higher levels of R&D management as well as for top management, but the ideas man and the entrepreneur are often separate persons operating in tandem. An R&D manager has, however, many other roles to perform and possibly the project-leader level is best suited to house entrepreneurs. On the other hand, the difficulties along the innovation process and the long time periods involved speak in favour of entrepreneurial responsibilities on high management levels, even on a top management level. It is tempting to think of providing seed capital, creating possibilities of shared financing, authorizing ventures, creating small innovation companies or some kind of business development units as top management responsibilities. However, it is also likely that, in Steele's terms, an anxious top management will starve a fledgling business to death:

> A common reason for bootlegging embryonic innovations is to avoid the spotlight of corporate attention and the concomitant endless round of reviews and presentations requested by corporate management. (Steele, 1975, p. 26)

It is beyond the scope of this study to recommend a scheme for stimulating entrepreneurship in managing R&D. To a considerable extent words like 'innovation' and 'entrepreneur' have a magic ring as if there was the possibility of not only a 'technological fix' but also a 'management fix'. All in all, it is argued here that the problem of managing R&D more entrepreneurially ought to be approached with the same philosophy of experimentation that has found application in R&D itself.

7.4 CONCLUSIONS

The boards of the corporations studied play virtually no direct role in R&D. A growing professionalization of corporate boards and an increasing degree of external R&D co-operation might change this. The room left for top management to exercize influence on R&D is, on average, utilized to a low degree. Top managers were also found to differ regarding their behavioural, financial and technological orientations. In general, different orientations in top management may be balanced through the composition of teams and as a long-term complementary alternative through a balanced succession of managers with different orientations. Examples of this were found as well as examples of corporate managing directors 'diving' in the corporation. In as far as R&D was concerned, this was one way to keep informed. Although inadequate intervention may also result, diving appears as an instrument in motivation and 'moving' the R&D organization.

The working roles of R&D managers above project level fell into the following categories in roughly the following percentages: management of R&D personnel (41 per cent); management of ideas, information, and projects (30 per cent); management of critical relations (15 per cent); 'Fayol' managerial roles (13 per cent). Roles in the Fayol typology are difficult to separate, but, more importantly, they do not emphasize crucial roles in R&D management, such as the handling of conflicts or deviant behaviour.

The R&D managers in this study did not emphasize the entrepreneurial role, although some of their roles in managing critical relations may be interpreted as having entrepreneurial elements. It is hypothesized here that fear of failure is a barrier to entrepreneurship in large corporations. A climate more benevolent to failure could stimulate corporate entrepreneurship, but at which level is an open question. As a general conclusion, the problem of managing R&D could to a larger extent be approached with the same philosophy of experimentation as applied in R&D itself.

Chapter 8
R&D AND CORPORATE ORGANIZATION

8.1 INTRODUCTION

This chapter will focus on the outer organization of R&D in the organization of industrial corporations rather than the inner or internal organization of R&D units. Also the focus will be on structure and structural changes rather than processes of organization and management. Especially the transition to a divisionalized organization will be described and the different possibilities and organizational ideas for accommodating R&D in large corporations. The relation between strategy and structure will, moreover be discussed.

The term 'organization' may be used for several quite different things in a subject/object-relationship. Thus, it may refer to the process of organizing, the manner by which something is organized, the object which is organized, or a body of persons organizing something. Although the term is sometimes used for the structure or composition of a non-human object, it mostly involves the work of human beings. To organize also has a basic connotation of forming a whole consisting of interdependent parts, co-ordinated to some degree for the purpose of doing some work.

Some distinctions of primary interest here are between structure and process, between organization and management, between an inner and an outer organization, and between a functional and a divisional organization.

The structure/process distinction is of ancient origin and could be elaborated upon, but for the present purpose it suffices to say that structure refers to 'the established pattern of relationships among the components or parts of the organization', (Kast and Rosenzweig, 1970, p. 170). A process on the other hand, refers to what goes on over time in an organization. A structure may also change over time and is thereby subjected to a process. The structure/process distinction is thus related to the perspective on time and stability.

Management, as distinguished from organization, in this chapter refers to formally established layers or bodies of leadership in the organization. The distinction between an inner and an outer organization requires the recognition of a boundary which delineates a whole with inner parts as a part of an outer whole. More simply expressed, and by way of illustration, the inner organization of R&D in a corporation refers to the organization of an R&D unit into departments for chemistry, metallurgy etc., while the outer organization of R&D in a corporation refers to the organization of R&D into different units within the corporation that perform R&D. (See Figure 8.1)

The distinction between a functional and a divisional organization refers to two types of organization. Normally, different functions in an organization, such as purchasing, R&D, production, marketing, finance and administration are discerned. Functions may, of course, be discerned on different bases and levels of

R&D and corporate organization

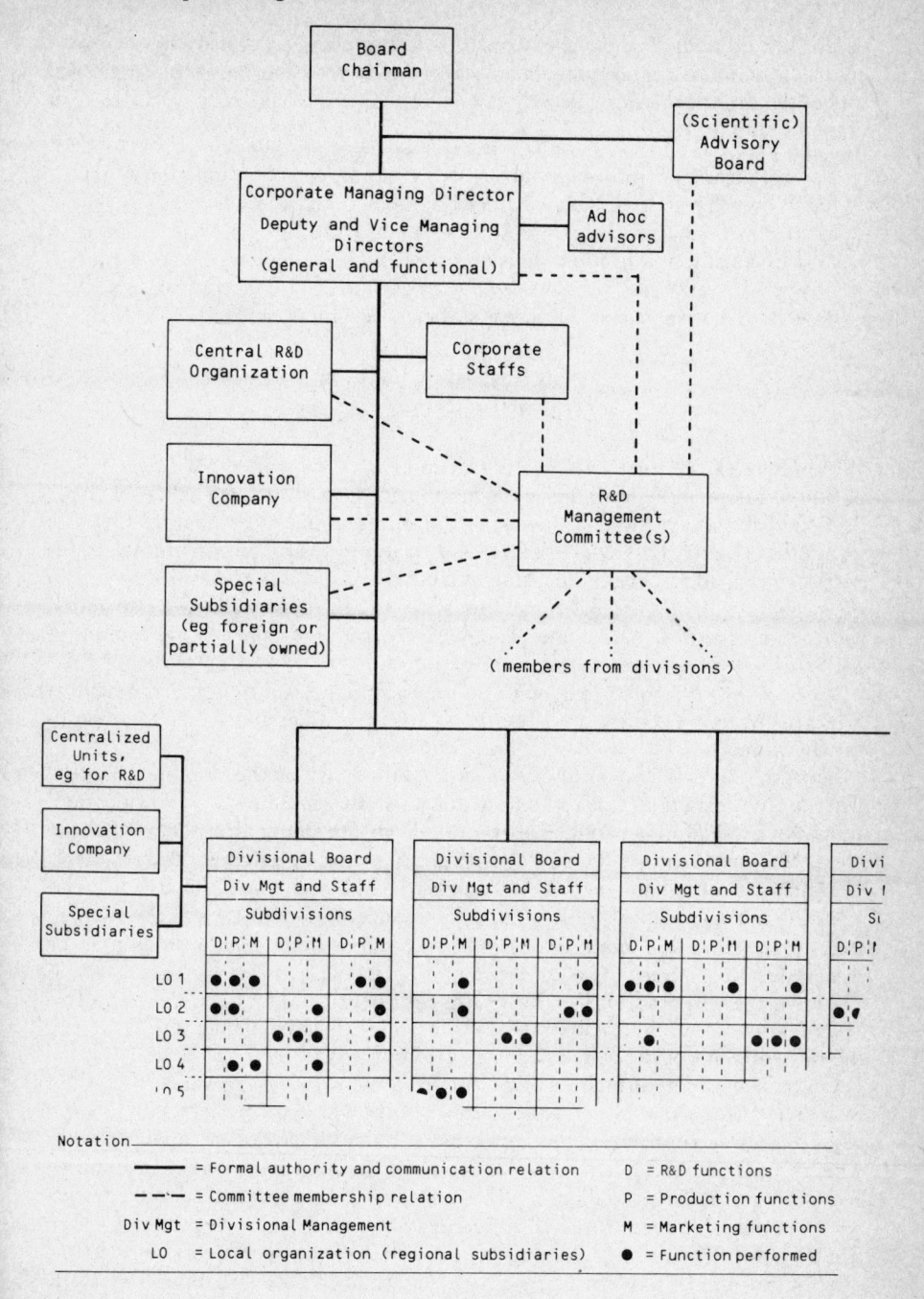

Figure 8.1 Example of a divisionalized corporate organization

detail, but a function refers primarily to a cluster of coherent activities in a process. A functional organization, then, has different functions as the principal sectors of the organization, while a divisional organization has divisions. A division is then defined as:

> an organizational unit with such a definable part of the total task of the enterprise that its goal has a composition and complexity which are closely aligned with that of the entire enterprise. In order for an organizational unit to constitute a product division or sector, it is required that it at least comprises marketing, product development, and economic control; that its result is measurable and that it has sufficient economic scale. (Bohlin 1976)

8.2 EMPIRICAL FINDINGS

Within about five years in the late 1960s and early 1970s, seven of the eight corporations adopted the multidivisional organization structure, regardless of variations in size, complexity, technology, environment and other characteristics of the corporations. This 'wave' of re-organizations restructured internal interdependencies and relegated the functional division of work to lower echelons in the organization. Figure 8.1 illustrates a full-blown divisionalized organization rather than a representative one. Table 8.1 shows the corporate organizations in 1975.

First, it may be noted that, with minor exceptions, all divisions are product oriented. Moreover, there are large variations in number and size of these product divisions.

Second, there is almost always a dominant division, the dominance being derived from tradition, size or internal attitudes. By separating into product divisions newer or minor product operations from the dominating ones, one can more easily redistribute the strategic emphasis between different product areas. Certainly, this has happened at Alfa-Laval, SKF, Boliden and Volvo. The principal inter-divisional relationships are dominance, autonomy, vertical coupling, mutual coupling and matrix couplings, but many more relationships may be discerned of an input/output or a synergetic nature.

Third, the corporate staffs have grown considerably. The 'pure' divisionalized organization with minor corporate staffs often seems to be just an initial stage in the development of divisionalized organizations.

One of the leading principles of divisionalization was to decentralize operations into divisions, each one amenable to short-range economic performance control while retaining centralized strategic control in the hands of top management, which was thus freed from operative decisions. In such a system of decomposed economic control, one could organize R&D according to several options. A variety of options for the outer R&D organization was actually employed, as seen from Tables 8.2 and 8.3. Among the corporations there are variations in the distribution of R&D work internally or externally. This distribution of R&D work may be more or less temporary and more or less a result of a conscious strategy. Some rationales for external allocation of R&D work are advantages of

Table 8.1 Corporate organizations in 1975

KemaNobel	Ten product divisions plus five partially owned producing subsidiaries. Large variations in size. Mixed interdivisional relations. One R&D intensive division. Small corporate staff. One innovation company.
Philips	Thirteen product divisions with mixed interdivisional relations. International matrix organization. Multinational R&D organization. Large corporate staff.
Alfa Laval	Four product divisions plus special subsidiaries. Two divisions are mutually coupled through deliveries, one is traditionally dominant. International matrix organization. Multinational R&D organization. Large and growing corporate staff.
SKF	Four divisions, of which three are international area divisions. The fourth division accounts for a variety of products and has a strong forward coupling to the other divisions, which have a traditional dominance. The fourth division also has an assigned responsibility for diversification. Multinational R&D organization. Large corporate staff. One innovation company.
Boliden	Two product divisions plus four producing subsidiaries. The traditionally dominant division has a forward coupling to the other. Small corporate staff.
Iggesund	Three product divisions plus two producing subsidiaries. One product division has a forward coupling to another product division. Small corporate staff.
Astra	Three product divisions, one of which is highly dominant. The dominant division has domestic and foreign subsidiaries with R&D and marketing integrated on the subsidiary level and production centralized. Multinational R&D organization.
Volvo	Ten product divisions with mixed interdivisional relations and some separate production units. One product division has traditionally been dominant. International matrix organization developed to some degree. Domestic R&D organization. Large corporate staff.

Table 8.2 Summary of corporate organization of R&D resources in 1975

Variable	KemaNobel	Philips	Alfa-Laval	SKF	Boliden	Iggesund	Astra	Volvo
Small innovation company at corporate level*	Y	Y	N	Y	N	N	N	N
Small innovation company in some division	N	Y	N	N	Y	N	N	N
Central† R&D laboratory	N	Y	Y	Y	N	N	N	Y
Central† R&D budget	N	Y	Y	Y	Y	N	N	Y
R&D performed in three or more countries	N	Y	Y	Y	N	N	Y	N
Divisional R&D laboratories	Y	Y	Y	Y	Y	Y	Y	Y
Special R&D intensive division	Y	Y	N	N	N	N	Y	N
Collective R&D of essential importance‡	N	N	N	N	N	Y	N	N

Notation: Y = Yes, N = No.
*By innovation company is meant a clearly detached organizational unit with the main purpose to develop inventions.
†By central is meant on the corporate level, detached from the divisions.
‡By essential importance is meant a subjective rating of importance relative to other comparable forms for performing R&D.

R&D and corporate organization

Table 8.3 Summary of corporate organization of R&D management in 1975

Variable	KemaNobel	Philips	Alfa-Laval	SKF	Boliden	Iggesund	Astra	Volvo
Scientific advisory board at the corporate level*	N	N	N	N	N	N	Y	N
Scientific advisory board in some division	N	N	Y	N	N	N	N	N
R&D management committee at the corporate level†	N	Y	N	Y	N	N	N	Y
Separation at the corporate level of management of product R&D/process R&D	N	N	N	Y	Y	Y	N	Y
R&D management committee in some division‡	Y	Y	Y	Y	Y	Y	Y	Y
Corporate project control system§	N	P	P	Y	Y	N	Y	N
Development centre concept is employed¶	N	Y	N	Y	N	N	P	N

Notation: Y = Yes, N = No, P = Partially
* A permanent body mainly composed of external R&D specialists.
† A committee composed of central and divisional R&D managers or technical directors, possibly also including marketing people.
‡ As†, but committee members come mainly from within a division.
§ An administrative system for establishing, profiling and reviewing R&D projects on a corporate basis.
¶ Permanent (or indeterminate) responsibilities for product or process development in different areas of corporate interest are assigned to specific R&D units.

scale, co-operative advantages exceeding competitive advantages, access to complementary knowledge, the creation of an intermediate stage to internalizing, resource flexibility and small risks. Reliance on a permanent external performance of R&D work requires inside scanning, controlling and receiving capacities, but this is at most marginally reflected in the outer organizational structure. Moreover, it is conceivable that the absence of innovation companies or other internal units for new product development is at least partially caused by reliance upon takeovers of external initial developments.

Second, there are various ways of distributing R&D internally. This is more clearly reflected in the organization structure. Divisionalization reshaped large technical departments into central and divisional R&D. Some rationales for a central R&D unit are to take advantage of scale and atmosphere, to perform R&D of an interdivisional nature, to perform R&D on radical technological substitutions, to perform R&D of corporate interest that is not clearly of interest to some existing division, and to perform services that are complementary to R&D and of corporate interest. Often a central R&D unit is also thought of as providing fundamental science and technology knowledge and performing long-range or high-risk R&D aiming at new products or processes. A flow of results from research and inventive activities into the divisions is then supposed to be achieved. Central R&D is sometimes thought of as a pipeline for new products or technical solutions to the divisions as well as a connection to the science and technology community.

The absence of central R&D at KemaNobel, Boliden, Iggesund and Astra is a result of top management attitudes, being in an initial stage of divisionalization, and the absence of interdivisional synergy, among other things.

Small innovation companies may have several modes of operation and their rationales also vary. At KemaNobel and SKF they have been formed around inventive people and inside inventions. There are also companies which had as a part of their original business idea to search for external inventions to acquire. The main rationales are in some respects similar to those of R&D laboratories, but in addition there is the notion that certain inventive people and activities are to be separated also from other forms of R&D, especially 'traditional' R&D. Sometimes, however, the creation of these innovation companies appears primarily as achievements of individual R&D advocates with access to the confidence of top management.

Concerning R&D management positions and bodies, a scientific advisory board is a manifestation of the need, mostly perceived at the general management level, to keep close contact with the science and technology community. However, many general managers feel that these boards tend to be too general in scope or just of temporary value (see Section 7.2). Committees and administrative systems for R&D management at the corporate level have intra- and inter-functional co-ordination of the R&D function and transfer of R&D results as main rationales. Co-ordination between functions is increasingly emphasized at the divisional level. The presence of interdivisional synergy is naturally influential, but on the other hand some top managers want to have a 'pure', decentralized organization, at least in the present stage of the organization. Moreover, strong forces are working against co-ordination of R&D at the corporate level,

R&D and corporate organization

which sometimes reduces the directive influence to a consultative, informative, or even just a nominal influence. The autonomy of divisions and subsidiaries is defended by both general managers and R&D managers at this level. The presence of central R&D resources, financed through the divisions, may facilitate interdivisional co-ordination, but even more crucial is the support from top management for this type of co-ordination.

In summary, the following may be stated about the shaping of the outer R&D organization:

— technical and R&D managers have had a minor influence compared to that of top management in the initial shaping of outer R&D organizations;
— acquisitions, local management ambitions, interdivisional synergy, and problems with transfer of R&D results have created a need for R&D co-ordination at the corporate level;
— some general notions or organizational ideas about the outer and inner organization of R&D are influential together with manning considerations in the shaping of an R&D organization.

Examples of general organizational ideas about R&D indicated in the interviews are:

— R&D is not amenable to decomposed economic control to the same extent as other operations.
— Product innovations emanate from a flow of results transferred from idea sources through R&D, production, and marketing functions. This flow must be 'streamlined', and coupling of functional activities is stressed. Thus, functional integration and transfer of results have high priority.
— The creation of the new is in its early stages always hampered by the existence of the old. Thus, R&D activities aiming at radically new inventions, ideas and discoveries should to some extent be separated or protected from the current organization, yielding central laboratories, external new ventures, innovation companies, appropriations for exploratory work, acceptance of guerilla R&D, externally supported R&D etc. (Sometimes status considerations are infiltrated. A small unit aiming for the new, with direct connection to the top, is a nice thing to demonstrate internally and externally.)
— The distribution of R&D results is very skew, yielding an elitist view. Thus the R&D organization should be centred around highly productive individuals rather than follow some formal pattern. This idea is widespread but manifested mostly in the informal organization.
— Large, diversified multinational corporations should utilize effects of scale, synergy and multinationality. Thus R&D activities should be co-ordinated functionally, divisionally and geographically, yielding integrative devices such as policies, networks of committees, guidelines for standardization and conferences. To some extent this idea is modified when stages of organizational development are taken into consideration.
— Research is one thing, development another. A sharp distinction between these kinds of activities is attempted, and they tend to be treated differently

when organized. This idea may be differently applied, yielding central 'R' organizations with divisional 'D', or external 'R' with internal 'D'.

Conceptions of growth and size effects of an R&D unit are sometimes determining the initiation and grouping of R&D activities. Assumptions about optimal size vary from the conviction that small R&D groups are 'the only thing' for creative work to the necessity of a large critical size (minimal rather than optimal size) for R&D (see Chapter 3).

8.3 DISCUSSION

8.3.1 Empirical summary

Within about five years in the late 1960s and early 1970s, seven of the eight corporations adopted the multidivisional organization structure, regardless of corporate characteristics. In general, product divisions were formed, among which one was often dominant. A variety of options for the outer R&D organization was employed, such as central and divisional R&D laboratories, innovation companies and external R&D institutes. Also the structure of R&D management varied considerably among the corporations. While largely the same organizational idea for the corporate organization was adopted, a number of different organizational ideas about the outer R&D organization were identified.

8.3.2 Corporate organization

The adoption of a divisionalized organizational structure and the simultaneity with which this took place are two outstanding features in the organizational history of the corporations studied. Horváth (1973) shows a similar simultaneity in a larger sample of forty-seven Swedish corporations, which in the early 1970s had adopted a divisionalized structure. At least 60 per cent of these corporations had divisionalized during 1966–70. Horváth found no relationship between time of adoption and size of the corporation, but the propensity to divisionalize tended to increase with the degree of internationalization and even more so with the degree of diversification. In the present study the corporations differ considerably with respect to size, degree of internationalization, and degree of diversification. All of them except for one, adopted the divisionalized structure within a period of a little more than five years in the late 1960s and early 1970s. Although the simultaneity may in this case have to do with the small size of the sample or the way it was chosen, the qualitative impression remains that the adoption of a divisionalized structure might just as well be explained in terms of other variables than size, internationalization and diversification.

A well known theme in literature about divisionalization is the relationship between strategy and structure, as originated by Chandler in his work on divisionalization in United States corporations. Chandler (1962) has spurred investigations about the strategy and structure of corporations in a number of countries, and the strategy/structure pair of concepts has been widely used.

Chandler, in short, advocates the view that strategy not only precedes, but is explanatory to, structure. This is especially so concerning the strategy of growing through diversification, he claims. While the concept of structure, defined by Chandler as '. . . the design of organization through which the enterprise is administrated', is uncontroversial, the concept of strategy is not. Chandler's concept of strategy includes the determination of basic long-term goals, the adoption of courses of action, and the allocation of resources for carrying out these goals, that is to say that a strategy includes both pre-conceived behaviour and actual behaviour. In a strategy/structure study of British enterprises, Channon goes one step further for reasons of methodology and confines the concept of strategy to mere observable behaviour of enterprises in product-market terms (Channon, 1973, pp. 6-7). Obviously, the question as to in what sense strategy precedes structure is contingent upon to what degree pre-conceived behaviour is included in the concept of strategy. The trouble with Chandler's inclusive concept of strategy is that it is hard to assess the precedence relation. If, in a stereotyped case, an enterprise decides to diversify and, in order to carry out that strategy, employs a divisionalized structure and then actually diversifies, it is incorrect to say in Chandler's terms that structure follows strategy. It is thus possible to interpret Chandler's cases differently. If the concept of strategy is confined to preconceived behaviour, which is a conceptual standpoint not necessarily favouring the structure-follows-strategy hypothesis since the actual behaviour does not have to be preconceived at all, it seems fair to say that—for example, in the case of DuPont—structure followed a strategy of diversification. At least, this was so during one period of its history. In the case of General Motors, on the other hand, divisionalization was not a response to the adoption of a diversification strategy (Chandler, 1962, pp. 43-68).

Based on the sample in this study, however, it can hardly be concluded that in general the adoption of a divisionalized structure was a consequence of an adopted strategy in the preconceived behaviour sense. Many factors may account for the reorganization of the corporations studied here and of Swedish corporations in general. The simultaneity in the adoption of a divisionalized structure suggests factors external to specific corporations. Thus, it is conceivable that rapid growth, which was a common feature of the 1960s, rather than size paved the way for reorganization. Also, a rapidly increasing complexity, which puts pressure on management and the organization, could bring about a reorganization. Especially a contemporaneous increase in pressure on the corporations and their top mangement to perform in product innovation required decentralization and strengthening of interfunctional co-ordination regarding products.

Compared to United States corporations, there was a lag in Swedish corporations in the adoption of the kind of managerial innovation brought about by the divisionalized organization. A possible cause of this lag was that the implementation of the new organizational concept required supporting organizational developments (for example, concerning systems for budgeting and accounting). The diffusion of the concept of divisionalization may also have been considerably speeded up by Chandler's work, possibly aided by the fear of a gap between the United States and Europe, not only in the field of technology but also in management and organization. The role of external organizational consultants in this diffusion process was also important, in Sweden as well as in England (see Channon, 1973, p. 239).

Finally, it should be noted that it is possible to differentiate between corporations regarding the relationship between strategy and structure. In some companies, structure tends to precede strategy, while in others strategy tends to precede structure. However, Asplund (1975) treats relationships between environment, strategy and structure and has a differentiated view on the interplay between different organizational levels and functions in the strategy formulation process, a view which comes close to disposing of a simple relationship between strategy and structure.

8.3.3 R&D organization

There is a considerable variety among the corporations concerning the outer R&D organization and management structure. The variations between corporations concern, for example, reliance on external and co-operative R&D, the presence of central R&D, innovation companies, corporate R&D management committees and scientific advisory boards. Also, there are variations for a specific organizational structure — for instance, with respect to location and degree of corporate control. Finally, there are variations over time within a specific corporation, as well as variations between different divisions. There are not many comparative studies of outer R&D organizations, and those which exist point to similar variations without very clear explanations.

One may ask whether the adoption of some of the options in Tables 8.1 and 8.2 is correlated with corporate characteristics such as:

(a) size measured as total sales;
(b) degree of internationalization (measured as number of employees abroad/total number of employees);
(c) degree of diversification (measured as sales outside largest product area/total sales);
(d) R&D intensity (measured as R&D cost/total sales).

One may also ask whether some measure of structural variety in and managerial integration of the outer R&D organization is correlated with such variables. If structural variety (or structural pluralism) is simply indicated by the number of employed options (Table 8.1) and managerial integration by the number of employed options (Table 8.2) numerical correlations could be calculated. (Partially employed options are counted as 0.5.)

The state variables size and internationalization are found to be positively correlated with structural variety ($r = 0.84$). (The significance limits on 5 per cent level for the correlation coefficient is ± 0.62.) Internationalization is also positively correlated with managerial integration ($r = 0.68$). However, managerial integration seems to be disrupted by a high degree of diversification ($r = -0.69$) as well as by increases in size and increases in internationalization. Structural variety, on the other hand, does not seem to be affected by changes in the state variables considered here.

The sample is unfortunately too small to allow extensive statistical analysis. Regarding the adoption of specific organizational solutions, one may note that corporations with central R&D laboratories are highly internationalized. Such relationships, however, simply provide a superficial basis for analysis in the light of all the qualitative information from each corporation. Several ways of explaining organizational variations are conceivable.

People experienced in designing organizations have found that manning considerations are crucial. Thus, an important source of organizational variation could be a variation in the manning situation of different corporations. This indeed accounts for some variations in the corporations studied. Major structural variations in the outer R&D organization, however, can be more easily derived from another explanation, which has to do with general organizational ideas and their interpretation and implementation by top management in the specific situation of the corporation. A variety of undifferentiated ideas on how to organize R&D then tends to multiply through the experience and preferences of top management with a variety of corporate situations, including corporate histories and manning possibilities, but also including corporate strategy and type of technology and markets.

Regarding explanations for internal versus external integration, Nyström (1979) found that external orientation in his terminology was associated with a higher level of technological innovation than was internal orientation. A common theme regarding R&D is that the genesis of those innovations which imply a high degree of diversification, is within research or outside the corporation, especially if it is a large corporation. However, one may, in fact, discern two processes with respect to radical diversification based on R&D. One process involves external idea sources such as external inventors, university research, or joint ventures, and the susceptibility of the organization and its management to external ideas and impulses. The other process involves primarily internal sources of ideas and a kind of evolutionary entry into new businesses, provided the organization is elastic enough to accommodate these developments. The crucial factor in these two processes, however, is a kind of (two-way) permeability in the organization, rather than purely internal or external integration or orientation.

Considering the distribution between central and divisional R&D, some of the organizational ideas in divisionalization are hazardous to R&D when carried to the extreme. For instance, the organization of all R&D aiming at new products in the form of a central laboratory for semi-autonomous research, the results of which are to be transferred to divisions, suffers from a misconception about at least two things:

(a) that research is the dominant source of innovations, and
(b) that research results are readily transferable to divisional operations.

The critics of the 'innovation chain' have demonstrated the insufficiency of assumption (a). Contrary to assumption (b), transferring research to divisions encounters many difficulties (see Steele, 1975). Thus, in such an organizational solution the potential of a source is overestimated and the effects of a barrier are underestimated.

Another example of hazardous thinking about R&D in divisionalization is to locate all R&D in product divisions organized as profit centres. The tendency to disregard the investment nature of R&D on the part of divisional management, leading to a concentration on short-range 'variations' R&D, has, however, been widely recognized.

The outer organization of R&D has not been extensively dealt with in the literature on divisionalization. Sloan (1963) certainly describes difficulties in relations between central and divisional R&D in the history of General Motors, and Chandler describes how chemical R&D played a role in the diversification strategy of Du Pont, which led to a central laboratory as a structural feature of the organization. The lack of a systematic assessment of the nature of R&D and its amenability to different forms of divisionalization, however, seems in some cases to have contributed to unawareness and inadvertencies in reorganizations. For instance, the divisionalization idea originated in the non-military industry. The ideas about the nature of R&D and the innovation process, on the other hand, were — at least formerly — largely influenced by military-industrial R&D, and it is conceivable that the combination of these ideas became misleading. Schon (1967) points out that an excess of resources for R&D, which is not infrequently the case in R&D for national prestige or military purposes, tends to make the innovation process more linearly ordered and possibly more amenable to rationalistic management and organization.

Admittedly, organizational solutions in divisionalization have seldom been carried out in extremes. New concepts for corporate R&D organizations have been formulated such as the concept of strategy centres presented by Wright (1973). Also, in practice, performance evaluation and resource control based on yearly profits have been de-emphasized and supplemented by more strategic thinking. Moreover, the possibility to 'take out' R&D results and create new venture units or the like is a possible response to problems in transferring R&D results to divisions. The organizational ideas behind a venture organization emphasize the need to integrate R&D and initial marketing and at the same time separate venture activities from the current organization. These ideas are in sharp contrast to the idea of transferring a project from central R&D to an existing division in the delicate phase of market introduction. Also a venture group is composed of a small number of individuals with single assignments in contrast to a project organization, in which individuals divide their efforts between several projects (see von Hippel, 1977; and Hlavacek and Thompson, 1973, for further readings about venturism). The innovation companies of SKF and KemaNobel have increasingly adopted these ideas and are becoming comparable to venture development companies, that is companies with the mission to organize and develop ventures.

8.4 CONCLUSIONS

The validity of the strategy-precedes-structure hypothesis is contingent upon the degree to which preconceived behaviour is included in the concept of strategy. The adoption of a divisionalized structure was in this sample of corporations hardly a consequence of an adopted strategy in the preconceived behaviour sense. Rather, rapid changes in size and diversity of operations paved the way for adopting a newly available organizational concept, the diffusion of which was aided by external organizational consultants.

Major structural variations in the outer R&D organization appear to depend especially on the intepretation and implementation of general organizational ideas by top management in addition to manning considerations. Some of the organizational ideas in divisionalization are hazardous to R&D when carried to the extreme.

Chapter 9
TECHNOLOGICAL CHANGE AND SUBCULTURES

9.1 INTRODUCTION

In this chapter some underlying patterns of the social context in which technological change takes place in a corporation will be analysed. It is possible to discern some significant social clusters or categories, as distinguished from significant actors and individuals in key positions. The observations will be presented in the framework of subcultures as identified among people engaged in science and technology and marketing in the corporations studied.

The vagueness of a concept and the use of a concept as a kind of residual explanation often go together and the concepts of 'culture' and 'technological change' are frequently used in this way.

Here the term 'culture' will be dealt with in its sociological meaning. In a standard textbook in social psychology, one reads the following definition of culture:

> The pattern of all those arrangements, materials or behavioral, which have been adopted by a society as the traditional ways of solving the problems of its members. Culture includes all the institutionalized ways and the implicit cultural beliefs, norms, values and premises which underline and govern conduct. (Krech *et al.* 1962, p. 380)

As to the 'subculture' concept, simply speaking a subculture is 'a culture within a culture'. It should be noted that the term subculture has some overtones of deviant behaviour and inferiority. These are not intended here. The word will be used in a strictly neutral sense, although it may involve 'deviant behaviour', a term which should also be interpreted in a neutral sense.

Increasing professionalization in industrial society not only accompanies an increasing fragmentation of knowledge and responsibilities, but also tends to create interprofessional barriers to communication and co-operation. A specialized occupational perspective in science and technology may, on one hand, contribute to technological development. On the other hand, 'disciplinarian imperialism' and competition among professions in colonizing areas of inquiry may arise. In particular, conflicts will arise from beliefs in the existence of an indisputable truth or from beliefs in the unification of science through reductionism.

It is natural that each profession characterizes its professional to some extent. However, differences in individual behaviour do not have to be strongly patterned according to different professions, and in some cases it may be exaggerated to talk about cultural differences between professions. Moreover, professions and individuals change and differences may be smoothed out. However, when differences of a cultural nature arise (i.e., differences in basic elements such as beliefs, norms and language) there is often little awareness and understanding of the causes and effects of such differences. Moreover, to use an anthropological analogy, there does not seem to be any breed (or profession) of investigator who is able to 'travel' among subcultures in the contemporary industrial society, and who can thereby gain and diffuse cross-cultural understanding.

9.2 EMPIRICAL FINDINGS

9.2.1 Subcultures within science and technology

9.2.1.1 Pharmaceutical industry

Within the pharmaceutical industry there has been a transition from chemistry orientation to biology orientation during the last few decades. This transition means that recruitment patterns have changed in favour of biologists, pharmacists, pharmacologists and people from other medical sciences. It has also changed the status and power of chemists. To a large extent they used to be 'generators' in R&D, and their thinking and attitudes about the biological impact of chemical substances dominated in large parts of the pharmaceutical industry. Today, biological concepts and principles have 'taken over', while the chemists' role has been geared towards synthesis. The transition is also said to have brought new ethics and a value orientation to the pharmaceutical industry. The former engineering approach to, and traditional economic value judgement of, new pharmaceuticals have to some extent been superseded by the professional ethics and values among physicians, pharmacists and pharmacologists.

The pace and extent of this transition have not been homogeneous throughout the pharmaceutical industry. Some corporations, such as Astra, re-oriented early, while others still are 'chemistry-oriented'. A partial explanation of why different corporations are in different stages of transition may be that the corporations have had different roots in the chemical industry. Some of the large pharmaceutical corporations diversified on a chemical basis early. Others, like Astra, have been in the pharmaceutical industry throughout.

A second, apparently crucial, part of the explanation is the succession of corporate managing directors and their thinking and behaviour. To break the influence of an established professional subculture in a corporation seems to require sustained efforts from the corporate managing director in concordance with changes in the professional power structure and recruitment and promotion patterns. Historical evidence (not only from Astra) support this proposition. At Astra several factors were concurrent, and these can only be briefly accounted for here. Investigations in the 1950s pointed in favour of R&D and internationalization and the location of subsidiaries close to medical schools; communications with external medical expertise paved the way for a transition. The corporate managing director played a role in this stage as well as in later stages, when recruitments and other investments had to be made and the R&D along the new lines had to be protected from established professionals in the rest of Astra. People at Astra-Hässle (where a pharmacist was the R&D manager) were treated as non-professionals and parochialists for a long time. It is interesting to note that the corporate managing director did not influence the choice of R&D lines as long as they were consistent with the new overall orientation. (In fact, these lines were rather randomly established. If the sequence of initial contacts, advice, minor successes and failures had been slightly different, probably Astra-Hässle would have been working along entirely different lines today.) One may add that the new professional subculture probably also was strengthened by the struggle against established professionals. Although 'the new professionals' received protection and support from the corporate managing director, this was of a non-professional nature, and they had to prove their case to 'the old professionals'.

A third factor in explaining the pace of a transition of this kind is the recruitment situation. In the case of Astra-Hässle, recruitment took place at a recently formed medical school, and it was therefore a new generation of academic researchers with which Astra-Hässle came in touch. They were not strongly influenced by the traditional values among academic medical researchers that research in industry is 'dirty'. In this respect the pharmaceutical industry, as well as many other sectors of industry, had to face the cultural values and beliefs of academic researchers, especially talented ones. Thus, there was both external and internal resistance, and the pace of transition was influenced by the way this resistance was managed. An inadequate supply of talented biologists was lowering the pace of Astra-Hässle. Routes of action employed by corporations in similar situations are to broaden the recruitment base to adjacent disciplines (such as chemistry in this case) or other countries (as with Philips), or alternatively to retrain internally. Thus, the connection to graduate education and university R&D is strong, not only in terms of supply but in terms of subcultural formations, which create barriers to transitions both inside and outside the industry.

In this case it is justified to talk about a transition from dominance of one professional subculture to dominance of another with respect to R&D and technology. Naturally, many internal and external factors of varying generality influence such a subcultural transition in a corporation or an industry. Furthermore, the transition is incomplete in a corporation, and the interpretations of what has happened and where one stands in the corporation in turn are affected by differences in thinking and perspective among people involved.

9.2.1.2 Raw-material based industries

Raw-material based industries constitute large and traditional parts of Swedish industry. Traditionally, at Boliden authority and status have surrounded people engaged in mining and production operations. Recruitment and promotion to leading management positions have favoured mining and production people. People engaged in chemistry related to the marketing side have experienced scepticism from other professionals. The securing of raw-material sources and plant capacity has been perceived as more crucial to business than marketing operations, integration forward and product or environmental R&D. Long-range planning and risk taking traditionally characterized mining people, but selective attention to sources of uncertainty has favoured the opening of mines and investments in new plants rather than new business ideas or concern about technological side effects. The mining and metallurgy professionals identify themselves with the corporation as a mining corporation and beliefs about what business they are in, what customer problems to solve, what parameters to judge product quality on, etc. are affected by their knowledge about mining and metallurgy. In the words of an interviewee, 'There has been an unwritten policy to stop at the pure metal.'

The metals in the ores of Boliden are chemically bound to sulphur. When new technological possibilities to utilize the sulphur content emerged, it took time before attention was paid to this development in influential circles and action initiated. An acquisition in the heavy chemicals and fertilizer industry came about in 1963. Recruitment and promotion to leading management positions have favoured mining and production people. However, the promotion of 'a mining man' to top manager of the acquired company was made partially with the intention that he should learn the chemical side and be able to 'lift it up' in balance with mining and metallurgy.

In this case a professional subculture has been connected to a segment of a refinement chain. Integration forward has required new professionals such as chemists and marketing people and the confrontation with several new subcultures. The main route to forward integration has been acquisition of companies. Thus, the company subculture in acquired companies also is involved in the transition.

9.2.1.3 Engineering industry

The engineering industry constitutes another large part of Swedish industry. Alfa-Laval provides several examples of subcultural change, although not drastic ones. In the 1960s the new corporate managing director changed recruitment and internal competence in favour of economists, administrators and marketing people. Alfa-Laval earlier had a high proportion of engineers, and clashes occurred between graduate engineers and economists, who — by the way — were and are educated in different types of universities. Perceptions of problem priorities ('what the company really needed', etc.) differed, and gaps in competence were mutually seen as causing mistakes and failures. Agreement could sometimes not be reached that failures actually were failures, at least not that they were 'failures in the long run'. Incidentally, this conflict superseded the social stratification between graduate engineers and technical college engineers. However, the subcultural change did not run as deep through the corporation as the one at Astra.

A simultaneous transition in Alfa-Laval from 'component thinking' to 'systems thinking' took place in the 1960s. On the level of post-rationalization such a transition may sound artificially related to subcultures in the corporation, but in fact, the connections are deep. Massive but selective attention was directed to concrete components such as separators, milking machines and heat exchangers. The traditional competence was centred around these components, and so was the stock of problems and the improvements that were called for. To introduce and base technological development on such abstract concepts as systems and functions took time, and 'systems thinking' diffused slowly and heterogeneously in the corporation. 'At a conference as late as 1966, it was discussed whether or not we sold components or systems'. Moreover, a higher degree of a systems nature in technological development and marketing involves more competence and professionals. Partly for this reason, partly because of trouble with products and processes and partly because of general advancements in science and technology, new technologies became relevant for Alfa-Laval during the late 1960s. The mathematics in the corporation was modernized at the same time as computers came into use. Because of this a temporary conflict emerged between, on one hand, empiricists and established mathematicians in the corporation and, on the other hand, mathematicians with a background in operations research and computers. Furthermore, automation technology based on electronic rather than mechanical components rose in relevance to the corporation. Alfa-Laval was slow to embark upon this general line of technological development. The slow pace was due partly to the dominance of mechanical engineers, partly to conflicts. A turning point occurred when a foreign subsidiary 'jumped off the corporate line' and started to buy and develop independently. A re-orientation in the corporation followed, and a competence in electronics was built up. Conflicts between professionals remained, however, and different ways of solving problems in process control and automation persisted. As a response, an independent organizational unit for automation technology was created in 1974, but the new technology has had difficulties in gaining acceptance within older parts of Alfa-Laval.

Generally speaking, the transition from mechanical to electronic solutions for engineering problems is usually well documented. The pace and extent with which this transition has taken place, have largely affected the competitive position. Many factors have been involved in specific cases, but professional subcultures have played a large role. The frames of perception are different in mechanical and electronic engineering and they give rise to different ways of solving technical problems. As a matter of course, people also identify themselves with their solutions, emotions and conflicts are built up, managers involve themselves more and more, anxiety about changes in power based on competence arises, informal coalitions are formed, etc. The traditional influence and status of mechanical design engineers were not voluntarily abandoned or shared, partly since it was not in their own interests but partly also because these engineers did not think it was in the interest of anybody. The latter point is representative of a professional subculture. Its shared values do not just encompass the survival of the profession but also the value of the profession to others (the corporation, industry, society).

Regarding Alfa-Laval, more representative cases are provided. The products and strategy of the corporation have brought it in contact with various other disciplines within chemistry, biology and agriculture. Again, the pace of the use of such competences was slowed down by traditional problem-solving behaviour, although no clashes or deep-running transitions or conflicts occurred. As a traditional manufacturer of machines and components in various processes, including food processing, Alfa-Laval had experienced successes largely based on trial and error methods. When ambitions towards systems technology emerged at the same time as the complexity of customer processes increased, mechanical engineering and problem solving by trial and error became inadequate. Product trouble and customer complaints may aid in pointing out such inadequacies, but the usual response is then to apply or marginally expand the existing competence and to 'search locally' for solutions. A global search, if one is initiated, corresponds to the hiring of a new kind of professional. This has been done gradually by Alfa-Laval, but it still has to amalgamate new values, frames of perception and professional norms. The food and agriculture sector of industry provides a slight parallel to the pharmaceutical industry in this respect, in that veterinarians and agronomists are said to be in the position to bring in new values among engineers and economists, just as medically trained personnel did in the pharmaceutical industry.

9.2.1.4 Forestry

As can be seen from the above, there are several examples of how biologists have diffused into different sectors of industry. Iggesund provides another example. Within forestry there has been a period of dominance by mechanical engineers. The selective attention to certain advantages of scale and ignorance of some long-term biological side effects promoted the development of forestry machinery and methods that later on called for biological competence. Mechanical engineers could more easily demonstrate benefits of their way of conducting operations and gained management support. The 'success' of this demonstration hinged not only upon management preferences for short-term corporate economy but also on difficulties to perceive, assess and understand possible side effects of a biological nature. Biological 'thinking' had only penetrated the industry marginally except for certain specific tasks. Contributing factors to the slow pace in the change of frames of perception of managers and engineers were, moreover, the delay in biological effects and the continuous character of technological change: 'Continuous development is not so easily noted'.

Thus, problem solving by a familiar approach appears to involve an underestimation of risks. The opposite also seems to hold, that is problem solving by an unfamiliar approach involves an overestimation of risks. For example, one response by Iggesund to scarcity of timber was to transplant a fast-growing Canadian pine. Top management perceived the experimental procedure by which this type of tree was introduced as a strategic decision involving high risks, while biologists perceived the decision making as a sequence of 'ordinary' decisions.

9.2.1.5 Formation of generations

The formation of generations within a professional discipline should be contrasted with the formation of subcultures. As advances in science and technology proceed and environmental changes occur, professional thinking and behaviour are naturally changed. Sometimes these changes are accommodated within a discipline, sometimes a differentiation of disciplines occurs. A renewal process within a discipline is sometimes not only markedly wave-like but also connected to a new generation. For example, within electrical engineering there have been transitions from vacuum tubes to transistors, from electromechanics to electronics, and from analog to digital technology. Philips has experienced such transitions and difficulties with differences in fundamental thinking between older and younger engineers. Within KemaNobel four epochs of chemical R&D may be discerned. The fourth and present one concerns polymer technology, while earlier there were 'old carbide engineers'.

Transitions between generations take place at different paces and extents in industry just as in the case of transitions between disciplines. However, changes among professionals in the corporation due to—on the one hand—changes between professional disciplines, and—on the other hand—changes within them, differ in one respect. The latter 'within changes' constitute more of a true transition, while the 'between changes' generally mean just a transformation of the mixture of relationships. However, the conceptual boundaries determining 'within' and 'between' are vague, which is shown by the presence of many names for disciplines and professions.

A word of caution is appropriate here. Changes within a discipline or profession may be so gradual and may not involve value changes deep enough to justify the term 'subcultural change'. Moreover, a subcultural change does not by definition require that new people supersede old people, although such a change is also often involved. Finally, subcultural changes by generation shifts are to be distinguished from a new group of people who just have a cohesive pattern of thinking and behaviour.

9.2.2 Subcultures within marketing

First, one should note that marketing people are not to be identified as non-technical professionals. In fact, several corporations have a high density of technically trained people in their marketing departments. This situation may result from a perceived necessity to have it that way and deliberately strive for it, as for instance at Alfa-Laval and SKF, while in some industries and corporations it seems to result rather from an attitude that marketing may be handled by technologists as well.

Except for the general categories economists and engineers, subcultures among marketing people seem to be more weakly associated with the structure of professional education than was the case among science and technology people. One should note, however, that education in marketing is not so well developed as education within science and technology.

Thinking and behaviour among people involved in marketing are naturally influenced by the thinking and behaviour of customers as well as by the thinking and behaviour within their own corporation around the products sold. This influence from external communication does not seem to breed subcultures to the same extent as does the external communication of corporate science and technology professionals.

9.2.2.1 Producer and consumer markets

Concerning marketing on producer and consumer markets, several corporations, such as KemaNobel, Philips and Volvo, are working in both kinds of markets, often with very much the same basic technology. One crucial feature is the competence of customers as professional buyers. With competent customers it is possible to foster a technological development with the aid of mutual communications and similarities in language and value. Under such circumstances marketing people are used to reduce uncertainty and distribute risks in the seller–buyer interface by mutual communications in a professional language concerning values of technical and economic performance. In consumer markets, or rather in markets with non-professional buyers, marketing people tend to place emphasis on the perceptual, cognitive and emotional behaviour of the customer in the buying process rather than on assessment of improvements in customer economy.

Both types of marketing behaviour may be 'need oriented', but for the latter type greater attention is paid to 'irrational' needs and weaknesses in consumer behaviour. Moreover, customers—and sometimes competitors—in consumer markets are often numerous and unstructured. Many factors on this type of markets create thinking and behaviour about technological development and beliefs about consumer behaviour and needs that differ substantially from those of marketing in producer markets. This is reflected in different traditions in doing market research.

There have been many failures in diversifying into consumer markets without previous knowledge about that type of markets. Naturally, economic and other circumstances are important, but also past experience, beliefs, and attitudes, which sometimes prove to be markedly inadequate. Often too high a value is placed on advanced technology to solve customer problems, which is not compatible with customer preferences. Within the corporation one commonly explains it in terms of 'being ahead of time', 'immature markets', or plain stupidity of customers. It is, however, a question of how to compromise between, on one hand, the company's perception of customer problems and 'rational' ways to solve them and, on the other hand, the way customers perceive their situation. At Alfa-Laval 'profitability for the customer' as a basic aim has been questioned on these grounds. To sell barn equipment to farmers involves buyer competence and behaviour that is far from always aligned with customer economy and profitability. For some chemical products it is 'more a matter of selling the can than its content'. Cars, clothes and home appliances sell to a varying extent on appearance in combination with performance. For a science and technology professional with his training in analytic thinking, it is hard to understand customer concern about microwave ovens. 'There has been no proof' is a common statement concerning possible side effects outside the field of a professional. Curiously enough, one sometimes encounters a confusion among science and technology professionals about the difference between unproved and disproved factors. Even if this issue is settled, an attitude often remains that the burden of proof rests mainly on the customer or bodies that are distrustful or frightened about risks.

9.2.2.2 Military markets

Related to marketing on producer markets is marketing of military products. The culture in this seller–buyer interface is well developed and highly important on a global level. The notion of the 'free' world ranged against evil powers has been fostered in the military-industrial complex in Western countries. The people at Volvo Flygmotor engaged in aerospace technology for military purposes point out the remarkable openness in Western countries concerning science and technology. Sweden is officially neutral but is considered to be Western-oriented, which is beneficial for Volvo Flygmotor in the development of United States technology. There are, to a large extent, shared values and beliefs among businessmen, military people, R&D personnel and governments about the necessity of defending the politico-economical system with a technology-intensive defence. Admittedly, some businessmen do not care — at least not very much — as long as they can sell; some military people entertain the idea of a labour-intensive defence; some R&D personnel may not consider it as part of their responsibility to question the values, or they become reconciled to them, and some people in government circles clearly express different opinions. Moreover, local authority interests and labour union interests often tie themselves to the interests of the military industry, at least in the short run 'until alternate production may be secured'. Despite many variations in ideologies and adaptations to situational logic, military technology is further developed, and this development takes place in a context that encompasses two basic cultural phenomena, namely collective pride and collective anxiety.

To explain some of the cohesiveness of the military culture, one may point to the long tradition, the ties to national culture, the military educational system, the organizational system and the instrumentality of collective anxiety and pride as well as of secrecy. In the interface to industry there is much professional education, many extensive studies and a considerable amount of research concerning military needs and technologies; there is also interface mobility between the military and industry and a regulated economy which consciously fosters a viable domestic defence industry. All this makes the military customer a generally competent buyer with knowledge about the role of technology in defence economy (with offshoots such as war economy and combat economy), a concept which is analogous to customer economy. Moreover, the military subculture diffuses and is reflected in, the corresponding parts in industry. Corporations which have for a long time been doing business with the military, such as Philips-Sweden and Volvo Flygmotor, develop a corresponding corporate subculture. Among its characteristics is that value is placed on advanced science and technology, analytical thinking, and management methods for solving problems. (Incidentally, many management concepts and methods have diffused from the military to the civilian spheres such as strategic planning, logistics, thinking in product life cycles, project planning and operations research.) Being tied to a single, competent customer, members of this subculture solve problems of market uncertainty in quite a different way than is common for civilian industrial customers. Similar traits, although not so pronounced, occur in other instances of a single, competent customer, usually a government body.

In the eyes of other people in the corporations, the military subculture is perceived as 'heavy' and 'very special', which is in contrast to a more 'moderate' self-image within the subculture. This image of 'the military side' in the eyes of others affects organization and management. The pressure upon Swedish military industry to diversify into the civilian sector has raised the need for management to modify the military subculture within the corporations. In the mid-1970s Philips-Sweden chose to locate civilian and military parts of the organization geographically close to each other, aiming at changing the communication pattern. Transfer and turnover of management and personnel could also have changed communication patterns in favour of civilian diversification, and new responsibilities for product work could have been assigned as well. Instead, a 'softer' way was thus chosen. Naturally, there were more reasons behind the move, and the ambition 'to strengthen the civilian leg' arose earlier in the 1960s and has been pursued by other means as well.

9.3 DISCUSSION

9.3.1 Empirical summary

There are several bases for the emergence of subcultures in and around a corporation. Such subcultures may thus be oriented around a product, a profession, a market, or an organizational unit. Here the focus has been on subcultures within science and technology and marketing. Typically, such subcultures are established in the corporation during a long period of time and are then opposed and subjected to a transformation. Table 9.1 summarizes some examples found in the corporations. (The list of factors of primary influence must be considered as a subjective and non-comprehensive summary.)

In addition to the examples in Table 9.1, the diffusion of biological thinking into different sectors of industry has been described, as well as differences in thinking and behaviour in the marketing of consumer and producer products. The culture in the military-industrial complex has been pointed at as a noteworthy example of an established culture in a seller-buyer interface.

9.3.2 Cultural structure

It should be pointed out that the culture associated with science and technology, which is sometimes presumed to be homogeneous, is heterogeneous with several subcultures that are sometimes in conflict with each other. Scientists and technologists certainly share some basic values and beliefs about the benefits of their work and their methods and what is legitimate in thinking and language. On the other hand, differences in these respects between disciplines, as well as between generations, are marked as described in the preceding section. Such differences within an overall science and technology culture seem to produce intermittent re-orientations rather than smooth, cumulative evolution. Individual scientists and technologists build up conceptions that ossify and obstruct intellectual reorganizations. Science and technology groups are formed on the basis of similarities in educational background and shared conceptions and language. Individuals tend to socialize in at least one group, their social skills improve, they become tied to interests, and they defy fundamentally new conceptions. As a result, disciplines expand and contract, amalgamate and split up, and this is accompanied by generation changes, breakthroughs of new knowledge and, not least, by conflicting interests.

The empirical observations point to science and technology cultures associated with, for example, chemists, biologists, mining engineers, mechanical engineers, and electrical and electronics engineers. These categories correspond to the structure of graduate education, as well as to the structure of industrial branches or sectors. The formation of subcultures also seems to take place to a large extent

Table 9.1 Examples of subcultural transformations

Change involving a subcultural transformation	Factors of primary influence
Astra	
Transition from a chemistry orientation to a biology orientation	Corporate origin Top and R&D management behaviour Recruitment Technological change
Boliden	
Integration of chemistry into the mining orientation	Top management behaviour Recruitment and promotion Corporate strategy Technological change
Alfa-Laval	
(a) Integration of economics into the engineering orientation (b) Transition from component orientation to systems orientation	Top management behaviour Recruitment Corporate strategy Internal conceptualizers Technological and market change Product troubles
(c) Integration of electronics into the mechanics orientation	R&D management behaviour Independent subsidiary action Recruitment Technological change
Philips-Sweden	
Reorientation from military markets to civilian markets	Corporate strategy Location Market changes

during graduate education or in the early years of professional life when large parts of an individual's professional '*Weltanschauung*' and language are formed.

The subcultural features formed during graduate education are then often reinforced when the young professional goes into a corporation, due to the structural correspondence between universities and different sectors of industry. The inertia of the educational system in universities then produces a strong and enduring sectoral barrier to change in industry. This circumstance may partially explain the phenomenon of innovation by invasion as described by Schon (1967), that is, how whole sectors of industry are invaded by new technologies outside their traditional fields.

9.3.3 Cultural change

Social differentiation into different cultures is neither hierarchical nor permanent, and an individual or a corporation may be associated with several cultures with multiple and temporary connections of various strength. An individual may belong to a subculture in science and technology but also to a corporate culture and to a regional culture. His cultural memberships may change as well. Individuals are also carriers of culture, and a corporate culture may be altered as the result of changes within individuals and among corporate personnel.

In considering cultural change, three connected processes are of relevance here:

(a) the formation of change of cultures;
(b) the association of an individual with a culture;
(c) the association of a culture with a corporation.

To discuss each of these processes in depth would be beyond the scope of this study. The role of graduate education has been noted above. In a second-order analysis, one may take as a starting point the observation that social differentiation is clustered (i.e., social differences are not evenly distributed but patterned). The clustering of social differences in language, beliefs and values in problem solving among professionals is influenced by the individual's need to reduce uncertainty in connection with his pattern of communication, which he can only partially influence. Interpersonal variations are a great source of uncertainty and this may be reduced by conforming to a certain language and to certain standards and norms of behaviour. Consider, for instance, the use of mathematical logic standards of reasoning among science and technology professionals or the standard way of assigning the burden of proof to the one who makes a statement or proposes a change. Individuals, however, differ in their capacities to process information and handle uncertainty associated with interpersonal variations. Their needs to reduce uncertainty differ, as well as the manners in which uncertainty is reduced. Moreover, different needs of different individuals become dependent upon each other, which may mutually reinforce a social clustering.

Thus, there are several determinants behind the formation of cultures and the association of an individual with different cultures pertaining to different segments of his life situation. The strength of this association differs between individuals and also changes with time. A high learning capacity makes a professional less dependent upon his discipline-oriented knowledge as acquired by formal education, and may therefore permit him to be more problem oriented and less inclined to associate with a certain professional culture. A university researcher may feel associated with science and technology in general but with academic research in particular and even more with academic research within his field. Problems in connection with too weak an association of university researchers with the culture of industrial R&D are often witnessed. Although not so frequently mentioned, the opposite may also occur, that is, an individual leaves the university and in a way overassimilates into the industrial culture, thereby distinguishing himself from his university colleagues.

The third process, the association of a culture with a corporation is of main concern here. The focus is especially on change associated with professional subcultures, as encountered in the corporations studied. On one hand, a corporation is associated with different cultures through its personnel. On the other hand, a specific corporate culture is often formed, a culture which may retain its basic characteristics even if turnover of personnel is high. Since a culture reduces variations and uncertainty for its members, it may be instrumental in coordination and communication. A culture may also be instrumental in preserving a power structure. Management has possibilities to influence language, ideology, beliefs and myths in the corporation and thereby influence the corporate culture to the benefit and convenience of themselves. Thus, there are several motives behind the formation of a corporate culture. However, a culture may also act as a barrier to change, as can be seen from the cases studied.

Focusing on changes of professional subcultures in the corporation as summarized in Table 9.1, one may discern twelve factors of primary influence behind such changes. Although it is extremely difficult to separate such factors and assess their influence, certain indications are worthwhile considering. The most frequently encountered factors are, on one hand, technological and market changes and, on the other hand, top management behaviour, corporate strategy, recruitment and promotion. The latter group of factors directly involves top management. This indicates that top management plays a primary role in cultural change in the corporation and that strategy formation, recruitment and promotion are important instruments in bringing about that change. In this sense a top manager in a large corporation may act in an important manner as a cultural entrepreneur. This does not always have to be the case, though. In some cases a corporate managing director has hindered or slowed down a cultural change initiated internally or externally.

Concerning the instruments for bringing about a cultural change, strategy formation, recruitment and promotion certainly are important. These instruments may, or course, be used in different ways. Thus, for example, Boliden promoted a mining man as head of the new chemical part of the corporation to be able 'to lift it up', while SKF, instead, promoted a steel man as manager of the corporate R&D laboratory, to be able to up-grade the steel side of R&D in traditional areas. Astra heavily relied on recruitment of new competence, which was natural considering the total dominance of chemists. (It is a fundamental fact that a specialized professional in one field cannot be converted into a specialized professional in a different field overnight or even over some years.)

A cultural entrepreneur may use other instruments as well. To restructure communications through organization and location is a tangible way of acting. He may also act in a more intangible way on the level of fundamental elements in a culture, such as influencing language and values, creating symbols and rituals, strengthening ideologies and nurturing myths.

However, the dynamics of cultural change as discussed here, involves more factors than just a cultural entrepreneur, which is often used as a handy explanation. Although there are instruments for management which influence a culture, it would be naïve to consider a culture as something which could be created and managed totally at will. Cultural change has, for instance, a pre-history in which external changes and internal conflicts are influential. The whole process of change, which may last over some decades, is characterized by disorder and uncertainty and the outcomes may vary. Starting from the situation of a dominant culture in a corporation, with a new culture emerging, four types of outcome may be discerned:

— amalgamation of cultures;
— transition to new dominance;

Technological change and subcultures 143

— ordered co-existence;
— rejection of emerging culture and regression to old culture.

Of the above, amalgamation (for instance, at Alfa-Laval), transition (for instance, at Astra) and the role of new generations of professionals are important. A new generation may change and amalgamate values and beliefs previously associated with two subcultures or disciplines, and a new generation may be needed to subdue an old subculture. Ordered co-existence of two subcultures (for example, at Boliden) may be accomplished both by hiring new professionals with weaker subcultural association and by structuring organization and management.

Finally, some comments may be made about the general trend to incorporate biological competence in industry. It is a response partly to threats from technological side effects and partly to opportunities in the advancing life sciences. Neglecting, for the moment, the many confluences of scientific disciplines in advanced natural sciences, one may make the following rough description. Chemists and others have been engaged in designing resistant compounds, they have been utilizing 'aggressive' methods and have applied rude measures to achieve certain effects and suppress others. To a different extent biologists utilize processes in nature (for example, by enzyme technology, microbiological extraction, biological control in agriculture and genetic engineering) and by these means it is possible to tailor outcomes, although in most cases industrial use is barely economically feasible so far. A naïve but illustrative simplification would be to view the change as turning from fighting with, to manipulative co-operation with, nature. This change may lead to the establishment of a new subculture of biologists in parts of industry. Likewise the transition to electronics has led to the dominance of electronics people in parts of industry. If there were to be a confluence of biology and electronics (c.f. bio-chips) in the decades to come, it would probably cause resistance to change among these new subcultures. The reasoning behind such a forecast has been presented here in the form of similar historic cases and a body of supporting evidence in psychology and sociology concerning individual and group behaviour in information processing, problem solving and socialization.

9.4 CONCLUSIONS

This chapter has focused on the relationship between technology change and subcultures in eight corporations representing different sectors of industry. The general conclusion is that treating technological change as an autonomous or exogenous variable in relation to cultural change is incorrect.

There are several bases for the emergence of subcultures in and around a corporation, for instance, a product, a profession, a market or an organizational unit. Formation of different cultures is neither hierarchical nor permanent, and an individual or a corporation may be associated with several cultures with multiple and temporary connections of various strength.

The tensions between a business culture and a science and technology culture are apparent in many cases. The culture associated with science and technology is, however, heterogeneous with several subcultures not infrequently in conflict with each other. Examples are subcultures associated with chemistry, biology, mining, mechanical engineering and electrical engineering. The formation of these professional subcultures is strongly connected with the structure of graduate education. The subcultures, moreover, tend to produce intermittent re-orientations in corporations and sectors of industry.

A subculture may constitute a means of co-ordination as well as a barrier to change. Through a period of conflicts and disordered co-existence, a state with a dominant culture in a corporation may be transformed into one of the following:

(a) a state of amalgamation of cultures;
(b) a state of dominance of a new culture;
(c) regression to the old culture; and
(d) a state of ordered cultural co-existence.

Several factors account for the transformation of different cultures in a corporation. The role of top management as a kind of cultural entrepreneur is important, although cultural change cannot be managed at will. Such instruments include corporate strategy, recruitment and promotion.

Chapter 10
CONFLICTS RELATED TO R&D AND INNOVATION IN LARGE CORPORATIONS

10.1 INTRODUCTION

In this chapter an account will be given of conflicts encountered within the corporations studied in connection with R&D and innovation. Corporations are often viewed as homogeneous decision-making and policy-making bodies. Sometimes management is viewed the same way with the principal corporate conflict between management and labour. Conflicts are however, ubiquitous, but usually they are not talked about very specifically and are thought of as compromising for individuals and organizations.

The chapter will be devoted to the recognition of the significance of conflicts among professionals and managers. The focus is on social conflicts; conflicts within the individual will not be discussed. Also 'ordinary' conflicts in resource utilization will not be included due to their familiarity. This does not mean that these two kinds of conflicts are unrelated to other kinds. Strong ambivalence may grow within an individual as a consequence of external conflicts, just as easily as the ambivalent behaviour of an individual may cause conflicts around him in the organization. Similar interactions between resource conflicts and other kinds of conflicts exist. Shortage of resources, and especially shrinking resources tend to accentuate social conflicts, just as a breakdown in co-ordination may lead to a waste of resources.

'Conflict' may be used in a 'weak' sense for any dissonance in values, emotions or cognitions. In a 'strong' sense conflict denotes a similar dissonance, which, however, implies incompatibility that has to be resolved. Traditional literature on organization and management usually regards conflict as something negative, and therefore as something which has to be avoided or resolved. This is, of course, also dependent upon the definition of conflict. With conflict defined as a 'breakdown in the standard mechanisms of decision making so that an individual or group experiences difficulty in selecting an action alternative' (March and Simon, 1958, p. 112) conflicts almost by definition have some negative effects.

Here conflict will be used to describe a state of a social relation that involves:

(a) a mutual awareness of a dissonance in values, emotions, or cognitions; and
(b) a readiness from at least one party in the relation to act against the preferences of the other party.

Thus, there are two graded scales, one pertaining to the magnitude of perceived dissonance, the other to the magnitude of incompatible action. The conflicts may be judged, at least qualitatively, in such terms as size, growth, duration and distribution. Being a state, a conflict may also be described in terms of diagnosis, causes, effects and treatments.

Conflicts related to R&D and innovation present special problems to an organization and its management. This kind of conflict has not been recognized to a degree corresponding to its importance. In addition, this kind of conflict involves conflicts within and around elites. It is probable that the development of an organization is influenced by the relations within a small elite. This is, however, extremely difficult to judge.

10.2 EMPIRICAL FINDINGS

The empirical findings will be presented in the following way. First, conflicts are viewed statically, and groups of conflicts are presented and typical significant conflict relations pointed out. Then, a dynamic perspective is applied in that a case is given, which illustrates how conflicts emerge and change in these significant conflict relations. One more case is then given, which especially illustrates the dynamics in one type of significant conflict relations, namely relations among significant actors.

10.2.1 Groups of encountered conflicts

A classification of conflicts into overlapping groups has been made. The grouping is closely related to the one of barriers to innovation discussed later in Chapter 11, emphasizing the suitability of a conflict perspective in studying and managing innovation. Thus, the following groups of conflicts and conflict relations were identified:

— conflicts in external relations;
— conflicts within management;
— conflicts among organizational units;
— conflicts in relation to corporate history;
— resource conflicts;
— conflicts related to certain individuals and groups;
— miscellaneous conflicts.

It is not possible to be conclusive in quantitative terms about the frequency and effect of these conflicts. Even qualitatively it is hard to be specific, since a weighted judgement of the frequency and effects of conflicts of a certain kind has to be made in assessing their importance in some sense. However, on the basis of the observations some relations of importance to the innovativeness of a corporation seem especially susceptible to conflicts. Typical significant conflict relations in this sense were:

(a) relations among significant actors (e.g., among top managers, technical managers, and R&D managers);
(b) relations associated with a traditional part in the corporation;

Conflicts related to R&D and innovation

(c) functional relations (e.g., between R&D, production, and marketing and their sub-functions);
(d) relations between central and local authorities;
(e) relations among professionals and among their subcultures.

On an operative level, pressures to achieve speed, quality and low cost in development work typically produced conflicts, especially when transfers between geographical and organizational borders were involved. Another well known issue, which also typically involved different opinions and interests, was resource sharing and budgeting. When resources are divisible, solutions by negotiation, adjustment and compromise may be attempted. However, opposition to permanent resource sharing or departures from practice typically produced conflicts. Cuts in R&D budgets have at some time been made by several corporations. This is also an example of the common conflict between short-range and long-range behaviour.

As already mentioned, the groups of conflicts displayed above are not independent. A conflict displays a complex of differences in the perception of values and causality. Several conflict relations exist latently and clusters of them become activated. Thus, for example, a conflict relation between central R&D and a traditional division may become activated when technology is about to be transferred. The conflict may then develop into a complex of subconflicts, including conflicts between professional categories, and conflicts between individual managers. The manifest causes may concern project priorities, inadequate solutions to technical problems and disputes over resources, while latent causes may concern old aggression, defeats and revenge feelings, competition for promotion, threats from young managers with current knowledge etc. All this is mixed together in a multitude of complex relations, and any discussion about a conflict of a specific kind with a specific cause is likely to be oversimplified.

10.2.2 Dynamics in typical significant conflict relations

A conflict complex changes with time. A conflict with a customer, for example, easily diffuses into the organization aided by distorted attributions. Marketing people 'hunt' production people, who blame a designer, who in turn claims he was forced to a sloppy design by time pressures put on him by management, including the marketing manager. Resources may then be redistributed to take care of immediate product problems, but grudges between individuals may remain as a net effect of social transactions and may become activated at a later time. The possibilities of diffusing blame are large in a large organization, especially when uncertainty is involved (as in innovative work). Nevertheless, social relations tend to become 'infected' by such a diffusion, and a scapegoat may have to absorb the blame and save the relationships between, and images of, others. An organization puts pressure upon individuals to co-operate, and self-interests, competition, and aggression have to be disguised to some extent. Memories of injustices, injuries, grudges, betrayals, and similar relational events cumulate in the organization, each individual having his own 'cumulative profile': as someone stated '[A] could never forget that he was passed by [B] for promotion.'

Thus, correlated with the stability in the personnel portfolio, conflict potentials are continuously being built up. Any relation attains a potential for conflicts. With some probability then conflicts are born, they grow or deepen, diffuse among people and relations, mature or are phased out, possibly by aggressive action or reshaped relations in some other way. For instance, as a feature of a corporate culture, individuals aiming for promotion have to display a combination of competitive and co-operative behaviour. This naturally creates a potential for conflicts within individuals and within the organization. Positional goods, moreover, cannot be shared, so there is a win-lose conflict potential tied to that kind of resources. Conflicts related to positions may be accommodated if the competing parties are not strongly dependent on each other. But if they are, resulting conflicts may grow out of control and have to be 'violently' resolved. Promotional conflicts between functional managers of R&D, production and marketing with dependence between the functions is one example of this. Thus, one effect of a reorganization from a functional organization into a divisionalized organization with semi-autonomous divisions is that the conflict potential is reduced regarding the position as corporate managing director.

Case 10.1 Astra

The last two decades of the history of Astra provide several examples of conflicts. As a result of strategic considerations in the 1950s, R&D was built up in a decentralized manner in subsidiaries located close to medical schools. The corporate managing director played a central part in the initiation and support of these ideas but was non-directive in issues concerning the content of R&D. The R&D manager of Astra-Hässle was a pharmacist and initially met strong resistance from the central R&D establishment of Astra: 'They wouldn't touch me with a ten-foot pole'. People from Astra-Hässle were accused of parochialism and non-professionalism. With the aid of external consultants, the support from the corporate managing director, and an ability of the R&D manager of Astra-Hässle to recruit and build relations with professional people, R&D was built up at Astra-Hässle. This phase (in the late 1950s and early 1960s) involved a change in the originally negative attitudes of academic researchers towards the pharmaceutical industry, a slow-moving transition from chemical to biological competence with accompanying shifts in professional power and values, and a more or less continuous struggle for corporate resources.

In the mid 1960s decentralized and regionalized R&D within Astra had considerably grown in size and content, and there was a call for corporate co-ordination, which was contrary to the corporate managing director's belief in decentralization. A corporate research mangement committee was formed, which started to function as a pressure group and a forum for communications. By this time, conflicts between Astra-Hässle and the central R&D establishment had faded somewhat, but criticism remained regarding the direction of R&D at Astra-Hässle. External events and signs of failure, such as pharmaceutical side-effects and advances by competitors, were also producing conflicting views, as well as jumps in resource requirements as R&D progressed. Moreover, Astra rigidly adhered to a principle of budgeting R&D in relation to turnover, and Astra-Hässle required resources for R&D that were above the average.

In the latter part of the 1960s, R&D at Astra-Hässle started to bear fruit after activities that were close to 'crash programmes'. The new product was, however, a 'slow starter', and success was not obvious. At the same time conflicts emerged among the subsidiaries, since their R&D territories started to overlap. A controversial profiling of R&D among the subsidiaries was carried through in the latter part of the 1960s. Conflict potentials among subsidiaries still existed in the mid-1970s, and within the parent company one even perceived a pressure from the subsidiaries to have central authorities as conciliators among the subsidiaries.

In the late 1960s a policy conflict emerged. Simply expressed, there was a question concerning the degree of leadership and whether or not to have R&D aiming for significant therapeutical advances. Involved in the conflict were also relations between a central R&D manager and the R&D manager of Astra-Hässle concerning the question of autonomy or control, the question of the value of R&D in industry, and differences in chemical and biological approaches to problem solving.

In the early 1970s the situation was under control in the sense that key people had largely adjusted to each other, the transition to dominance of biological competence was completed, the basic ways of conducting R&D were established, good external relations had been built, and R&D at Astra-Hässle had proved successful. Basic threats to Astra-Hässle, its R&D, and autonomy had largely disappeared. By this time a more constant but accepted pressure was exercised by the co-ordinating research management committee. A top researcher, recruited by the R&D manager of Astra-Hässle, had transferred to a position as corporate R&D manager. He showed signs of wanting to decrease subsidiary autonomy, signs which were carefully watched by the subsidiaries. However, he died and his position was not filled.

A conflicting issue in 1976 was the development of a third generation of products along one of the original lines of R&D at Astra-Hässle. This development was favoured by the R&D manager of Astra-Hässle, but scepticism had arisen in the committee. The issue of corporate control was also activated by the recruitment of an external top researcher as division manager. His competence and authority were widely accepted and respected and at the time it was hoped that he would 'control through his competence'. Moreover, the growth of subsidiaries and their R&D again brought up issues of corporate control such as profiling R&D among subsidiaries, determining a proper scale of subsidiary R&D, and determining whether diversification and risk distribution through R&D should take place on a subsidiary or divisional level.

In the parent company Astra-Hässle had appeared as homogeneous and 'able to keep their conflicts within the house. One can understand that some of their researchers are very independent boys'. There had certainly been internal conflicts within Astra-Hässle as, for example, in 1976 concerning the successor to the R&D manager. However, the relations between R&D and top management and between R&D and marketing have apparently been free from conflicts at Astra-Hässle.

[End of Case 10.1]

In summary, the conflicts at Astra and Astra-Hässle show that:

(a) a diversity of conflicts existed for a long time within and around a subsidiary that eventually proved successful;
(b) the size and duration of conflicts did not grow to impairing proportions by personification;
(c) at Astra-Hässle the absence of conflicts in crucial internal relations and the presence of external conflicts, to some extent controlled by corporate top management, is probably part of the explanation of success;
(d) part of the success is attributable to the good relations between subsidiary top management and R&D management and the ability of the R&D manager of Astra-Hässle to recruit and utilize top researchers, to manage internal conflicts, and to build good external relations.

10.2.3 Dynamics in relations among significant actors

A conflict is just one kind of state in a relation between two significant actors; it is also a simplified one. In any sociogrammatic representation, the binary relations between individuals are simplifications of dislike, avoidance, esteem, conflict, competition, agreement etc. The relations may be asymmetric, their states may fluctuate over time, and — not least — the relations are contingent upon situations. Perhaps especially when describing relations among significant actors with sophisticated ways of relating to each other in different situations where the pictures of their relations usually are distorted, one is in danger of over-simplification. Nevertheless, an example will be given that should convey a little of the essence of the interplay and 'personnel chemistry' among significant actors in a large corporation. A distinction has to be pointed out at this stage. There are significant actors and there are positions in an organization, which have been equipped with possibilities to exert influence. Different representations may be chosen to describe the relations among significant actors and significant positions over a period of time as well as the 'professional trajectories' and to show how the positions are created, changed, and eliminated. The following notation of general applicability will be used:

Position

CB — chairman of the board; MD — managing director; TD — technical director; SD — staff director; RM — R&D manager; DM — design manager; EC — external consultant.

Level

C — corporate level; D — divisional level; S — subsidiary level; v — vice-.

Change

↑ — promoted; →X — recruited from the outside to the position as X; X→ — left the organization from the position as X; ↘ — retired; † — died.

Subscripts denote one chosen enumeration of organizational units and posi-

Conflicts related to R&D and innovation 151

tions. Superscripts denote one chosen enumeration of successors. (The superscript changes notation from position to occupant.)

Examples

(a) →D_3MD^2 denotes a person who has been recruited from the outside as managing director for division number three and who is the second occupant of this position.
(b) vCMD denotes a position as vice managing director on the corporate level.

Case 10.2 The X Corporation

The X Corporation (anonymous here) was re-organized into divisions in two steps in the late 1960s and the early 1970s. The time focused on here is roughly a five-year period between and including these two organizational changes. Some specific information has had to be left out, making more exact representations impossible.

A sociogram or a matrix of relations could be at least partially constructed as in Figure 10.1. However, a verbal account must be given in order to do better justice to the dynamics of the relations. Moreover, the relations are not exclusively binary. Personal relations are complex: coalitions and inner circles are formed, reorganizations are discussed, and consideration for individuals and the organization are shown, and maybe most of all, it is hard to gain access to an overall, unbiased picture. It is hoped the importance of the subject justifies the simplified and somewhat fragmentary account below.

In the late 1960s, the top management constituted a very good working team. Arvid was a vigorous, authoritative corporate leader, who also competently engaged in technical matters, although only in his favorite field. Christer was a gifted production man; he was calm and judicious and was also said to be able to 'moderate' Arvid. The relation between Arvid and the technical director David was not the best. David was a talented technologist and had built up a kind of 'empire'. He was said to be unobtrusive but stubborn and was working in an old-fashioned way. He had some backbiters around him, and there was a conflict with a marketing manager and with the design manager, Ivar, who also was a talented technologist. The first step in the reorganization, in which Nils played a central role, involved the destruction of David's empire. David moved stepwise into a central managing position, in which he adopted a rather timid role.

The re-organization created new positional resources, but in general new people were recruited, and old people were moved to corporate positions so that corporate staffs grew. A corporate R&D manager and a divisional R&D manager were recruited from outside. The corporate R&D manager, Johan, did not succeed in establishing productive relations and esteem from his environment in the organization. As an outsider he had to face much resistance from internal cliques among old '[X]-men'. Moreover, he lacked adequate personal skills to relate to people and was perceived to be 'extreme' in certain respects. Johan was recruited by Arvid but was afterwards considered as 'a hell of a mistake. It was a pity because he was a nice guy'.

The divisional R&D manager, Karl, also created non-productive relations around him due to personal behaviour and circumstances in the organization,

Name of person	Sequence of positions
	────▶ Time
P 1 Arvid	↑CMD, CB
P 2 Bertil	→dCMD, CMD
P 3 Christer	dCMD+
P 4 David	CTD, CRM¹, CSD→
P 5 Erik	↑CSD,
P 6 Gunnar	↑D₂MD¹, dCMD
P 7 Holger	↑D₁MD², CSD
P 8 Ivar	DM, D₁MD¹+
P 9 Johan	→CRM²→
P 10 Karl	→D₁RM
P 11 Lars	↑CRM³
P 12 Magnus	D₁DM→
P 13 Nils	EC

Note:
+ denotes a positive relation on an average
− denotes a negative relation, ranging from skepticism to conflict
Omitted arrows denote neutral relations or missing data.
Superscripts are deleted when possible.

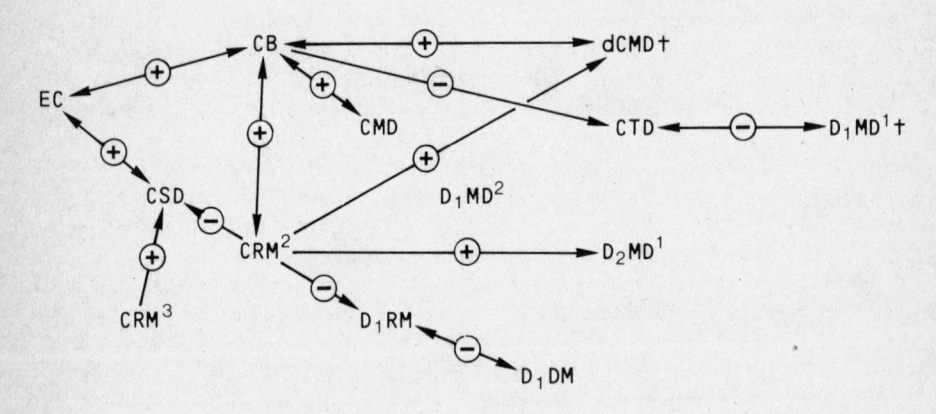

Figure 10.1 Simplified sociogram of significant actors with respect to R&D and innovation in the X-Corporation

particularly a management conflict between R&D and design in that division. Karl was recruited from a competitor on the recommendation of Christer but was not prepared to lead an organization of that size. Shortly afterwards, the company lost David to a competitor; the same year Ivar died, and thereby many old relations ceased.

The following year Christer died also, which was a severe loss. Moreover, Bertil succeeded Arvid as corporate managing director that year. Bertil represented a younger and 'modern' management style, perceived as more democratic. Bertil initiated the second step of reorganization. Profitability had declined, and costs were 'hunted'. The organization was further decentralized into product divisions and central staffs. Erik embarked early upon the new organizational ideas, while Johan made resistance. Johan had also lost a valuable relation in Christer, and the support from Arvid for a resourceful central R&D unit had weakened. Johan experienced a period of contradictory information and decisions and had to watch 'his' resources being grabbed away. Finally, Johan left the X Corporation. The remaining central R&D resources were put in charge of Lars, who was said to be 'Erik's man', and Lars had to rebuild internal morale and relations. Erik moved upwards and has since became a member of the corporate management, a post that Gunnar was appointed to also. The other divisional manager, Holger, who succeeded Ivar, had problems in leading his division and has since been 'put aside'.
[End of Case 10.2]

Much more could, of course, be added to the case description. More actors have been involved, events and external circumstances have been influential, the relations have evolved in a more complex manner, and many 'small' factors have interacted. For example, Sweden is a small country; people know each other; they socialize with each other; they have family relations; they live close to each other; they have been schoolmates; they meet in the military service and professional organizations; they have worked for competitors.

In what respects have the relations among different actors been significant to R&D and innovation within the X Corporation? First, one observes that the technical leaders in the 1960s, including Arvid, favoured one specific product area and others were handled with 'the left hand'. The first step of the reorganization in a way released the other product areas from suppression. Gunnar was esteemed as a competent leader and technologist and could manage his division with a new degree of independence and freshness in relations. His authority also enabled him to control conflicts within his division. Similarly, the authority of Arvid had suppressed conflicts in the traditional product area.

Secondly, there was a period of high turnover of technical leaders. Two technical leaders died (Christer and Ivar), one left (David), one moved to a less influential position (Arvid), and two new ones were hired (Johan and Karl); these two were unsuccessful appointments as was the managing director for the traditional division (Holger). The relations became turbulent and non-directed, and technological development declined. Whether or not to install a technical director at the corporate level long remained an issue. Advocates for doing so included Arvid and Nils, but within top management one feels that what was needed was a 'technical authority' within the traditional product area. To install a corporate technical director would not have fitted in with the present phase of decentralized organization. This, however, does not rule out the technical competence being provided by top management. Incidentally, one reason behind internationalization in the X Corporation was to broaden the base for recruiting managers. As we have pointed out, Sweeden is a small country, and it is hard to find suitable personnel for specialized positions, who do not create unfavourable relations.

10.3 DISCUSSION

10.3.1 Empirical summary

All conflicts involved people, issues and relations as basic elements. Some conflicts were inherent in issues, others in organizational relations, and still others in personal behaviour and ambitions. A number of significant conflict relations were identified. Conflicts appeared in interdependent complexes which changed over time. Conflict histories developed in the organization, and some corporations were for some period of time more afflicted than others. Examples were given which illustrated conflicts related to the establishment of new R&D-units, the incorporation of new technologies, the up-grading of non-traditional operations and stagnation of traditional ones, subcultural changes, reorganizations, and the behaviour of significant actors. The examples showed that conflicts may be instrumental in innovative work and that conflicts among significant professional actors have severe effects and are difficult to handle.

10.3.2 Conflicts and their effects

On a high level of aggregation, the following simple facts about conflicts in large organizations may be stated:

— conflicts are ubiquitous;
— a variety of kinds of conflicts exists and conflicts of different kinds are often linked together in complexes;
— conflicts and conflict complexes change over time;
— conflicts may have good, as well as bad, effects in an organization.

The ubiquity of conflicts is in contrast to the lack of conflict perspective in management, at least where management of R&D and innovation in large organizations is concerned. The fact that conflicts may have good, as well as bad, effects in an organization has not been a common view. Normally, conflicts have been looked upon as bad, both in an organization and in organization literature.

The effects of different conflicts encountered in this study are difficult to evaluate, partly because of an inadequate time perspective, partly because of a lack of information and partly because of the uncertainty related to R&D. However, it may be stated that:

(a) There are a number of tensions around R&D, which are 'in the nature of things' and which cannot be considered 'unhealthy' in due proportion. Such

Conflicts related to R&D and innovation

tensions exist, for instance, between interdependent functions, between central and regional operations, between traditional and new operations, between short-range and long-range perspectives, and between autonomy and control.

(b) Internal competition above the individual level concerning different orientations in R&D and innovation may have good effects. Examples were found in Philips, Alfa-Laval, SKF and Astra. The interdependencies between competing parties must not, however, be highly mutual or sequential.

(c) Personal conflicts among significant actors (managers, professionals) generally have severe effects.

Some implications for management may be summarized. To generate ideas and to provide alternative views are vital elements in R&D in a corporation, and here conflicts may be instrumental. But there also have to be mechanisms which in some way regulate the outcomes in order to avoid underselectivity, disintegration, personal conflicts, deadlock and similar effects. Regulation may also be inadequate and produce new conflicts and barriers to innovation. Nevertheless, there are strong cases against a Darwinistic, non-intervention approach to conflicts. Sensitivity to, and awareness of conflicts around, R&D — where they are, how they develop, when they 'go too far', etc. — are needed in general management, as well as a readiness to act when opportunities arise, even though conflict management may be time consuming. How to deal with conflicts related to R&D and innovation and conflicts among professionals seems to be an underdeveloped aspect of management.

10.3.3 Causes of conflicts

The complicated interplay between people, issues and relations over long periods of time makes it difficult to discern special causes and the conceptual categories of explanations have to be rather broad.

10.3.3.1 First-order analysis

A first order analysis of different cases gives a generalized set of relevant factors to consider (see Table 10.1). The roles of growth, reorganization, and change of significant actors are dubious. Growth involves a resource expansion but may also involve overloads and misfits in organization and management. Both contractions and expansions of an R&D organization have limits beyond which conflicts arise. Reorganization and change of significant actors rearrange relations but do not necessarily decrease a conflict potential. On the other hand, the pattern of conflicts may be changed, and the negative effects of conflicts may be redistributed. Thus, divisionalization released operations in non-traditional product areas from the dominance of traditional product operations, at the expense of some conflicts in central–divisional relations. Divisionalization also relieved the pressure on the corporate managing director, while creating conflicts between divisional and corporate perspectives. Moreover, interdependencies on a corporate level were changed, in that sequential dependence between functions

Table 10.1 Factors affecting conflicts related to R&D and innovation in the corporations studied

Factors tending to increase the conflict potential	Conflict-regulating factors	Factors with varying impact on conflicts
Rise of complexity	Smooth resource expansion	Growth
Unstable profitability	Dominant leader	Reorganization
Problems in external relations with multiple interpretations	Submissive behaviour	Change of significant actors
New technologies competences, and professional skills becoming relevant	Dominant issues	
	Reduction of uncertainty	
	Multiple communication channels	
Changing emphasis on traditional operations	Mediating individuals or bodies	
Faltering policies for organization and resource allocation	Weakening of interdependencies	
	Time	
Troublesome relations between different management levels		
Troublesome relations between interdependent functions		
Selective attention of top management		
Low relation-building abilities among managers and professionals		
Competitive behaviour		
Personified issues		
Subcultural differences		

was substituted for a pooled dependence between the product divisions constituting the parts of the corporate whole. However, in several cases interdivisional dependencies preserved a sequential dependence relation, or even a reciprocal one, on a corporate level.

10.3.3.2 Second-order analysis

The frequent occurrence of conflicts around R&D and innovation has to be explained in the light of:

(a) the characteristics of relations in large corporations;
(b) characteristics of issues in R&D and innovation; and
(c) the characteristics of people involved in innovative processes.

Conflicts related to R&D and innovation 157

By definition, large corporations involve many relations. Large corporations are, moreover, generally complex and have many critical interdependent relations, many sources of information and much ambiguity, many hierarchical levels, and communication patterns may involve infrequent contacts, time lags, distortion etc. Many people develop attitudes and preferences, make decisions and act on order, on a consensus basis, or on a consultation basis, or they act independently, and each mode of action in the organization may create conflicts at some stage with a higher probability the larger the organization is. There are certainly more positional goods available, as well as possibilities of diffusing a blame. However, careerism, status, elitism and small margins between success and failure are constituents of the culture of a large corporation, yielding tensions in interpersonal relations.

Several characteristics of issues in R&D and innovation tend to increase a conflict potential. Uncertainty yields multiple interpretations, as well as anxiety and tensions. Parallel approaches and selection are natural features in R&D work and long time spans put strain on patience and resources. The exposure to clear failures and difficulties makes innovative work a target for suspicion and distrust, new technologies threaten the established professional power structure, innovations lead to change and substitution of some kind etc. Many of the conventional ways of handling conflicts do not work very well in an R&D and innovation context. First of all, it is hard to recognize the effects of a conflict in this context and mobilize efforts for conflict resolution. Then, diffuse alternatives and fluid decision situations may obstruct resolution through problem solving approaches. Resolution through coercion may yield a guerrilla development or underground behaviour, and focusing on external threats or a dominant issue or appointing a scapegoat may have only temporary effects.

Characteristics of people involved in innovative processes provide still more factors that increase conflict potentials. However, one has to be careful when describing a category of people so heterogeneous as the one considered here. Ideas about certain human types are indeed long lived once they have been established and found useful, no matter how incorrect they may be. Burns and Stalker (1961) discuss the legendary view of inventors as highly intractable individuals. Thus, as long as it refers to innate characteristics of inventors, no doubt many individuals in innovative work have found this view convenient and adapted their behaviour accordingly. Similarly, the energetic aura of entrepreneurs is appealing to some managers, who in the legendary view of entrepreneurs find a means of excluding themselves from adherence to rules and organizational conventions, and this may also add to their reputation and career. Thus, the myths about those involved in innovative processes are to some extent self-reinforcing and in that respect they are important.

It is not hard, in the literature, to find lists of epithets commonly applied to innovators (e.g., describing them as being dominant, independent, assertive, self-sufficient and having little interest in human relations). The affiliation of R&D people with a professional subculture with other goals than those of the corporation is another characteristic as is the lack of managerial abilities. Moreover, this kind of people tend to be territorially oriented, emotionally involved and have a skewed distribution of personality features, implying a mixture of cultivation and primitive spirits (see Chapter 11). All these human characteristics increase the conflict potential in an organization.

Similar conclusions may be drawn when considering the common view of entrepreneurs as ambitious, hard-driving, goal-oriented, independent etc. An obvious rejoinder would be that the entrepreneurial spirits in large corporations actually are very scarce, and this may or may not be the case. It is clear, however, that conflicts among managers involved in innovation are frequent and highly significant. Moreover, these managers may have conflict-evoking characteristics; for example, they are ambitious and hard-driving and may be competing for power and striving to increase their independence. That socio-political skills do not correlate with inventive skills and professional competence is important to note in this context. When professionals move up in the organization, this is correlated with a higher share of managerial duties. The risk of promotion failures in the form of 'losing a good engineer and getting a bad manager' is perhaps adequately recognized although the reverse situation, when mediocre professionals compensate for a lack of professional competence by developing socio-political skills is not usually discussed. Managers, thus promoted, are likely to become detrimental to innovative work, not only because they de-emphasize competence aspects of work and act as 'plugs', more or less concealed, but also because they tend to create personal conflicts with other managers.

10.4 CONCLUSIONS

A conflict perspective in the study of R&D and innovation proved fruitful in the sense that a high frequency of conflicts of various kinds was encountered. Typically, significant conflict relations were relations among significant actors, relations associated with a traditional part of the corporation, functional relations, relations between central and local authorities and relations among professionals. A number of tensions surrounding R&D are natural and may be beneficial to some extent. Internal competition above the individual level concerning different orientations in R&D and innovation may have good effects, depending upon such things as the kind of interdependence and the mode of evaluation. Personal conflicts among significant actors generally have severe effects. The ubiquity, complexity, dynamics and mixed effects of conflicts suggest, as an overall conclusion, that conflicts in corporations cannot be completely resolved; they can only be regulated, and to some extent they are desirable.

Many conflicts emerged in connection with divisionalization, which rearranged interdependencies and relations among managers. General explanations of the high frequency of conflicts pertain to the characteristics of large corporations, characteristics of R&D and innovation and characteristics of people involved in this kind of work.

Chapter 11
SOURCES OF IDEAS AND BARRIERS TO INNOVATION IN LARGE CORPORATIONS

11.1 INTRODUCTION

Large and/or old organizations are commonly conceived of as hampering creative and innovative work. The aim of this chapter is to explore this issue on the basis of perceptions of people involved in innovative work. Thus, representatives of principal functions, levels, positions and professional categories in the corporations have been interviewed specifically regarding this matter. The aim has been confined to providing recognition of and insight into the multitude of barriers to innovation in particular. No attempts have been made to assess the frequency and severity of different types of barriers in other than qualitative terms.

In this context the word 'source' pertains to a stage of an information and communication process, a stage that significantly changes the information content. It is far from clear cut how to identify a source, and networks of sources without beginnings and ends are possible. Usually, however, there is in a given context a consensus about where to stop in the identification of sources. The concept of the 'idea' has a rich history of philosophical thought. Here, however, the 'idea' will just signify a coherent conceptualization of a possibility. The word 'barrier' refers to obstacles in a process or a course of events. These obstacles may alter, delay, aggravate or prevent a certain outcome.

11.2 EMPIRICAL FINDINGS

11.2.1 Sources of ideas

Sources of ideas, as stated in the interviews, have been grouped in the following overlapping groups:

(a) external sources;
(b) sources on management levels;
(c) sources in organizational functions;
(d) sources relating to history;
(e) miscellaneous sources;

and are explained herewith:

(a) *External sources*. External R&D at universities and institutes is seldom mentioned as a source of specific product ideas for the corporations, at least not in the engineering industry. External inventors are often mentioned as a valuable source of such ideas. However, the corporations do not consider it necessary to actively seek these people, since these corporations are often approached by them and 'the name of the corporation is enough'. Each corporation has a loosely structured 'satellite organization' of independent inventors, consultants and advisors who are regarded as external. Aside from being a flexible resource and a possible recruitment source, this satellite organization may be a productive way to relate to individuals on the fringes of the proper organization.

Concerning the 'corporate neighbours', that is customers, competitors and suppliers to the corporation, their ideas generally filter through some organizational unit in the corporation such as a marketing or an R&D department. Qualified customers may act as important sources of product invention depending upon the 'balance of knowledge' between customer and supplier concerning technology and customer production economy and needs. A similar argument applies to suppliers as a source. This balance of knowledge varies in different industries. Bulk producers do not have customers as important sources of invention — while, for example, the defence industry does. Suppliers of machinery account for many innovations in the processes of their customers. Suppliers may also have information about competitors, but that kind of source is mentioned marginally. Naturally, competitors substantially affect innovative work, although not by being explicit sources of ideas and information. The information exchange among competitors differs from one industrial sector to another. Companies within the mining industry are said to be traditionally very 'closed' to each other (but opening up), while the automotive industry is very 'open'. The exchange of ideas and technological information, partly formalized through licensing, may become very complicated, especially in technologies that are expensive for the individual companies such as jet engine technology.

(b) *Sources on management levels*. When speaking of sources of ideas at different levels of management, it is hard to distinguish between sources of 'genuine' ideas, on one hand, and sources of significant influences on the shaping of ideas, on the other. Mainly the levels of top management and R&D management will be treated here. Top managers differ somewhat concerning their actual role as idea generator and 'pusher'. 'Pet ideas' from the top are not hard to find historically, although their frequency seems to have declined. At present, most top managers are not — and do not regard themselves as — idea generators for innovations. Sometimes their ideas and initiatives for innovation concern acquisitions or joint ventures. Top managers with a technical background want to take an active part in stimulating and reviewing innovative work to varying degrees. Their overview and basic technical knowledge may enable them to make combinations of ideas, knowledge and productive factors and initiate pre-studies and co-operation.

Comments similar to those above about top management's role in idea generation apply to R&D management above project management level (see Section 7.2.3). Although influential in many corporations, this level of management seems to be more selective and directive than generative. Specific areas of interest and/or competence allow R&D managers to make certain contributions, but in general their role in idea generation is indirect and managerial rather than substantial.

(c) *Sources in organizational functions*. Here a distinction will be made between the basic functions R&D, production and marketing. These functions may be separated and integrated in different ways into the organization, but as sources of ideas they are in general recognizable. Ideas for product innovations from marketing people sometimes concern 'wild' but technically unrealistic ideas. Mostly, however, their ideas concern marginal improvements of a short-range nature, while R&D people are said to account for the main part of the more radical ideas with long-range implications. Marketing people, and especially sales people in close contact with customers, are said to have difficulties in raising their vision over the immediate customer needs, as perceived through complaints, desires, trouble-shooting and the like. This opinion is held by people in marketing and R&D as well as general management positions, especially at Alfa-Laval and SKF, which have engineer-intensive marketing. On the other hand, similar opinions are delivered about R&D people, who are said often to go on with mostly refinements of some original ideas.

Sources of ideas for product innovations within the production function are rare, while production is the main internal source of process innovations. This is especially so in heavy process industries, for example, at KemaNobel, SKF, Boliden and Iggesund, where the production function traditionally has attracted technically talented people.

The distribution of sources within the three functions is generally considered to be very skew. Almost always there are only a small number of individuals prolific in ideas. Every R&D manager pointed out the skew distribution of ideas among people. Key inventive people are not, however, necessarily tied to an R&D department. Thus the distribution of sources within the organization may be very much affected by the distribution of key inventive people within the organization.

(d) *Sources relating to history*. Often ideas have evolved in the past; then they have been shelved and finally considered again in more or less modified versions ('brushed up'). In this way there may be a continuum between renovation and innovation. Advances in supporting technologies, maturing of markets, supply shortages, or changed price relations may revive old ideas or technologies. Also current and completed projects as well as products on the market are sources of ideas or may be viewed as such. Such 'spin-offs' are an important factor in self-perpetuating developments, while spin-offs in unexpected areas are rather rare. In industries with traditional directions along which improvements are made, such as the steel and certain engineering industries, the continuity in project successions is high and they may sometimes be described as 'eternal projects'.

Zeitgeist may sometimes be referred to when the pattern of sources is diffuse, or 'development is in the air' or 'everybody is running for the ball in a way'. To name the individual or the corporation that is first out to 'put together the key pieces' as a source of invention during such circumstances is somewhat misleading.

(e) *Miscellaneous sources*. Sources of information may often be appointed sources of ideas. This includes many conventional sources such as literature, travels, *ad hoc* contacts, colleagues, conferences and fairs. For instance, work on further improvements is considered to be largely a question of being aware of the existence of knowledge and this brings in literature as an important source.

Ideas may also emanate from active search and stimulation through campaigns, permanent 'suggestion boxes', the application of some specific design or method of idea generation, the use of outside consultants etc. Most corporations have at some time tried something of this kind. Certainly, temporary efforts and suitable communications will tap people's ideas, of which a small fraction then turn out to be usable. Specific sources of this kind have not been mentioned as yielding significant innovations.

A comment upon the so-called gatekeeper and new product searcher is also justified. A few corporations have people with such roles more or less formally assigned. There are so far no examples of these people having generated or transmitted ideas for innovations. It is, however, hard to be conclusive about such formally assigned roles because of the short time perspective in the cases involved.

11.2.2 Barriers to innovation

The identification, separation and classification of barriers to innovation are at least as difficult as for sources of ideas. Roughly 140 such barriers were indicated in the answers. However, sometimes interviewees skip 'the conventional barriers' and identify some of more specific interest to them.

There are many ways to classify the barriers. The presence of perceived barriers more or less all the time everywhere has made a grouping similar to the one of sources of ideas suitable. Thus, the barriers to innovation are grouped in the following overlapping groups:

(a) external barriers;
(b) management barriers;
(c) organizational barriers;
(d) historical barriers;
(e) resource barriers;
(f) people barriers;
(g) miscellaneous barriers;

and are discussed more fully below:

(a) *External barriers.* The relations with external R&D people may involve barriers (for example, in recruiting talented people). Industrial R&D has sometimes had a low status among academics (for example, in the pharmaceutical industry).

Among customers there may be a fear of 'letting people in' to study their problems. Or they simply do not have time, for instance, in a boom when there is no opportunity for a supplier to make experiments using the production equipment of his customer. Conservatism among customers varies: low technology industries or customers with a small scale of production such as in the food, agriculture, or graphic industries are considered to be conservative, while the situation is different in, for instance, the energy or computer industry. Different nationalities also vary in this respect. 'Customers in the United States are very conservative, Japanese customers are more progressive, and the Russians are even bold when they finally buy'. Customer conservatism also varies within industries or groups of customers. Progressive customers may even stimulate an innovation which finally finds a small market, since progressive customers may not be representative customers. It is not just that 'the market was not mature'; the market was perhaps never there, with the exception of a few 'advanced' customers.

Barriers in relation to suppliers are mentioned only in exceptional cases. Shortage or uncertainties of supply may even breed innovations. (Germany during World War II provided classic examples of shortage-induced substitutions.) Shortages of raw materials gave incentives for developing new or improved processes or products at, for example, Boliden and Iggesund. A limited supply of human material for experimental work in the pharmaceutical industry is another example of a supply-oriented barrier to innovation.

Competitors may create barriers to innovation by several defensive actions such as pricing out small inventive companies, creating barriers to market entry, 'squeezing' by vertical integration, buying and 'freezing' patents or companies. Mostly, however, competition is referred to by interviewees as promoting innovation.

Another area of perceived barriers is societal action and reaction. Legislation, consumerism and environmentalism are sometimes said to hamper innovations. Broadened responsibilities for quality control of products and processes make innovative work more costly while at the same time the returns on development costs are doubtful. Process industries (Boliden, Iggesund, KemaNobel, SKF) and consumer industries (Astra, Volvo, KemaNobel, Philips) have been affected particularly. For large corporations the competitive picture is said to be at most marginally changed by environmental regulation. The profitability picture may sometimes change in favour of more expensive and profitable products, which meet raised standards, but no competitive advantages are considered to exist in developing products that outdo environmental and safety standards.

(b) *Management barriers*. It is easy to complain about managers and regard them as too passive, active, negligent, careful, slow, conservative, opinionated, misinformed, rigid, preferential etc. As mentioned before, higher levels of management are directive and selective rather than generative towards innovations. It is then natural for people involved in operative work to regard management's selective action as barriers rather than sound selections in some sense. On the other hand, managers may just as easily complain about operative people not generating good ideas or coming up with results fast enough: 'There will always be money available if good ideas come up'. The conceptions of 'good' may vary, however.

Conflicts between managers are also seriously harming innovation (see Chapter 10). Personal traits of managers vary considerably and many times barriers are more related to a specific person than to a group of people in a similar management position.

First, there is the issue about managers' competence regarding technology and markets. There are examples of top managers overestimating their technological knowledge and pushing their pet ideas. This is a very effective barrier to innovation. Other projects will suffer, and at the same time, as people do not believe in the project, its chances of success will be reduced. Mostly managers' unawareness of their own obsolescence will also prejudice their opinion of the ideas and work of others. Some managers will act as plugs in the organization, and if they affect recruitment and promotion around them, the barriers tend to be reproduced. The possibilities to take detours around such barriers or put them aside in the organization are greater on lower levels. Such possibilities may also increase as time passes. In other words 'the last resort is just to let time work for you'.

One is inclined to conclude that the ability to appreciate and couple knowledge in different fields, among which one is a specialty, is rare among technical managers. There are many examples of conservative effects due to this phenomenon, sometimes reinforced by promotional preferences.

The case of competent but domineering managers is sometimes also mentioned. Their ideas and work are good, but there is little room for initiatives from people around them. After some longer period of time they will be surrounded by people who accept a domineering manager. Some old and highly esteemed engineers tend to create such regimes, which may work very well until the day they leave. Moreover, the distribution of power and influence among management levels is affected by promotion or reorganization. Promotion of a domineering manager may leave a 'hole' in the organization, or decentralization may create too powerful managers on the level below. Instances of this were caused by, for example, divisionalization.

Second, there is the issue about managers' competence to handle people and relations. Judging people and ideas in combination is essential. Also the judging and handling of deviant behaviour is considered important in innovative work. Inability to identify and handle the inventive and entrepreneurial elite and the relations those people create around themselves clearly acts as a barrier to innovation. Management's attitudes in this respect vary, however:

> It is like football. Either you let everybody pass to the elite player or you take him out of the team. (Subsidiary Managing Director of Astra-Hässle)
>
> These researchers should not become prima-donnas. (Corporate R&D manager)

The manager just above an inventive person may be important as a provider of support and protection. However, examples are also given of managers on this level who do not tolerate subordinates who are more competent than themselves.

The career system is pointed to as a barrier since it favours individuals rather than groups. When positional goods are scarce, people will tend to compete or leave. People in organizations involve themselves in a mixture of competitive and co-operative behaviour. A divisional manager with problems of competition and conflicts among his sub-managers said that he was trying to create a climate of evaluation that favoured the ability of a manager 'to make the whole work'. However, it was 'his' own whole he referred to, and at the same time there was competition about the corporate managing director position involving the divisional managers.

The third subclass of management barriers concerns management action in making policies and decisions. Generally, managers are accused of passivity, slowness or conservatism in these respects. The degree of specificity in directing innovative work is often low on higher management levels (see Chapter 5). On the other hand there is the obvious effect of a policy that it will tend to favour action 'within' and discourage action 'outside' its delineated area of application, thus in itself acting as a barrier. Higher management's provision of timely resource decisions is sometimes pointed to as inadequate. Of course, resource decisions imply risk-taking. If the distribution of risks has a peak among managers in a decision-making process, a delay is likely. It is not only a matter of total risk to the corporation; it is also a matter of perceived ego risks by engaging in a decision. It is a well known fact that it is easier and involves less ego risk to say 'No' to a proposal, even if inaction involves a large risk to the corporation.

Conservative recruitment policy is mentioned as a barrier. This is related to the management's perception of what kind of competence is needed. Traditional industries often favour their traditional professional categories, in both recruiting and promoting. Some managers are also overly cautious in reacting to proposals to recruit qualified personnel.

Attitudes to and climates for innovation in the organization are substantially influenced by higher management. They affect it by their mere behaviour and not only by making proclamations and emitting signals. People learn the preferences of higher management and increase the probability of receiving support for different initiatives and proposals. Management attitudes towards open communication and co-operation, enthusiasm, creativity etc. tend to be reflected and reproduced in the organization. Managers may be unaware of how their behaviour is interpreted and how they affect the taking of initiatives at lower levels. Here the absence of indicated barriers is an ambiguous sign.

If a policy towards innovation is enunciated, it has to be demonstrated. Top management at both SKF and Alfa-Laval point to projects which have been accepted partially on the merit that they are somewhat odd but show people in the organization that there is room for such projects. (Similarly, there are internal PR projects that work the other way around, that is, some projects are created at lower levels so that higher management easily understand and appreciate them.) Thus, top managers may want to avoid the demonstration of total rejection of radical innovative ideas, since that might harm the climate for all kinds of innovation.

(c) *Organizational barriers*. This group of barriers is not very well separated from other groups. Here we will deal with barriers that are related to the characteristics of an organizational structure. A common conception is that the size and complexity of an organization will act as an important barrier. This pertains to both structure and behaviour. It is rather common to conceive of large corporations as possessing a large amount of inertia. Caution, resource orientation, conservative selection of people, defensive attitudes, established structures, etc. are all attributed to large organizations as distinguished from small ones. The small organization, on the other hand, is said to be flexible, creative, responsive and so on.

Some structural features related to size and complexity, which have been mentioned as barriers, are:

- long, critical paths of evaluation and decision making concerning ideas and projects;
- diffuse areas of responsibility;
- many lines of communication;
- departmentalization;
- rigid structure of salaries, promotion and status.

Repetitiveness of certain operations is also a feature of large organizations, a feature that works also in favour of an increased level of bureaucracy. Problem solving behaviour focuses on incremental innovation and the making of small refinements whose effects will multiply. Routines will be established, specialization will increase, and the organization will get settled in a rigid network of behaviours. To create and implement radical change close to dominating and traditional operations is generally thought of as meeting barriers. Processes of selective attention work in favour of existing operations and resources. Moreover, attitudes, status patterns and behaviours evolve that reinforce the traditional 'core' of the large organization. As opposed to small and young ones, a large organization generally has a history of growth, experience and pride of achievements. All this will act as selective barriers outside the mainstream of existing operations and ideas for their improvement. One must, however, remember that some behaviours in large organizations with mature products are simply rational or practical. The long periods of time before even minor changes in high-volume products may be introduced on global markets are necessary for several obvious reaons and are not just due to some kind of unavoidable inertia. Sometimes changes are also collected and introduced batch-wise, giving rise to product generations.

The critical assets of an organization are potential barriers in the sense that they absorb attention and resources. The defence of large market shares, concern about production economy in a capital-intensive industry, concern about raw material sources, and defence of important products against technological substitution are examples of actions that are mentioned as barriers to radical innovation in the corporations. Excessive 'cost thinking' or 'profitability thinking' are also frequently mentioned as dangerous for innovations.

Large resources and innovations interact, as has been the case at Alfa-Laval. High prices have been needed in order to give a yield to the large resources of the corporation. High prices need in turn innovative or high-quality products, which in their turn require still larger resources and thus a vicious circle is created.

The phrase 'organizational barriers' may lead the thoughts exclusively to the interaction across boundaries in the organization. Many such barriers are mentioned, but mostly they are well known due to their prevalence. A simple list of boundaries important in this respect would include boundaries between:

- R&D - production - marketing;
- different levels in the organization;
- project organization - line organization;
- central - regional operations.

Ideas and innovation in large companies 167

Finally, the now famous 'not-invented-here effect' is often mentioned as a common and powerful barrier to innovation as well as to transfer and co-ordination and 'NIH-effects exist everywhere'. This effect works across every organizational boundary but especially around R&D groups. Ideas from 'the field' or from external inventors are said to be subjected to NIH-attitudes from internal R&D, and people in some corporations criticize themselves for being self-sufficient.

(d) *Historical barriers*. Examples of barriers related to history are the traditions and conservatism within and around the corporation. To some extent this has been dealt with above, and this group is another means of describing and emphasizing these barriers. Historical experience tends to be selective towards new ideas. People in some sectors of industry and some corporations develop notions of what does not fit that particular industry or corporation. The arguments and the selection of supporting evidence are refined and difficult to argue against. Also success experiences are easily reinforced. Some engineering corporations have successfully employed a trial-and-error approach to R&D and innovations and persist in this behaviour until concrete signs of inadequacy show up.

The existence of a large traditional part in the organization as a product of historical growth has also been mentioned above. References to this part as producing barriers to radical innovations are frequently made. All traditional products such as passenger cars, separators, ball bearings and metals have at some time acted as barriers to work on radically different products. The same holds for those corporations which have one predominant customer, such as a defence department, or which have one predominant professional category, such as mechanical engineers.

Original innovations frequently develop into barriers to future innovations in this way, and not only in traditional industries. Both individuals and organizations get more or less stuck in a line of development for some period of time. This is not unexpected; however, the corresponding barriers become reinforced and tend to be permanent until eroded by external rather than internal forces.

(e) *Resource barriers*. It is possible to treat most barriers to innovation as resource barriers. Resources will here mean time, money and personnel in the conventional sense used in budgeting. Generally, the barriers in this group are related to the level, the change of level and the distribution of resources.

Resource limits are inhibiting in later stages of development but not necessarily in the earlier ones. Idea generation and desk work may not necessarily suffer from shortness of money, time or personnel. Phrases such as 'motivation by starvation', 'the need is the mother of invention', or 'time pressures give the best results' point in this direction. Also, it may be argued that such shortages will keep development personnel from overachievement in technical perfection and having 'the best as an enemy to the second best'. Acting on the basis of such arguments is two-edged, though, and certainly long-lasting pressures or permanent struggles for critical resources will act as barriers to innovation.

Time, money and personnel are to a certain degree substitutable resources. There are, however, strong non-linearities in resource substitutions in innovative work. Time cannot be stored and used at convenience, and often additional money can buy just marginal extra time. Two or more average researchers or inventors do not add up to a top one and 'hiring and firing' is seldom a great possibility. The inability of managers and operative people to understand that not only money but time and qualified people are needed to produce innovations is also listed as a barrier. Time is a resource that attracts much attention. Complaints of lack of time for idea generation, preliminary studies, following up spinoffs etc. are more common than complaints of lack of money and personnel for similar tasks. Day-to-day operations absorb attention and lead work away from possibly radical innovative work. A certain proportion of time budgets (mostly 10–20 per cent) is set aside for explorative R&D, preliminary studies, or just 'free' work in some cases. It is, however, hard to live up to this intention, especially since people assigned to that kind of work constantly tend to be in demand for other tasks.

Short-sighted thinking as a barrier is a variation on this theme. Short pay-off times, fast feedback of results and adaptive behaviour are manifestations of both a psychological and an economic nature. This 'local orientation' in time and space prevails on the group and department level as well as on the corporate level. The allotment of resources on the basis of the immediate past and the immediately foreseen future performance may, of course, reflect economic fluctuations in a harmful manner. R&D budget cuts or reassignment of talented R&D people in difficult times are common. Of course, the reverse also happens. Recent loss of market shares, a perceived threat of technological substitution, soaring quality problems, or a sudden discovery of a loss of leadership may up-grade innovative work. What is generally said in this respect is that over-reactions and drastic changes in resource levels are detrimental to innovation. Barriers due to sharp budget increases are perhaps not seen immediately but there are limits to the growth rate of an R&D organization (see chapter 3). Above these levels it will be difficult to keep up the average quality level of people, and newcomers will either absorb most of the time of others for their introduction or they will essentially be idle, which destroys morale. There will be small opportunities to assimilate newcomers into productive teams, management will be distracted, and — not the least important factor — resource excesses will raise envy and criticism in the surrounding organization.

Finally, there are the effects of resource distribution. Again, this is obviously a case of balancing somewhere in between. The merit of having very many or very few projects is doubtful, although synergy has to be considered as well. The assignment of people to projects and activities shows similar features. The splitting of the time of individuals on many activities is pointed to as harmful. The time required for intellectual 'set-ups' or 're-starts' is considerable, and some tasks simply have to be completed in 'a large step'. Both the indivisibility of some intellectual tasks and a limited time-sharing capacity of many inventive people speak in favour of concentration. On the other hand, changes in work assignments are stimulating to a certain degree, and new people on old projects may provide new angles of thought and action or break a standstill.

(f) *People barriers*. A list of barriers in people could again include almost anything. Those barriers which clearly fall in this category are surprisingly many.

Ideas and innovation in large companies

Moreover, they do not constitute a very 'nice' picture of people involved in innovative work. Just as the distribution of achievements is skew among different persons, the distribution of personality features is skew among high achievers. Unbalanced talents, specialized abilities, strong emotions, high sensitivity to criticism, vanity and egotism are not uncommon. A rough subgrouping has been made below of cognitive and emotional barriers.

Examples of cognitive barriers are a lack of abilities to raise vision, to listen to ideas without having a visible hardware, to work creatively, to understand the problems and ideas of others, to communicate, to break habitual thinking, to think globally, to look far ahead, and to identify needs and opportunities. These cognitive barriers are also attributed to groups and departments. A whole generation of technicians may have difficulties in a transition to new technologies or new thinking in a field (for example, in a transition from tubes to transistors). Professional categories create language, norms and values that act as barriers (see Chapter 9). Different groups of people 'don't understand', and individual filters conform to group filters.

Emotional barriers have an animalistic resemblance. Superficially they may show up as cognitive barriers, since such barriers are much more *comme il faut* in an organization. That 'technologists easily fall in love with their solutions' may show up as an 'inability to understand and evaluate alternatives'. Nevertheless, cognitive and emotional barriers are hard to separate. The propensity of people involved in innovative work to identify and value themselves in relation to their work is deeply integrated in their whole psyche.

People also embark upon and push an idea or line of thought if this can favour their position. Perhaps it is not just a lack of clear-sightedness that makes some people dismiss certain ideas and stick to others but a vanity of being in the forefront and reaping the benefits from that. This feature facilitates invention and diffusion of new concepts, ideas and methods but may hamper necessary co-operative action towards implementation and innovation.

Although not a typical emotional barrier, secrecy is an important barrier around some people, who 'hold on to their ideas' and cautiously communicate them to others. Naturally, protection against leakages may be needed around innovative work both internally and externally, but internal secrecy and claims to being the originator appear to be in excess. The patent institute is intended to provide incentives and remove secrecy of ideas and knowledge. Similarly, procedures for internal recognition and compensation for inventive ideas may loosen up internal secrecy. Some idea and innovation search exercises simply function this way. It should also be mentioned that secrecy in some cases is used merely as a way to add to somebody's prestige.

A final comment will be made about the ageing process as producing cognitive and emotional barriers to innovation. It is commonly thought that individuals lose creative talents as they get older. This has proved to be a truth with many exceptions. Long-standing experience in a field will probably decrease the ability to 'think along new tracks', but selective attention may be just as fruitful. Also the confrontation between long experience and new problems or fields may produce creative thinking. Moreover, social abilities come later in life, abilities which are highly needed in innovative work. On the other hand, counteracting social abilities may be at least as powerful. What is really disastrous is when creative, intelligent and socially able people are engaged in mutual sabotage.

No attempt will be made here to pursue an analysis of individual ageing and the emergence of emotional barriers. There are indications that important barriers of that type develop over a lifetime. Experiences of success and failure may develop into egotism, overcompensative action or bitterness over the years. People's need structure changes and so do their prospects of life as their future shrinks. People attain invisible assets they care about such as reputation, social relations, contacts and position. They attain more recognition, which increases their sensitivity about their images. In other words 'people get big and sore feet over the years'. Moreover, if they attain power, regulating criticism around them may cease. Dissenters leave or become silent and 'after forty, one does not risk the job to point out bad conditions'.

(g) *Miscellaneous barriers*. Most indicated barriers of some generality have already been accounted for, since the chosen groups have been both broad and overlapping. Perhaps what was unexpectedly missing deserves a comment. For instance, references to location as a barrier were seldom made. This does not mean that the benefits to communication of geographical closeness are not appreciated. There were more complaints about scattered locations than about a single remote location. Scattered locations hamper co-ordination, and especially in multinational operations it is a problem (see chapter 4). Locations remote from large cities or universities are not perceived as barriers to innovation in those corporations that have such locations. Location in small communities in which the corporation is regionally dominant is said to produce some benefits to innovative work such as 'people think of their jobs also in their leisure time'.

A remote location may hamper the recruitment of R&D people and managers. However, corporations with traditionally remote locations such as Boliden, Iggesund and parts of SKF and KemaNobel encounter no specific difficulties in recruiting from educational categories that have traditional connections with the corresponding regions. The engineering industry, on the other hand, sometimes experiences problems in recruiting qualified personnel to remote locations, and the pharmaceutical industry has deliberately located their R&D operations close to medical schools in large cities. Closeness to universities and communication possibilities have similarly influenced the location of R&D in parts of KemaNobel.

11.3 DISCUSSION

11.3.1 Empirical summary

A diversity of sources of ideas was found. Each corporation had on its periphery a loosely structured satellite organization which provided some inputs to innovative work. No corporation was self-sufficient in this kind of work, but external orientation and the dependence upon external sources of ideas varied among the corporations. It is difficult on the basis of the data here, to try to explain this variation, except to say that some corporations are more rigid in outlook and self-sufficiency.

Sources of both radical and incremental innovation were found both internally and externally. Moreover, the sources of ideas among people are skewly distributed with a few individuals as dominant sources of invention. Top management generally does not constitute a source of ideas for innovation. The role of higher R&D management is also more selective than generative. Historical activities are an important source in the sense that there is a high degree of continuity in innovative work. Not infrequently, there is a global contemporaneity in technological change, making sources of ideas diffuse and creating a sense of *Zeitgeist*.

Perceived barriers to innovation have an even greater diversity than sources of ideas. The most frequently mentioned barriers were related to management, organization and people.

Each industry seems to develop unique complexes of interacting barriers, yielding different patterns of innovation, for instance, in the automobile industry, pharmaceutical industry, food industry and process industries.

Perceived barriers among managers are partly due to the nature of managerial functions and partly due to inadequate competence and behaviour of managers. Many hierarchical layers and a 'tall' organization jeopardize innovations. Managerial risk is an additional risk dimension in innovative work.

Barriers are commonly attributed to the size and complexity of an organization as well as to behaviour in large organizations in general. Organizational barriers mentioned are rather conventional, and the same comment applies to barriers associated with traditions, conservatism and resource allocations.

People barriers are most frequently mentioned, especially barriers related to emotions. Specialized interests and cognitive abilities among individuals seem to correlate with a skewness in other personality features. The role of ageing is important in the development of cognitive and emotional barriers.

11.3.2 Pluralism, competition and co-operation

Several of the empirical findings above are supported by other studies (see, for example, Jewkes *et al.*, 1969, p. 228). A pluralistic outlook on sources of ideas, and especially an increased degree of external orientation, appears to be of value at the corporate level. The same may hold for certain forms of internal competition, but competition also tends to create barriers. Internal competition at the individual level seems to be of particularly negative value in innovative work, while internal competition on a project or R&D unit level may be productive.

An emphasis on historical continuity and the accumulation of incremental innovations has been found by several authors, including Jewkes *et al.* (1969). Barriers to innovation may both increase and decrease continuity in this respect. The pace at which genuinely new developments are conceptualized and materialized is smoothed and slowed down by several of the barriers encountered. On the other hand, the complex of barriers in a certain industry may shelter it from developments in different technologies until a breakthrough occurs. The innovation by invasion phenomenon, described by Schon (1967), which some traditional industries have been exposed to, is an example of this.

The continuity of technological change and the incremental nature of innovations have an important implication for management. It might well be that a manager with an aim to encourage innovations overlooks the potential of alterations in on-going work. At the same time it is true that work on improvements has a tendency to centre around certain parameters and established standards of improvement, which act as barriers to innovation. The point is that a manager looking for radical innovation excessively, but well aware of this said tendency, will hinder any kind of innovation. The finding by Marquis (1969) that small incremental innovations with internal sources contribute significantly to commercial success, is supported here.

A contemporaneity of technological advances in certain fields is indicated by the data. Contemporaneity in innovative work also has an implication for management. It does not necessarily imply a 'rat-race' policy, but if inventive leadership is not aimed at, a rapid catch-up must be built on a relative advantage in the absence of barriers.

That barriers associated with management, organization, and people are frequently mentioned may seem natural where large corporations are concerned. However, neither the grouping of barriers, nor the distribution of emphasis here is in accordance with the findings in the report published by Arthur D. Little Inc. and the Industrial Research Institute Inc. in 1973. The latter study is also based on perceptions of barriers to innovation as expressed in interviews. The perceived barriers are divided into seven groups, namely barriers relating to:

(a) markets;
(b) corporate organization and behaviour;
(c) existing government policies;
(d) finance;
(e) lack of 'seed capital' for independent entrepreneurs;
(f) technological factors; and
(g) labour unions.

The specific complexes of barriers in different industries are also pointed out. The important barriers are found to be related mainly to marketing but also to finance, corporate organization, government policy and the lack of seed capital.

Several explanations of the difference in emphasis between this report and the present study are relevant. First, there are some differences in method and focus. The 1973 report focused on public policy. Interviews were conducted with 120 key executives in seventeen large and seven small industrial firms as well as with officials in government, financial, and labour institutions. Besides, a preliminary list of groups of barriers provided a pre-selected focus on marketing, finance, organization and government policies. Thus, a broader context for innovation than the corporation was focused on. References to 'people problems' in innovation became subsumed under corporate organization and behavioural perspectives, and further research was suggested to illuminate such internal corporate barriers. In the present study, on the other hand, perceptions of market-related barriers are classified as external barriers, while barriers related to lack of (external) marketing ability are treated under management, organizational and people barriers.

These explanations do not seem to compensate adequately for differences in emphasis, and further explanations must be sought. It might very well be the case that perceptions, interpretations and classifications are valid and that the results reflect differences between corporations operating in the United States and Sweden. The principal differences indicated would then be that market-related barriers are more emphasized in United States corporations and people-related barriers are more emphasized in Swedish corporations. Explanations of such a difference would then have to consider differences in problem awareness and internal versus external orientation and/or differences in the extent to which these types of barriers exist in the United States and Swedish corporations and/or differences in the propensity to explain barrier effects in terms of market-related factors or people-related factors. In a competitive and individualistic American culture one may be more sensitive to market conditions and less inclined to associate barriers with lacking abilities of people to cooperate. It may not be totally the other way around in Sweden, but co-operation certainly is a valued feature in the corporations.

Concerning implications for management, the diversity of barriers is again an argument for pluralism as was the case with diversity of sources. The singularity of many critical relations and positions in a traditional organizaton, in which hierarchy after all is a strong and basic feature, is conspicuous. Organizational features such as clear boundaries, clear lines of authority and communications and well-defined and stable goals and subgoals, conforming behaviour, regulated processes and comprehensive co-ordination, are all subjects of wide-spread and deep-rooted esteem, which almost form a kind of organizational aesthetics. Fluid boundaries, primary and secondary responsibilities, temporary structures, dual ladders for promotion, extended positional goods and detour possibilities, multiple lines of communication, and flexible and multiple goals represent a counter-aesthetics, involving fewer unproductive barriers.

The mere size of an organization in terms of turnover or number of employees should have a remote relation to barriers to innovation. With the exception of scale advantages in certain types of R&D, effects of size and complexity are mainly due to the chosen form of organization and management. New ventures, small innovation companies or business development units spun-off from a larger organization may be management responses to barriers associated with size and complexity.

The prevalence of people-related barriers puts a premium on behavioural skills, and an interplay between technological, economic and behavioural skills is a salient feature of innovative work in large corporations. This emphasizes an additional dimension of traditional entrepreneurship.

11.4 CONCLUSIONS

A diversity of sources of both radical and incremental innovation were found both internally and externally. A loosely structured satellite organization on the periphery of the corporation provided inputs to innovative work to a varying extent among the corporations. Sources of ideas among people were generally skewly distributed. Top management and also higher R&D management were selective rather than generative.

Among a wide variety of perceived barriers to innovation, the most frequently indicated ones were related to management, organization and people rather than to the resource situation or the business environment. These findings differed somewhat from those of the 1973 report (Little et. al.), the principal difference being that market-related barriers were more emphasized in United States corporations and people-related barriers were more emphasized in Swedish corporations. One out of several possible explanations could be the relative cultural differences in sensitivity to market competition versus internal co-operation.

Internal competition among individuals on both operative and managerial levels appears as a barrier in innovative work, while internal competition on a project or R&D unit level as well as external co-operation may have a positive effect on the rate of innovation. A general conclusion would be that the age and ageing of organizations are creating barriers to innovation and that the size of an organization *per se* is not creating barriers to innovation but that the principal determinant is the chosen form of organization and management.

Chapter 12
DISCUSSION

12.1 INTRODUCTION

The aim of this chapter is to synthesize the findings in the preceding chapters and to discuss them in a theoretical framework. The study has, however, been largely exploratory, and the different aspects have not been selected for the purpose of developing or testing some hypothesis or framework. It is therefore natural that the synthesis is partial, since the subject does not lend itself easily to a synthesis. It is also to be recalled that the different chapters in themselves constitute mostly self-contained pieces of research results.

The themes for a discussion integrating and synthesizing the findings have been chosen in retrospect. One theme concerns the management and technology factors and the discussion serves to clarify and emphasize the management factor viewed in parallel with the technology factor. The distinction between managerial and technological innovations is important in this respect.

Another theme concerns the question whether some form of management systems and internal organization is to be preferred to a market organization. The discussion of this theme has been aligned with the work of Williamson (1975).

12.2 EMPIRICAL SUMMARY

The empirical investigation presented in the preceding chapters has been concerned with R&D, innovation, management and organization in eight corporations. These corporations are large, diversified and predominantly multinational. They represent different industries and technologies — such as the chemical, electronic, engineering, mining, forestry, pharmaceutical and transportation industry. The data include several hundred interviews with people in R&D, marketing and top management positions.

The primary focus has been on strategic aspects and the relations between R&D and the rest of the corporation rather than solely on internal R&D. The focus of the different empirical chapters has shifted in several respects. First, there has been a shift from viewing the corporations as actors in a larger system of actors to viewing a corporation in itself as a system of actors. Second, there has been a shift in time perspective, in that the early historical development of the corporations has been treated, as well as their more current strategies. Third, aspects of behaviour, often associated with rational behaviour, such as policy making, decision making and organizing have been focused on as well as behaviour less associated with rationality, such as conflicts and the formation of subcultures. Finally, based on perceptions, managerial roles have been focused on as well as the source/barrier structure pertaining to technological innovations. Thus, the history, strategy, structure and behaviour have been studied in relation to R&D and innovation in large corporations.

Chapters 2, 3, and 4 constitute the historical part of the study. Among the empirical findings are the following:

— Industrialization and the rise of large corporations in Sweden was to a large extent based upon domestic raw materials and domestic inventions, supplemented by foreign capital, technology and managerial influences.
— The 'classical' Swedish innovations were product improvements rather than radically new products. Managerial achievements in connection with invention-based internationalization through direct foreign investment were conspicuous.
— Historical continuity has characterized corporate development. In general, the corporations have grown, diversified and internationalized to different extents, primarily depending upon whether they were based on raw materials or product inventions.
— There has been a mutual interplay and a give-and-take relationship between R&D and corporate development. Particularly, large internationalized R&D operations were associated with large internationalized corporations, while R&D was loosely associated with diversification, at least radical diversification.

Chapters 5, 6, 7 and 8 deal with aspects of strategy and structure. Among the findings are the following:

— Strategies for R&D and innovation were in general vague and loosely coupled to corporate strategies.
— There was a low frequency of strategic decisions made with respect to R&D. However, an assessment of the strategic, tactical or operative nature of R&D decisions was difficult.
— Top management was often evasive in policy making, sometimes in combination with policy-seeking behaviour in the organization regarding R&D. On the other hand, top management was active regarding organizational structure and manning.
— The multidivisional form of organization was adopted by the Swedish corporations in the sample within a period of about five years, regardless of variations in size and degree of diversification and internationalization.

Chapters 9, 10 and 11 deal with specific aspects of behaviour in relation to technological change, R&D and innovation. Among the findings are the following:

— Several corporations have experienced the formation and change of subcultures associated with different professional categories. Typically, such subcultures were established in the corporation for a long period of time and were then opposed and subjected to a transformation.
— There was a high frequency of conflicts of various kinds in connection with R&D and innovation. To some extent certain conflicts were instrumental,

but personified conflicts among professionals and managers had severe effects.
— A diversity of sources of ideas and barriers to innovation was found. The most frequent barriers were directly related to human characteristics and organization and management.

12.3 TECHNOLOGY AND MANAGEMENT

12.3.1 Technological and managerial innovation

In constructing explanatory frameworks it is customary to make conceptual decompositions into causal factors. Throughout this study there has been a focus on management and technology, and it is natural to try to assess the explanatory potential of these factors. In particular, this section aims at recognizing the potentiality of management as an explanatory factor, which ought to be considered in parallel with technology in both practical evaluations and theoretical analyses.

Needless to say, the role of both technology and management in economic development has been recognized, but in widely different ways and with varying emphasis. Consider first the well-known production function approach in economic theory. A measure of output of a collection of firms is related to measures of different input factors considered to be of relevance in the industrial production process. In the last few decades the decomposition into a set of input factors has, to an increasing extent, explicitly taken technological change into consideration. Sometimes aggregates of R&D outlays have been used to represent technology as an input factor. Often, however, the residual factor, besides labour and capital, has simply been labelled technology and has come to reflect changes in the quality rather than the quantity of labour and capital, as well as changes in additional input factors. To the extent that management is a factor of relevance in explaining say, productivity differences between nations, time periods, sectors of industry, or individual firms, it has been subsumed in a statistical residue, sometimes under the heading technology.

The heterogeneity of the residue has, of course, been observed. In addition to the distinction between product and process technology, the technology factor has been further decomposed conceptually into factors reflecting industrial structure, learning and different managerial activities, for example organization and marketing. There have been attempts at quantitative modelling of the management factor, but analytical tractability seems to disfavour the management factor, at least when it comes to incorporating different qualities of management rather than quantities (the latter expressed, for instance, as cumulated salaries to managers).

The following questions may now be asked: 'How can management be distinguished from technology?' 'For what purposes could a distinction between technology and management be a valuable analytical tool?' 'How can the relative importance of technology and management be assessed?'

Several authors include management in technology by using a broad concept of technology. When talking about innovations, Schumpeter used a broad definition of innovation which he first referred to as 'any "doing things differently" in the realm of economic life', and which then was defined as 'the setting up of a new production function', (see Section 1.3). Moreover, Schumpeter used a narrow concept of management as referring to the organization and administration of running operations, while he reserved the term 'entrepreneur' for an individual who carried out an innovation. (As may be recalled, 'management' in the present study is taken to include entrepreneurship.) Thus, Schumpeter does not specifically distinguish between technological innovations and what is here called managerial innovations, although he recognizes the latter as well. Many authors who first define 'technology' and 'innovation' in a broad sense, in using these terms seem to have industrial products and processes in mind most of the time rather than management and organization. This is in contrast to Nelson and Winter (1974), who define innovation as a change of existing decision rules, thereby tying the concept of innovation directly to managerial behaviour.

It would be wrong to say, however, that Schumpeter does not emphasize what is called the management factor here. On the contrary, he emphasizes the carrying out of innovations and subsequent imitations as the basic events causing economic change, events which are directly associated with entrepreneurial or managerial behaviour.

A slightly different way to decompose industrial production into input factors is to focus on information or knowledge and/or skills in general. Difficulties in finding suitable representations of knowledge make production function modelling harder, and the analysis often becomes qualitative. When a knowledge perspective is used, the problem of conceptual separation also arises: how to distinguish certain skills from labour, certain types of knowledge from capital, etc. To separate managerial knowledge from technological knowledge is difficult both conceptually and quantitatively. Again, there is a tendency to focus on technological knowledge of a non-managerial kind, although different types of knowledge may be explicitly recognized by the authors.

Now the focus may be shifted from aggregate production functions to the level of the firm as described in neo-classical economic theory. At this level of theorizing, the management factor enters only as an assumption about managerial behaviour as maximizing something, usually profit or some more general utility measure. The crucial inadequacy of this assumption is neither that managerial behaviour is equated with a maximizing algorithm, nor that profit or some utility is maximized, but that it fails to consider the uneven distribution of managerial knowledge and skills. In fact, an assumption which associates an extreme trajectory in an abstract space with the behaviour of the management of a firm is flexible enough to deal with a wide range of objections based on notions of satisfying behaviour, limited rationality, imperfect information, multiple goals, sequential attention to goals and the like. But as long as all managers are assumed to be equally skilled in maximization with equal access to information and other factors of production, the theory will fail to explain differences among firms. This may, however, be done by varying the starting conditions of the firms in a dynamic model, by introducing differences in access to information, by varying the values used by management in maximizing or by simply introducing random elements

Discussion

to reflect pure luck. But what reason would there be then for not differentiating the qualities of management? It is to be noted that profit is clearly recognized by Schumpeter as an entrepreneurial motive in capitalist economies but at the heart of his argument is also the view that entrepreneurial talents are skewly distributed in a population.

It may be argued that much of the ignorance about the management factor in economic theory has more to do with a lack of empirical insight and difficulties in incorporating management qualities in quantitative analyses than with the level of analysis. To support the last statement, attention may be drawn to a few examples. In comparing economic performance among different nations, attributions to differing qualities of management in industry are not uncommon. (See Pratten, 1976, for example.) The shift in topics for public discussion during the 1960s from a technology gap to a management gap between the United States and Europe illustrates this point, as does the discussion of Japanese methods of management. In addition to management styles, management education and research may also be compared at an international level (see Singh, 1971). At the sectoral level, the notion of innovation by invasion may illustrate different qualities of management in different sectors of industry. At the level of the firm, there may be a skew distribution of entrepreneurial talent as Schumpeter claims, which could imply a tendency of the same firms to be pioneers through innovating. However, there does not have to be a similar distribution of managerial talent in a wider sense since imitators may be just as economically successful as innovators as may late adopters in relation to early adopters of an innovation.

If quantitative modelling is disregarded rather than the management factor, what could be gained in an analysis? To indicate this, management will be viewed in parallel with technology in a knowledge perspective. That is to say, knowledge (or, interchangeably, information), including intellectual skills, is considered to be at the heart of the matter and technological knowledge will be distinguished from managerial knowledge, in the same way as technologists may be distinguished from managers as knowledge actors (carriers, learners, generators, disseminators etc.). Needless to say, technologists and managers do not have to be different persons but rather refer to different roles.

Now a set of research questions concerning technology and innovation could be transformed into a set of similar research questions concerning management (and vice versa). For example:

— What are the impacts of managerial innovations on economic and social life?
— What are the sources of and barriers to managerial innovations? Do they emanate mainly from management research, from large corporations, from independent inventors, or what?
— What factors govern the processes of diffusion of managerial knowledge?
— What kind of managerial innovations foster technological innovations and vice versa?
— What is the role of significant actors in management and in technology?

Naturally, there are also salient differences between the two types of knowledge. Thus, for example, artifacts from technological knowledge ('hardware') differ from artifacts from managerial knowledge (c.f. the notion of 'orgware' in Dobrov, 1978). The production and distribution of the two types of knowledge differ, for example, with respect to possibilities of experimentation and reproduction, and it is not suggested here that, for instance, new managerial knowledge could or should be made patentable. The point here is rather that the distinction is useful in posing analytical questions.

The economies of managerial knowledge has been widely recognized for a long time, at least since Adam Smith, and associated with questions of the division of labour, co-ordination, resource allocation, competitive behaviour, size and efficiency, etc. Also, a division of management itself into different specialities, functions, roles and so on has long been recognized and notions about the corresponding economies attached to it. Thus Penrose (1959) includes marketing, financial and research economies in managerial economies. Also, there are managerial diseconomies, associated with limits to size, growth and diversification of a firm. This is a common view, and sometimes references are made to 'the law of diminishing returns of managerial control'. Such a 'law' then has implications for questions about market structure and limits of management. However, any implications of that kind would have to be modified when technological and managerial innovations are taken into consideration. Certainly the operations of a multinational corporation of today are more complex than those of a large firm a century ago, but managerial knowledge has increased and so has the stock of available management tools, including technological innovations such as the telephone and the computer. Management, therefore, has not necessarily become more difficult. On the other hand, the cumulation of knowledge and tools for management leaves more room for differences in utilizing available knowledge and tools among different firms. The skewness in the distribution of managerial qualities in industry does not necessarily increase as a result of such a cumulation, but at least the range of possible variation has increased.

Managerial innovations, together with technological innovations, could thus be viewed as dynamic factors in an economy, which not only change optima and limits of production but also change optima and limits of market structure and management itself. A new set of research questions could now be constructed by combining the aspects of management and technology.

Examples of questions in such a set would be:

— What kind of management is the most conducive to technological innovations?
— How will technological innovations facilitate management?
— Is the kind of management which promotes technological innovations also promoting managerial innovations?
— Could managerial innovations be substituted for technological innovations in achieving economic performance?
— Do different types of technology require different types of management and do the latter affect the rate of technological innovations differently?
— What are the differences regarding source/barrier structures of technological and managerial innovations?

Discussion

Table 12.1 Examples of major managerial innovations

Managerial innovation	Major characteristics of sources of innovation
Scientific management	A cluster of innovations made around the turn of the century in large companies by a well-educated inventor (Taylor) with operative experience. To some extent simultaneity was present in regard to similar innovations by the Gilbreths.
Multidivisional structure (M form)	An innovation originating simultaneously in two large companies (Du Pont and General Motors) and carried out by the top managers.
Linear programming	A cluster of innovations based on science and originated partially in a military context during and after World War II. The innovations have then diffused into civilian industry and numerous subsequent improvements have been made.

Sources: Taylor (1964), George (1968), Chandler (1962), Dantzig (1963)

— Does the generation of technological and managerial innovations compete for similar kinds of resources?

The knowledge about managerial innovations does not correspond to that about technological innovations. As Williamson puts it:

> The importance of organizational innovation to economic efficiency is poorly understood... The diffusion of organizational innovations—within industries, across industries, and across cultures—both in terms of the mechanics of the diffusion process and the economic consequences associated with organizational innovations of various kinds, ... warrants investigation. (Williamson, 1975, p. 262)

Any textbook on management gives a wide variety of management methods, techniques, concepts, tools and the like. Table 12.1 gives a few examples of major managerial innovations and Table 12.2 a few examples of major technological innovations in order to illustrate the parallelism. One may, for example, note that simultaneity as well as clustering may apply to both technological and managerial innovations. Also, sources and diffusion patterns of both kinds of innovations may be structured in similar ways.

The parallelism may be further illustrated by the different inventive approaches of Frederick Taylor and Charles Babbage (see, for example, Taylor, 1964; Babbage, 1832). The latter has mainly become associated with unsuccessful attempts to develop a mechanical computer, but he was also a brilliant observer and analyst of the economics and industrial organization of his time. It has been claimed that some ideas of Babbage (which by the way had little to do

Table 12.2 Examples of major technological innovations

Technological innovation	Major characteristics of sources of innovation
Detonator and dynamite	Research-based innovations made in the 1860s by a well-educated autonomous inventor (Nobel) with entrepreneurial skills.
Diesel-electric railway traction	An innovation with a main impetus from the R&D department of a large company (Kettering at General Motors). Improvement of existing technology for a new application.
Electronic digital computer	An innovation in the early 1940s based on science and originated through a United States government supported project at a university as a response to war-time needs. Rapid diffusion into civilian uses and numerous subsequent improvements.

Sources: Lundström (1974), Jewkes *et al.* (1969), Stern (1979)

with his ideas of a computer) preceded those of Taylor and such beliefs are not without foundation. But while Babbage was studying how to make manual operations amenable to automation (i.e., substituting technological innovation for human labour), Taylor was studying manual operations in order to make them more efficient and his managerial innovation was based upon this. Clearly, these innovations may substitute for each other to some extent in achieving economic performance. The illustration may also be carried a little further. According to Peter Drucker, the essence of Taylor's managerial innovation was that planning became distinguished from doing (see Drucker, 1977). The later innovation of multidivisional structure led one step further in that strategic planning became distinguished from operations and assigned as a prime responsibility to top management. The innovation of the computer in turn has provided means to facilitate the management of a complex organization.

12.3.2 Management of R&D and technological innovation

While it thus seems clear that technological innovations influence management and may partially be substitutable with managerial innovations, one may ask how management influences technological innovations. Would not, for instance, the computer have been invented and put into operation regardless of any managerial innovations and qualities? The question may be refined to concern how the rate and direction of technological innovation may be influenced by management. This brings in the question of R&D management. It is therefore important in this context that R&D management is interpreted in a wide sense as influencing technological innovation through managerial action at different levels. R&D management is thus not just confined to, say, management at some

Discussion

Table 12.3 Examples of innovations in R&D management

Managerial innovation	Major characteristics of sources of innovation
PERT (Program Evaluation Review Technique)	An innovation originated in a large company in co-operation with management consultants in connection with a large-scale military R&D project (Polaris). Rapid diffusion into civilian uses. Simultaneity present to some extent with respect to other network techniques.
TVO (Technical Ventures Operation)	An innovation originated in 1970 in a large company (General Electric) as an effort to join advantages of large and small companies. Simultancity present with respect to other forms of venture management.
Technological forecasting	A cluster of innovations originated partially in military contexts during and after World War II. Slow diffusion into civilian contexts.

Sources: Finch (1976), Williamson (1975), Sabin (1973), Jantsch (1967), Twiss (1976).

department or laboratory level, and it is certainly not suggested that R&D and technological innovation may be controlled, which sometimes happens to be a connotation of the term 'R&D management'.

An immediate example of a managerial innovation with a bearing on technological innovation would be the patent institute. Doubts have been raised about its effectiveness, and it is debatable whether a temporary monopoly is conducive to technological innovation, but it is an example of an R&D management innovation, albeit at the level of an economic system rather than at the level of a firm. More examples are given for illustrative purposes in Table 12.3.

If both the technology factor and the management factor are important for economic development, their joining in the form of management of R&D and innovation should be particularly important. In a similar vein of somewhat simplified deduction, one could develop this idea and say that to the extent that large corporations are important in technological and economic development, R&D management in large corporations would be important. However, in the extreme, one may argue on one hand that R&D cannot be managed at all, and on the other that R&D can be managed just like any other industrial operation (see Bright, 1964; Blake, 1974). Admitting that there are both random processes and universal elements of management involved in processes of innovation, the more interesting question is how to assess qualities and the role of R&D management. There are several studies which deal with this question. Some of these studies have been referred to in the preceding chapters, but as a reminder one can cite the study of Burns and Stalker (1961) and their concept of mechanistic versus organic organizations, the study of Lawrence and Lorsch (1967) and their concept of differentiation and integration, the many studies of barriers to innovation, and finally the Schumpeterian emphasis on entrepreneurs and innovations in contrast to inventors and inventions.

The empirical material in this study adds to the recognition of qualities as well as limitations of R&D management as reported in the preceding chapters (see the next section for a summary). When it comes to the relative importance of managerial knowledge versus technological knowledge, some of the findings in the preceding chapters will be highlighted here.

In Chapter 2 it was found that the inventions on which a group of companies were based were product improvements rather than radically new products, while the managerial achievements, not the least in international marketing, were remarkable. To the extent that this is true, it emphasizes the role of management for corporate development rather than the role of radical technological inventions and flashes of technological genius. Similarly, the versatility of management in the initial corporate development is important for utilizing the often small competitive advantages offered by R&D under circumstances of initial sensitivity of the corporation to the environment (Chapter 3). This holds true also in the subsequent corporate development in the light of the kind of grassroots R&D mostly undertaken, the cumulative effects of which are of great importance (Chapter 3). However, it should also be noted that more radical innovations have occurred in the subsequent histories of most of the corporations studied, and the management factor has then not always been conspicuous.

Diversification and internationalization as two main features of corporate development offer another illustration of the relative importance of different types of knowledge (Chapters 3 and 4). Most, if not all, successful internationalizations have been based on a technological achievement, while many diversification failures may be attributed to failures on the part of management to appreciate the technological and marketing knowledge needed to enter into new product areas. Thus, it seems that differentials in knowledge about different national markets are less decisive for management than the differentials in knowledge about different product technologies. To some extent also, multinational co-ordination of R&D is possible, although such co-ordination is mostly reduced to intra-continental co-ordination (see Chapter 4). Whether multinational R&D in a single product area is less difficult to co-ordinate than nationally based R&D in multiple areas is likely but is largely an open question. It may also be observed that in market economies, multinational corporations based on a few technologically related products are more common than national conglomerates. That the extent to which this is true in turn depends upon the type of management is illustrated by the difficulties of Japanese multinational corporations in implementing the Japanese way of management in foreign subsidiaries (Yoshino, 1976).

The importance of differentials in technological knowledge is also illustrated by the emphasis in R&D policies on technological synergy, 'natural' or 'organic' extensions of competencies to adjacent fields of science and technology, etc. (Chapter 5). The difficulties in bridging technology differentials through management are further illustrated by the formation of subcultures and conflicts (Chapters 9 and 10). However, subcultures may be conducive to communication

Discussion

and co-ordination, and cultural entrepreneurship is a managerial possibility, so consideration of subcultures actually gives a mixed judgement with respect to the relative importance of management and technology. This can also be said about conflicts since they may be instrumental to some extent in the management of R&D and innovation.

Policy evasiveness on the part of top management, lacking strategic planning of R&D, inadequate top management involvement in R&D management, lacking entrepreneurial R&D management and managerial barriers to innovation (as described in Chapters 5, 7 and 11) may be intepreted as shortcomings or failures in the R&D management factor. With this interpretation one is inclined to believe in a possible up-grading of the management factor in relation to the technology factor. But to the extent that the observed circumstances are interpretable as unremovable limitations of R&D management or just as desirable states of R&D management, such a belief is unjustified. One may also note that both the actual and desirable pattern of decision making regarding R&D may be dependent upon the type of technology (see Chapter 6).

With respect to changes in organization structure, top management is actively exercising a decisive influence, and the structural variable is largely at their disposal, although manning considerations may influence the choice considerably (Chapter 8). To the extent that structure is of importance in managing R&D, the management factor is then up-graded, provided technology does not influence structure. This is, however, likely to be the case. If a market in itself is considered as an organization, its structure is not at the disposal of some central managerial authority (unless it is totally regulated). Managerial decisions in several firms then indirectly influence market structure, which leaves more room for the technology factor. This whole issue, however, is intricate but important, which will be seen when we return to it in the next section.

Finally, it may be observed that in a competitive economy with qualities of technology and management among the means for competition, an increased complexity in the corporate environment and an increased information load on management reinforce the effects of skewly distributed managerial talents. Part of this complexity derives from technological innovation, which thus up-grades the importance of the management factor. Schumpeter's view that the 'creative destruction' in the 'perennial gale' of technological change is the only important form of competition in the long run then places emphasis on R&D management (Schumpeter, 1976, pp. 83–85).

In conclusion it may be added that no significant managerial innovation appears to have originated in Swedish industry, with the possible exception of Alfred Nobel's creation of a multinational R&D organization in the 1880s. While the utilization of foreign technology in Swedish industry has been supplemented by significant domestic technological innovations, there has been an almost total foreign dominance, especially a United States one, regarding managerial innovations. Their diffusion patterns have also differed. For example scientific management diffused into Swedish industry quite differently compared to the diffusion of the multidivisional structure.

In summary, this section has demonstrated the parallelism between technology and management and attempts have been made to assess the relative importance of these factors. The multinational corporation based on technologically related products is a viable form of organization, while technological differentials appear to make organizational integration less efficient and likely. In the subsequent section the perspective will be shifted and an internal organization versus a market organization as two distinct forms of management in a wide sense, will be compared with respect to their effects on and influences from R&D and technological innovation.

12.4 MANAGEMENT AND MARKETS

As a point of departure, the following question may again be asked: 'What kind of management and organization is the most conducive to technological innovations and economic performance?' This question may be directed at different levels of the organization such as the R&D team, the R&D laboratory, the firm, the sector of industry, or the economic system. When discussed at the interfirm level, the concepts of management and organization have to be interpreted in a wider sense in order to include different types of market structure as special cases.

Obviously, the above question has been asked extensively with different levels as the prime focus. At the interfirm level it has been a matter of discussion among economists for a long time (see Kamien and Schwartz, 1975). A most coherent penetration is made by Williamson (1975). This work along with related ones, such as Phillips (1980), will be taken as a central framework in which this study may be viewed when synthesizing it in retrospect. This study is not an empirical comparative study of relative advantages of, say, management systems versus market systems. However, it provides empirical insights into management of R&D and innovation in large corporations, insights which may contribute to assessing the possibilities and limitations of management in relation to the treatment of management versus markets by other authors.

12.4.1 Review of Williamson's work on markets and organizations

What is sometimes referred to as 'the Williamson hypothesis' is the statement that an internal organization is superior to a market organization. Although Williamson argues that this is the case in a great number of circumstances, he also carefully points out several modifications, exceptions, limitations, weaknesses of empirical support and so on. Williamson sets out to examine a firm (or a hierarchy) and a market as alternative organizational (or contractual) modes (pp. 5, 253), rather than alternative economic systems (p. 39). He then assumes that 'in the beginning there were markets' and shows how organizational forms develop essentially by referring to the relative advantage accruing from performing transactions in an organization rather than on a market among autonomous parties. This transactional approach is consistently carried through by using such concepts as bounded rationality (referring to Simon), opportunism (that is, self-interest seeking, possibly with guile), uncertainty, information impactedness (that is, the effects of unequal possibilities of information access among the par-

Discussion 187

ties in a transaction) and the effects of a small number of parties. Among other things, the cost of information and the difficulty involved in carrying out negotiations and transactions are found to disfavour market-mediated exchanges, while—relatively speaking—an internal organization is found to benefit from such things as learning from transactions. The technology factor, which is often used to explain the rise of certain structures, does not enter into Williamson's framework other than to the extent it affects transactions.

Williamson then analyses limits to organization and management and thus avoids predictions of an indefinite evolution towards organizational integration and monopolies. Also, in relation to innovation, he modifies the stand that integration permits transactional economies to be realized. A systems solution is forwarded in which small firms, having a relative advantage at the early stage of innovating, complement large firms having a relative advantage at a later stage. Taking transfer disadvantages into consideration, this system is claimed to be superior to full integration. Finally, Williamson addresses problems of monopoly and oligopoly with anti-trust implications in mind.

Generally, possible and existing organizational forms are only partly integrated. The question is then to what extent will productive units be integrated? For example, a market could be viewed as a completely disintegrated collection of internally integrated firms. But if inter-organizational ownership relations are introduced, an element of integration arises, which may vary along a continuum. Also, the multidivisional structure (i.e., the 'M form in Williamson's terms) could be modified along a continuum of degree of integration. Certainly Williamson thoroughly examines the relative advantages and limitations of different organizational forms, including the market, and he also addresses himself to the question of optimum divisionalization, as well as a total system for efficient innovation. But his emphasis on markets versus hierarchies is recurring. That a vertically integrated firm or an internal organization is superior to the market organization is thus a tempting way to summarize Williamson's findings in a single statement, in spite of the fact that he himself treats the issue in a differentiated manner.

12.4.2 Review of Phillips' work on markets, organizations and R&D

Williamson's work pays considerable attention to R&D and innovation. The focus is on questions of size of firm, market concentration, barriers to entry and similar features of market structure, on the one hand, and resources devoted to R&D, productivity of R&D and different barriers to innovation, on the other. A system for innovation, in which large firms limit their integration backwards into R&D and small firms specialize in early-stage invention, is proposed, but in intra-firm terms little is said explicitly about the R&D function. The applicability of Williamson's framework and conclusions when R&D are explicitly introduced as a subsystem in the firm has, however, been treated theoretically by Phillips (1980). This work is summarized below.

Phillips analyses the confluence of internal organizational factors and external market organizational factors in a theoretical framework, with special reference to the functioning of R&D in different intra- and inter-organizational systems. These systems are composed of selling organizations S_i, manufacturing organizations M_i, and R&D organizations R_i, the latter in turn decomposed into exploratory research (R_i'), advanced development (R_i'') engineering development (R_i'''), and product and marketing development (R_i''''). The relationships considered between these organizational elements are whether they are separated, meaning that the market mechanism is used for transactions, or integrated to some extent vertically or horizontally.

By and large Phillips finds support for Williamson's hypothesis that vertical integration is superior to a market organization. In fact, Williamson's arguments, based on concepts such as bounded rationality, informational impactedness, opportunism, goal differences and costs of transactions through contracting, apply with increased strength when R_i is added to the analysis. However, there are several limitations of integration as well, both as understood by Williamson and in other respects such as the appropriability problem, effects arising from interdependencies among different technologies and organizational persistence.

When $R_i' - R_i''''$ are added to the analysis, a set of organizational dilemmas arises regarding the balancing of effects from horizontal integration, for example, through 'horizontal' professional associations, and vertical integration. These effects affect the probabilities for incremental versus radical technological change, which in turn affect the dynamic rather than static efficiency of the organizational structures. Different networks of market/contractual and administrative/integrative relations affect the perception and transmission of technology- and demand-related facts differently, and the framework presented by Phillips permits an analysis of the often obscured issue of technology-push versus demand-pull factors in technological change. Whether or not push or pull factors are effective in some sense, or information about threats or opportunities are transmitted, the efficiency inducing aspects of vertical integration are still largely valid. However, what is exactly the most efficient organizational form is not easily defined. As succinctly expressed by Phillips: 'Bounded rationality applies to the choice of organizational form itself.' (Phillips, 1980, p. 113).

Thus, to put it briefly, Phillips finds that problems of information arising from R&D strengthen Williamson's arguments, although some additional qualifications and limitations to integration have to be recognized. Without going further into Phillips' work here, comments similar to the ones above about Williamson's work also apply to Phillips', with the exception that Phillips does not use the term 'hierarchy'. With respect to R&D and innovation, Phillips' work further clarifies the usefulness of Williamson's framework and also penetrates issues not specifically dealt with by Williamson, such as the technology-push/demand-pull issue. On the other hand, Phillips does not treat Williamson's systems approach to innovation, although both decompose the R&D and innovation process in similar ways.

12.4.3 Findings in the present study regarding management and markets

In this section the findings from the present study will be examined to see how they strengthen, weaken or modify the arguments forwarded by Williamson and

Discussion

Phillips in relation to markets and industrial organization. A preliminary note on terminology is in order. While Williamson speaks about markets and hierarchies and Phillips about markets and organizations, essentially the same phenomena will here be referred to as markets and management. Markets and management represent two kinds of systems, sometimes also referred to as inter- and intra-organizational systems. Although recognizable as distinctive stereotypes, their actual differences are a matter of forms and degrees of integration. Integration, in turn, refers to connecting properties of relations among actors, especially contractual relations. Degree of integration then is contingent upon and indicated by several related factors, such as level of interaction, agreements, information flows, stability in transaction patterns, and co-ordinated behaviour.

12.4.3.1 Indications supporting the hypothesis about the superiority of an internal organization

Table 12.4 summarizes the findings of this study, which offer support for the Williamson hypothesis. Each of the indications in Table 12.4 may be treated quite extensively but will be done only partially here with respect to some of the indications and commentary rather than analysis offered for the rest.

(a) *Early corporate histories*. For expositional purposes Williamson assumes that autonomous contracting is initially ubiquitous. Then he raises the questions why such contracting might be supplanted by a non-market organization and what

Table 12.4 Summary of indications found in the present study that management and internal organization may be superior to market organization with respect to R&D and innovation.

Type/area of indication	Chapter(s)
Inter-individual integration of inventive and entrepreneurial skills	2
Rise of national invention-based monopolies (bearings, matches, explosives, among others)	2
Internationalization in product-invention-based corporations	3,4
Early diversification in corporations based on domestic raw materials and/or foreign technology	3
Systems orientation	3
Mixed strategies and structures as response to uncertainties	3,5,8
Global information processing capacity of multinational corporations	4
Development of corporate planning	5
Strategizing in certain technologies	6
Range of managerial functions and comparative advantages to market functions	7
The 'M form' as an organizational innovation	8
Internalization of R&D	3,8
Structural adjustments and experimentation	8
Communication and co-ordination structures	8
Formation of subcultures and cultural entrepreneurship	9
Regulation of beneficial conflicts (internal competition, for example)	10
Managing generative and selective processes	11

internal forms of organization will appear first. In short, his answer is that simple hierarchies will appear, possibly preceded by teams or peer groups, since these forms are more efficient in carrying out transactions. Bounded rationality and opportunism are decisive human factors in this progression, and these factors also explain further organizational developments into more complex hierarchies.

Williamson's treatment may be checked with respect to studies of corporate histories. Some qualifications must then be made on empirical grounds. First, Williamson's approach is analytically tempting but the starting condition is never one of full entropy. In the beginning there may be markets, but these are structured, and different resources such as managerial skills, capital, technology, labour and raw material sources are skewly distributed. However, this does not necessarily weaken the argument that simple organizations will arise due to realization of transactional economies when different skewly distributed resources and differentiated skills are pooled. In fact, the common inter-individual rather than intra-individual integration of inventive and entrepreneurial skills, as described in Chapter 2, is an example of a team which emerges in connection with the foundation of a firm. Different contractual forms naturally appear, but uncertainty, bounded rationality and opportunism all limit the possibilities of short-term, contingent claims or sequential spot contracting. It may then be argued, along the lines of Williamson, that teams of actors may realize transactional economies through the special contractual commitments involved in starting a firm, although the team may be bound together in additional socio-psychological respects as well (c.f. family-owned companies). Thus the formation of a small group organization, rather than a collection of autonomous contractors, in connection with the foundation of a company may be explained in the transactional framework development by Williamson. However, Williamson seems to have a worker organization much in mind, and when discussing the role of technology he does not make distinctions between hard and soft technology or between product and process technology. Some qualifications with respect to entrepreneurs, inventors and technology-based companies are therefore to be expected.

The inter-individual joining of technological know how and managerial skill and the build-up of mutual trust and adaptation of behaviour present a case of indivisible information. As Williamson points out, this does not necessarily imply collective organization, but rather that such an organization stems from transactional difficulties with market contracting.

The combination of productive factors in founding a company also presents a case of non-separability. Because of the multiplicative nature of this combination, the marginal productivity of each supplier of productive factors such as technological and managerial assets cannot be determined. Team production is involved, just as in manual freight loading, which Williamson cites as an example of worker non-separabilities. In the latter case, an internal organization is presumed to arise in the form of a manager, who:

> monitors the performance of the team and allocates rewards among members on the basis of observed input behavior. Shirking is purportedly attenuated in this way. (Williamson, 1975, p. 50)

Also, non-separability does not mean that collective organization results as a general rule. Technological know-how may be licensed on a long-term basis, patents may be sold, managerial know-how may not be patented but supplied through management agreements (see Chapter 4), raw material sources subjected to various forms of contracting for utilization, etc. Transactional difficulties do not necessarily prevent these contractual forms from supplanting collective organization. Rather, experimental behaviour in these respects occurs together with the emergence of certain standardized options of behaviour (for example, in connection with royalties).

Thus, a variety of combinations of productive factors, human characteristics, and situational conditions create a variety of contractual relationships and quasi-organizational forms. The team of founders in the corporations studied displays this variety of relationships (see Chapter 2). Heterogeneity at the outset is reflected in an initial variety of quasi-integrated forms of founding companies. The role of technology in forms and degrees of integration cannot be reduced to a question of physical indivisibility and non-separability in process technology. Transactional considerations are certainly at the heart of the matter. However, various aspects of technology, management and situation determine the transactional economy, which can be realized through different forms of contracting in the foundation stage of a company, a stage which resembles a venture or a project rather than a collective organization.

The rapid progression into hierarchical forms as a firm develops is a basic and important phenomenon. This may be explained in several ways. Theoretically, a hierarchical structure may be seen as a graph or a system structure with extreme properties arising, for example, from postulates about communication economy, control properties, management principles, or need structures in terms of power and autonomy. But as Williamson points out, a 'leading theoretical need is for additional work on the properties of hierarchy' (p. 261). An analysis of the empirical reasons for the rise of a hierarchy will not be made here other than to point out the importance of skewness in resource distribution, including a skew distribution of managerial talent. Resourceful individuals gathered people around them to assist in company operations, thereby taking advantage of hierarchical forms. As pointed out by Williamson, something of an elite or a group of significant actors in the organization thereby results, who have better access to information, capital and other significant actors in the environment of the firm. This gives the elite a strategic advantage in the organization. Thus, skewness at this point is reinforcing. As also seen from Chapter 2, there appears to be a coupling between the capacities and orientation of the significant actors on the one hand, and features of early corporate development on the other.

A strong case may thus be made that hierarchical forms eventually appear. However, it must be added on the basis of this study that there are imperfections in the rising hierarchy. The rise of an informal organization is well known but the imperfections at the top of the hierarchy are less so. A hierarchy that is imperfect at the top often arises from the initial quasi-organizational team formed at the foundation stage of a company. Sometimes it is obvious that there is one strong man at the top, integrating in himself inventive and entrepreneurial skills (this, for instance, was the case in KemaNobel and SKF) but more often than not there seems to be a hetereogeneous elite at and around the top, which makes the hierarchy a poor model.

(b) *Diversification and internationalization*. The management and technology factor in integrating a corporation in multinational and multiproduct respects has been dealt with in Section 12.3. Differentials in technological knowledge rather than differentials in knowledge about international markets are crucial for integration through the internal organization of a corporation. The rise of multinational corporations in itself offers support for Williamson's hypothesis in that internalizing operations substitutes for international trade. Similarly, support is offered through the internalization of operations in diverse product fields. This is not necessarily efficiency-inducing in overall respects since some managerial efficiency may have been sacrificed for managerial security in spreading business risks among different product areas. Diversification failures also indicate limitations to the internal management factor due to technology and market differentials.

(c) *Managerial versus market functions*. A market may be conceived of as an overall organization with functions to provide entrepreneurial incentives, to distribute risks, to process information through price formation, and to allocate resources. Similarly, managerial functions, such as motivation, planning, manning, information processing and resource allocation may be discerned, although in different ways and with varying emphasis (see Chapter 7). Relative advantages of markets versus management may be assessed to each of these functions, and a mixed judgement is the likely outcome. For instance, a market is at an advantage in providing entrepreneurial incentives in the form of autonomy and profits, which appeal to some individuals, while the prospects of organizational careers and power have appeal to others.

An internal organization economizes heavily on uncertainty and bounded rationality through sequential decision making and cumulation of managerial experience. Mixed strategies and structures in response to uncertainty, the possibilities of managerial experimentation, recruitment and promotion of individuals on grounds other than their proven economic successes, etc. speak in favour of internal organization. On the other hand, the rise of dynamic conservatism in an organization, managerial conflicts, and conversion of market risks to managerial ego risks disfavour internal organization compared to a market organization. This leads to the question of limits to management, which will be considered next.

12.4.3.2 *Managerial limits*

Although management and an internal organization may be considered to be superior to a market organization with respect to information processing, planning, co-ordination and learning, several indications of limitations on the part of management may be observed with respect to R&D and innovation (see Table 12.5). This has also been recognized in literature (see Table 12.6).

Williamson derives the limitations from basically human attributes, such as opportunism and bounded rationality, the latter implying limitations with

Discussion

Table 12.5 Summary of indications of failures and limits to organization and management with respect to R&D and innovation as found in the present study.

Type/area of indication	Chapter(s)
Diversification failures	3
Acquisition failures	3
Increasing costs and risks in advanced science and technology	3
Multinational co-ordination	4,8
Weak coupling between R&D and corporate strategy	5
R&D policies for incremental knowledge extension	5
Policy evasiveness	5
Impact of business cycles	5
Non-existing means/ends hierarchies	5
Policy evolvement in organizations	5
Incrementalism in decision making	6
R&D decision-making nature	6
Politicizing	6
Lack of entrepreneurial R&D management	7
Inadequate top management involvement	7
Non-precedence of strategy to structure	8
Externalization of R&D	8,11
Internal transfer problems	8,10
Persistence of subcultures in the organization	9
Reorganizational conflicts	10
Conflicts among managers	10,11
Conflicts related to R&D people	10,11
Individual needs for power/autonomy	10
Barriers to innovation in management, organization and people	11

Table 12.6 Some indications of limits to organization and management with respect to R&D and innovation as reported in literature[*]

Type/area of indication	Author(s)
Appropriability problems with R&D	Phillips (1979)
Range of implementation uncertainties associated with R&D	Phillips (1979)
Organizational persistence	Phillips (1979)
Bias towards minor innovations	Phillips (1979)
Limited adaptive responses to technological threats and opportunities	Phillips (1979)
Insufficient incentive system	Williamson (1975)
Organizational ageing	Williamson (1975)
Inadequate atmosphere for R&D and entrepreneurial elites	Williamson (1975)
Decline in R&D spending and productivity in giant organizations	Williamson (1975)

[*]Naturally such indications may be found in a wide variety of literature. However, only the literature particularly focused on in this chapter is considered.

respect to computational abilities and language. However, in the course of transactions, the number of parties will be reduced and organizational conservatism will arise. Thus, limitations will be built into the organization and derive from the nature of organizations rather than from solely human attributes. In fact, Williamson's assumption of bounded rationality and opportunism may be discarded and omniscient altruistic management with unlimited rationality assumed as a possibility. Limitations may, however, still be derived from limited channel capacities in processing information in combination with initial information asymmetries. Limited capacities to process information may be derived in turn from considerations of costs in transmitting information. Since unbounded rationality implies non-scarcity and zero opportunity costs of the corresponding managerial resources, such cost considerations will have to rely upon costs of time delays in transmitting information rather than distortion due to opportunism and limitations in node capacities. This serves to illustrate the limitations inherent in organizations in addition to limitations primarily attributable to individuals. Just as it is unimaginably improbable that all molecules in a room will concentrate in a corner and someone in the room will be choked to death through Brownian motion, it is improbable that all human action will be perfectly co-ordinated by random processes. Not even with an altruistic, omniscient manager will this be possible, since processing information for non-trivial co-ordination purposes will be time-consuming. (Limits analogous to Heisenberg's uncertainty relation are also conceivable.) The crucial underlying factors are uncertainty, information asymmetries and limited organizational capacities. Of course, limited human capacities add to this picture in reality, but this strengthens the argument.

Two factors in particular will be considered here in relation to managerial limits: the nature of R&D and technological change and the role of a heterogeneous elite.

Williamson argues that technology is important only in so far as it affects transactions. The universal nature of transactions gives strength to his argument, but at the same time attention is drawn from the role of technology and R&D. It will be argued that the nature of technology and R&D as well as the nature of a heterogeneous elite involved in the carrying out of innovations are major sources of uncertainty and imbalances in a system of transactional relations.

That uncertainty is involved in R&D and technological change hardly needs to be pointed out. In an important way, however, R&D does not reduce but increases the uncertainty. For one thing, it raises the awareness of new and previously inconceivable problems, but technological change also creates uncertainty with respect to other effects on a market (such as side-effects or new demands derived from technological change). It may be noted that basic human needs have remained rather unchanged, while market demands have shifted. It is also questionable whether satisfaction of some human needs have been raised on the whole due to technological change. For example, it could be argued that military technology contributes to the satisfaction of a human need of security, but military R&D may hardly be said to have had this effect globally. That human behaviour is a source of uncertainty also hardly needs to be pointed out. Limitations in disclosure of motives and plans, limitations in organizational transmittance of information and segmentation of communication networks

Discussion

through the formation of subcultures and elites also increase the uncertainty derivable from human behaviour.

Corporations, large and small, collectively account for a large number of technological developments. These developments often move rather continuously and contemporaneously where technological knowledge is concerned, while this pattern is somewhat disrupted where materialized technology is concerned. Technology, moreover, has the intrinsic feature of what will be called here latent economies and dis-economies. First, there is the economy associated with repeated utilization of technological information. In contrast to other productive resources, a piece of information is not being consumed or worn out when it is used. Technological information, therefore, has a non-depletable economic potential. (This does not mean that a piece of information cannot lose its value in a particular situation.)

The other kind of latent economy associated with technology is due to the causality structure of technological developments. If there were single causality chains such as

$$\to C \to E \to$$

each technological advance should have a closed and well-defined economic potential calculable from its single particular effect. However, technology, in general, displays complex causality patterns involving combinations and multiple effects such as the structure below

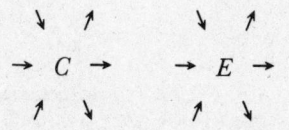

$$\begin{array}{cc} \searrow \nearrow & \searrow \nearrow \\ \to C \to & \to E \to \\ \nearrow \searrow & \nearrow \searrow \end{array}$$

If E is a desired effect (for example, local anaesthesia or food preservation) achieved by C (for example, a particular pharmaceutical or microwaves), then C and E also tend to give other effects as well. These other effects (side-effects and spin-off but not secondary effects in the normal sense) yield an economic potential (or potential difference more strictly expressed) either by creating possibilities for new advances and applications or by creating a need for new technology. When considering technological development over time rather than considering a set of isolated technological advances, there is a complex push-pull pattern leading to a particular state of technology. In this state of technology there is thus a potential of non-realized fulfillments or applications of technology. Economy is connected to this causality pattern in such a way that economic transactions are carried out for a limited set of steps in the causality pattern. This means that the size of payments related to technological innovations are not adjusted indefinitely according to new side-effects or applications. (Theoretically, such an adjustment would be indeterminable and, in fact, negotiating work would rapidly grow.) Thus, there is a fundamental source of imbalance in the way the economic system is connected to the structure of technological development.

The values, perceptions and behaviour of leading actors have been focused on in several of the empirical chapters. Two main impressions stand out. One is that technological advances and their exploitation are undertaken by an elite, the other is that this elite is heterogeneous. The skew distribution of intellectual output among individuals is well documented as are skew distributions of such things as managerial talent, power and capital. The heterogeneity of the elites, both within and among the corporations, is also conspicuous considering the formation of subcultures and the prevalence of conflicts. Thus, there is a second fundamental source of imbalance, this time of an empirical social nature.

Thus, the point may be made that R&D, technological change and a heterogeneous elite are disruptive to organizational integration and limiting its use. It is conceivable to think of fragmentation of large organizations when certain managerial limits to size and complexity are approached. In a sense then, limits are imposed on the level of interaction needed to achieve a certain degree of organizational integration. In fact, one may hypothesize a certain constancy of the average level of interaction times the size of the organization. The adoption of the M structure is a case in point here. It should also be noted that interaction is a wider concept than transaction. This leads to the next section on the Williamson hypothesis, namely its possible qualifications in the light of what has been said above and support from empirical findings in this study.

12.4.3.3 Further qualifications and the rise of quasi-integrated forms

The inclusion of considerations about R&D and innovation in an analysis along the lines of Williamson (1975) qualifies in several respects the hypothesis that management and an internal organization are superior to a market organization. However, there is also supporting evidence for the hypothesis from these considerations. As treated by Phillips (1980), bounded rationality applies particularly strongly to R&D and innovation, as do uncertainties about input/output-measures and information impactedness through increased differentiation in education and experience. In Phillips' view, problems with high transaction costs, appropriability and range of implementation, due to the nature of R&D and technological change are more efficiently coped with through integration than through markets. Thus, integration is seen to give advantages with respect to communication and favour responses to threats and opportunities.

On the other hand, Phillips clearly points out that integration does not solve all problems. Appropriability problems still remain, as do problems about the interactions between different technologies and their applications. Organizational persistence will arise, as well as a bias towards minor innovations, and there will be limits on adaptive responses. In addition, differentiation within R&D units, that is $R'-R''''$ in Phillips' terms, will increase information impactedness internally. The latter argument does not, however, necessarily imply that vertical integration of $R'-R''''$ is becoming inferior to a corresponding market organization. To the extent that professional specialization increases (for example, because of technological change), information impactedness problems will generally increase, but possibly less so for an internal organization. On the other hand, it should be noted that certain limits to vertical integration (see Table 12.6) have led Williamson to suggest the systems solution that early stage development is

Discussion

Table 12.7 Summary of indications found in the present study of quasi-integrated forms of organization with respect to R&D and innovation

Type/area of indication	Chapter(s)
Internal R&D competition	3,10,11
External R&D cooperation (various forms)	3,5,8,11
Temporalistic/pluralistic structures	3,4,8
Decentralized divisions with weak centralized strategic control	5,8
Formation of inter-organizational decision making complexes	6,9
Reliance upon innovation takeover	3,5,8
Collective R&D in certain technologies	3,8
Semi-autonomous innovation companies	8
Scientific advisory boards	8
Inter-organizational structures of corporate boards	7,8
Links to the environment through subcultures	9

carried out by small companies and then transferred to large ones, in spite of some market impediments to transfer.

When findings from this study are taken into account, there is some evidence that an internal organization may be superior to a market organization with respect to R&D and innovation (see Table 12.4). On the other hand, there are also extensive indications of organization and management failures and limits with respect to R&D and innovation (see Table 12.5).

It is not possible to make an overall assessment on the basis of these findings. Besides, such an assessment in terms of an internal organization versus a market organization, as two distinct alternatives, would by-pass possible intermediate organizational forms. In fact, it is not difficult to conceive of such forms theoretically, internal organization being multidimensionally integrated to a matter of degrees. Empirical instances of what would then be called quasi-integrated forms of organization are collected in Table 12.7.

Now some questions naturally arise:

— Are there common factors underlying the different kinds of indications and empirical observations?
— Do optimally quasi-integrated forms exist in some sense?
— Are there any observable trends towards some kind of quasi-integrated forms?

At this stage the empirical and explorative nature of the study does not seem to permit anything more than a few guidelines for further observation and hypothesizing.

First, the characteristics of different stages of an innovative process, together with transfer characteristics, may determine the proper form of integration as already mentioned in connection with Williamson's proposal for a systems solution. However, there are several conceivable variants of such a solution. Small innovative firms may be taken over by large firms, and there are examples of large firms that have this kind of acquisitions as part of their business ideas. Small firms may also be spun off from larger ones as new business development units or exist as a permanent semi-autonomous innovation company for the purpose of acquisition and early stage development of internal and/or external ideas for transfer or divestment in some form at a later stage. Although its operations are usually more narrowly defined, a central R&D laboratory could also function in this way. Another variant would be an industry-wide co-operative R&D laboratory. What determines the proper form of these variants of specialization by stages is difficult to say. For example, they vary regarding the extent to which the transfer of people takes place in connection with the transfer of results. Moreover, a transfer may involve a mixture of management and technology. One may also note that small management consultancy firms seldom are taken over by large industrial firms and that the latter seldom spin off the former type of firms, although it could be argued that instances of this are increasing.

Second, the characteristics or specific nature of different technologies may determine the proper form of integration. For example, rapid advances combining different technologies put a strain on integration, while engineering improvements in a stable set of parameters (or natural trajectories in the language of Nelson and Winter, 1977) may build up a potential for integration in a producer–user interface. It may be noted that the empirical findings in the present study show neither a significant correlation between R&D intensity and a certain form of outer R&D organization, nor a significant correlation between R&D intensity and an employed variety of organizational forms. Although the sample is small a variety of forms of outer R&D organizations within the same sectors of industry may also be observed. This, in fact, is in contrast to the intersectoral adoption of the M form.

By viewing management in parallel with technology, the specific nature of different management areas could be taken into account as well. The separability of managerial functions may be low, and one may ask why there exists general management in technologically specialized industries when the reverse situation is hardly to be found. On the other hand, managerial functions such as budgeting, planning and legislation may be carried out on a higher level of aggregation. In comparison with technological development, managerial development has so far not been characterized, measured and subjected to forecasting or assessment similar to technological forecasting or assessment.

There is an important interplay between managerial and technological innovations. (Take, for example, the computer or the principle of division of labour.) There is also an important interplay between the growth of managerial and technological knowledge and its manifestations as artefacts. (Managerial artefacts would include, for example, formal organizations, contracts and adopted policies or laws.) There are effects from learning by doing both regarding technological innovations (see Sahal, 1980) and managerial innovations. (See Section 12.3.1 for examples of managerial innovations that have originated in practice and in large firms, rather than from managerial research.) It is thus conceivable that experimentation and innovation lead to incremental adoption of quasi-integrated forms, the efficiency of which will change over time depending upon the state of management and technology. For example, contractual forms may be an area of future managerial innovations which could signify important changes in organizational forms.

Third, the concept of strategy might be complementary to transactional considerations in judging the rise of different organizational forms. For a concept of strategy to be valuable in this respect, it ought to include an element of preconceived behaviour, although admittedly at the expense of analytical as well as empirical tractability. Strategy formation relates to managerial behaviour, which does not have to be guided invariably by transactional calculations determining structure any more than it has to be guided invariably by profit maximization. The impact of cultures and values on structure is also important to consider — for example, with regard to the use of co-operative or competitive strategies.

Fourth, it is important to take randomness specifically into account. In fact, it is remarkable how much could be explained by models of random processes (see, for example, Price, 1963; Steindl, 1965; Williamson, 1975; Sahal, 1978). Stochastic models of technological developments, the development of firms and the development of structure may be used. Thus, it is conceiveable that a stochastic graph model of relations, whose degrees of integration are governed by, say, a Markov process, could be designed to describe and explain (in the language of the model) the appearance of quasi-integrated forms.

In summary, the presence of quasi-integrated forms in between pure forms of internal organization and market organization may be interpreted in different ways. Assuming a degree of managerial rationality influencing the emergence of quasi-integrated forms, their presence could be interpreted as an intermediate stage in a progression from one pure form to another. However, they could also be seen as resulting from managerial experimentation with organizational forms as well as resulting from technological innovation or from random processes.

Here an empirically based regression argument will be forwarded to indicate that quasi-integrated forms are responses to inadequacies of internal organization as well as market organization. The adoption of the M form in itself could be seen as a regression from an internal organization to a quasi-integrated form to the extent that decentralization is achieved and centralized strategic planning is diminished. Similarly, there are other cases such as the reliance upon innovation take-over and the creation of semi-autonomous innovation companies, which could be interpreted as regressions from organizational forms with a higher degree of integration. Reasons for such regressions are found in difficulties experienced in managing R&D and innovation in large, highly integrated organizations.

Whether there is a general tendency to employ quasi-integrated forms to an increasing extent is difficult to say (see Osers, 1972, for indications in socialist countries regarding R&D). Essentially, both managerial and technological innovations could promote such a tendency as well as its countertendency.

In addition, bounded rationality and opportunism in the choice of organizational form, which — when it comes to internal structure is a choice fairly open to management — will induce managerial experimentation with a variety of organizational forms. (It should be noted that managerial opportunism — that is, self-interest seeking, possibly with guile — is an extra factor, which in addition to bounded rationality, contributes to re-organization.) Certainly, evidence of the limitations to innovation set by large corporations is accumulating as is the evidence of limitations on market organizations that promote technological innovations that contribute to welfare. Thus, it might be hypothesized, albeit on speculative grounds, that organizational forms of extreme purity of the market or the internal organization type will decrease. The range of employed intermediate forms will, however, remain in a flux due to uncertainty, bounded rationality, opportunism and innovations.

In summary the entire study has explored various aspects of R&D and innovation in large corporations. These aspects refer to corporate histories, strategies, structures and behaviour. The findings have been synthesized and related on a higher level of aggregation to the hypothesis that organizational integration in a firm is superior to a market organization. This is described as the pure form of the Williamson hypothesis, since a leading work on this theme was published by Williamson in 1975. The findings which emerge from this study with respect to the hypothesis treated by Williamson are then:

(a) The inclusion of considerations about the organization of R&D in the context of a firm and a market qualifies the Williamson hypothesis as follows: there are intermediate quasi-integrated forms, and these are the most conducive to technological innovation.
(b) Experimentation with organizational forms, due to uncertainty, bounded rationality, opportunism and managerial innovation will create an ever-changing state of organization, which makes an arrival at stable, optimally quasi-integrated forms unlikely.

In addition, one may hypothesize (although on weak grounds) that:

— The quasi-integrated forms that are the most conducive to technological innovation are dependent upon the specific nature of different technologies and, moreover, change over time due to technological and managerial innovation.
— There is a movement towards employing quasi-integrated forms of organization, and convergence from market structures and totally integrated structures to quasi-integrated structures takes place in the sense that variety at the extremes is reduced. This movement is due to market and organization failures and is enforced by managerial and technological innovation.

12.5 MANAGERIAL IMPLICATIONS

The purpose of this study has been to provide insight into the varieties and subtleties surrounding innovation and to provide a sense of the contingencies involved in managing innovation and theoretizing about innovation. Managerial implications have been formulated in different chapters. These implications must be weakly formulated and interpreted with much caution. However, for the sake of clarity some of the normative findings of this study will be outlined below. They include the following:

(a) Internationalize through R&D-based specialization.
(b) Do not centralize all R&D for technology transfer to product divisions.
(c) Profit centres for R&D and innovation should be noted as dangerous.

Discussion

(d) Embryonic radical innovations should be separated into innovation companies, venture development companies, and the like. Premature transfer of technology should be avoided.
(e) Internal R&D competition as well as external R&D cooperation may favour technological innnovation.
(f) Integrate R&D into corporate strategies through interaction in the strategy formulation process.
(g) Perform collective or co-operative R&D in certain technologies.
(h) Vertical integration does not necessarily favour technological innovation in the long run.
(i) Integration of R&D and marketing is important.
(j) Apply pluralistic and temporalistic forms for the outer R&D organization.

The last point deserves to be elaborated upon.

12.5.1 A pluralistic R&D organization

Figure 12.1 depicts different possible organizational structures and Figure 12.2 shows different possible processes in innovation. What could possibly be said in a normative way about the best organization of R&D and innovation in a corporation in the light of the variety of solutions available and employed? Under what circumstances should one rely upon suppliers, co-operate externally, have an innovation company, centralize R&D, etc.? Internal and external uncertainty cannot be sufficiently reduced to advocate a certain choice between different solutions. Another approach is then to allow for multiple solutions, or what will here be called a pluralistic R&D organization. This approach is analogous to portfolio (or diversified) solutions in uncertain investment situations, as reported by Markowitz (1952) and others. A pluralistic R&D organization would then mean using mixed solutions such as having a satellite organization, performing co-operative R&D, having one or more innovation companies, having central as well as divisional and regional R&D, having multiple channels of communication, having dual ladders of promotion etc. The multitude of uncertain sources of, and barriers to, innovation speak in favour of such a pluralism, and so do general arguments about diversified solutions as a response to uncertainty. The effects of a poorly functioning R&D organization do not show up immediately, and the risks in relying upon one particular form of R&D organization, carried to the extreme, have also been described in Chapter 8.

Organizational features such as diffuse and/or multiple rather than single clear goals, fuzzy rather than sharp divisions of responsibilities, and loose rather than rigid structuring of work sometimes are advocated for R&D organizations. Although such features may be instrumental in certain situations, they may or may not be present in a pluralistic R&D organization and certainly do not characterize it. It is a question of having overlapping rather than unclear responsibilities and goals. If, for instance, a marketing department has the responsibility for doing market research in product R&D, it is quite feasible that the R&D department has a responsibility to make sure that the work is done in case the marketing department does not fulfill its responsibility. The overlapping respon-

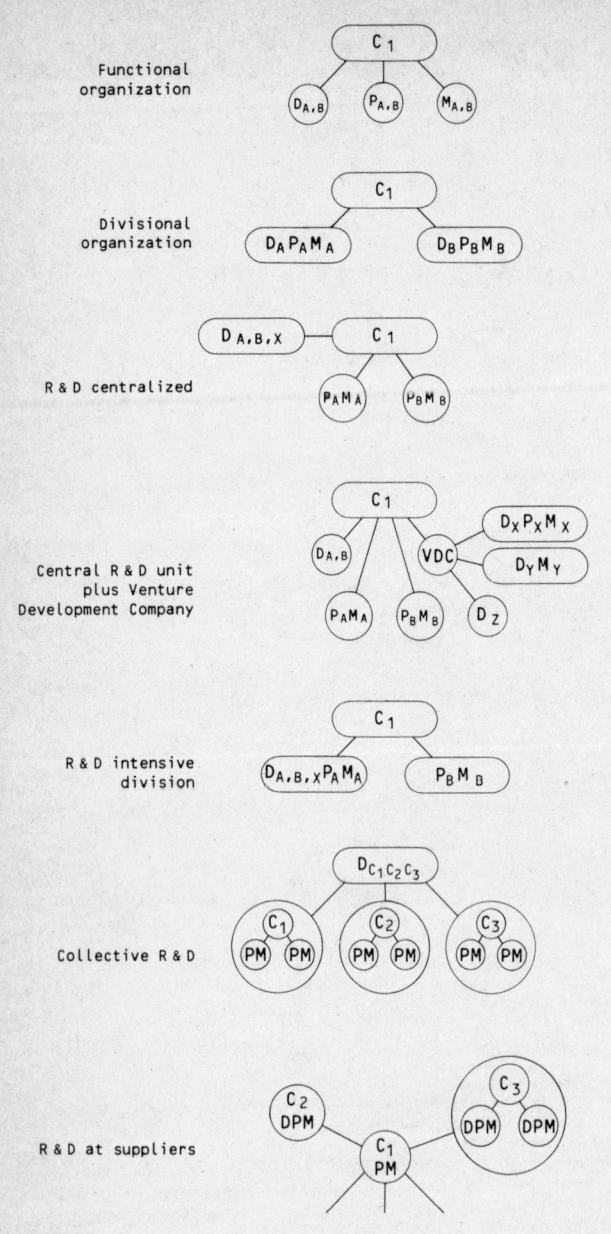

Notation:
$C_1, C_2 \ldots$ denote companies. A, B denote existing product areas and X, Y, Z new product areas. Functions are D for R&D, P for production, M for marketing.

Figure 12.1 Organizational structures for R&D and innovation

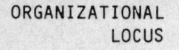

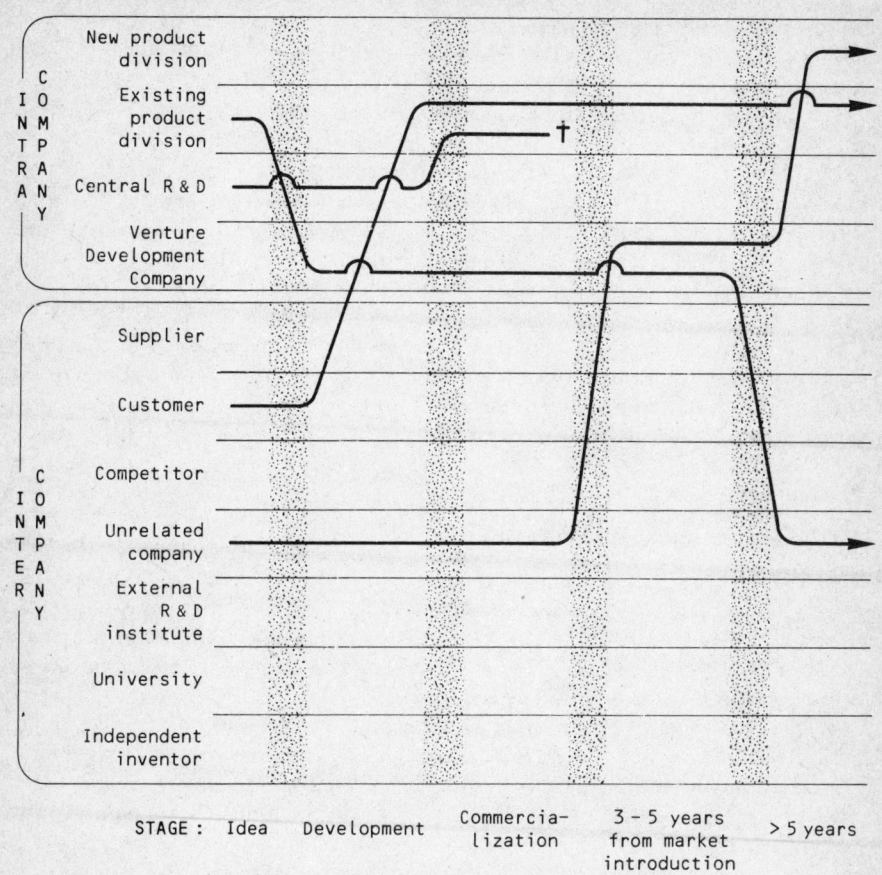

Discussion

Figure 12.2 Innovation and business development paths

Note: Simplified venture paths are shown. Multiple sources and paths are common in practice. Vertical movements denote a transfer, eg through licensing or acquisition.

sibilities do not, however, have to be vaguely outlined but may very well be clearly defined in terms of primary and secondary responsibilities, the secondary ones being in effect when the primary ones are not fulfilled.

One may argue against a pluralistic organization for at least two reasons:

(a) that such an organization would be too costly; and
(b) that it would create conflicts.

That a pluralistic organization is not suited to take certain advantages of scale is natural. Although there are scale advantages in certain types of R&D, regarding equipment, communication and personnel, they are often diffuse and may vanish when a threshold size is passed. It could therefore be argued that a large organization would be less sensitive to the advantages of scale than a small one, other things being equal and thus could better afford a pluralistic R&D organization.

Regarding the creation of conflicts through a pluralistic R&D organization, it is likely that role conflicts, territorial conflicts and internal competition will develop in a pluralistic structure. On the other hand, conflicts are prevalent in innovative work, and some of them are fruitful. Conflicts tend to have negative effects when they become personified, but not necessarily when they are issue oriented. It is, in fact, conceivable that institutionalized pluralism would weaken the tendency of conflicts to become personified. Nevertheless, internal competition in R&D is seldom fully exploited as a means of increasing innovativeness in large corporations. Thus, a pluralistic R&D organization places requirements on corporate R&D management, regarding both effects of scale and synergy and effects of conflicts.

12.5.2 Temporalistic R&D organization

When the organizational structure is discussed, the time dimension is sometimes collapsed in a static model and disregarded in the sense that a sequence of employed structures over time and the processes which take place in the structure are not primarily considered. It is conceivable to have a succession of solutions—for instance, to let a period of decentralization follow a period of centralization, rather than to seek a compromise as a permanent solution. The question of whether R&D should be integrated mainly with external science and technology or mainly with marketing could be resolved in this temporalistic manner. Admittedly, this is somewhat speculative but little attention has been paid to the possibilities of what may be called temporalism in organizing for innovation. It is not primarily a matter of adapting the organization to environmental changes or working with temporary assignments. Rather, it is a matter of creating long-term 'swings' in the organization, which may create positive effects from the change in itself and provide for a kind of dynamic compromise along conflicting dimensions such as degree of integration and degree of decentralization. It is true that continual reorganizations have negative effects and that innovative work requires a certain social order as Merton (1957) expresses it. But this speaks in favour of carrying out major reorganizations with long intervals of organizational stability in between. Besides, changes in the outer R&D organization may affect the social order to a lesser degree than changes in the inner R&D organization. There may certainly be a tendency to overestimate the positive effects of a change in itself, possibly leading to irresponsible reorganizing. On the other hand, an R&D organization is indeed ageing or ossifying. On the whole, an increased circulation and mobility of people involved in R&D are desirable in many large corporations in order to transfer know how and experience as well as stimulate the generation of ideas. This does not, however, have to be the primary aim of structural changes, nor does it have to be accomplished through structural changes.

12.5.3 A final comment

Knowledge about managing R&D and innovation has increased considerably during recent decades. It has largely been true that management theory has been lagging behind management practice, at least the best practice. It is also true that research in management seldom is a source of radical managerial innovations. Systematic, scientifically oriented empirical studies appear to be able to contribute more to the gradual improvements in management. By analogy with the increasing role of science in technological innovation, one may hypothesize an increasing role of management science (in a broad sense) in managerial innovation in the future.

Chapter 13
CONCLUSIONS

13.1 CONCLUSIONS REGARDING R&D AND INNOVATION IN LARGE CORPORATIONS

The presentation in this book has been structured in a way similar to the multidivisional organizational structure, and conclusions have been formulated in each empirical chapter. The major conclusions will be recapitulated here.

In general, large corporations have arisen from a variety of combinations of productive factors and local conditions. According to the dominant element in the original business idea, two slightly overlapping groups of corporations could be discerned—raw-material based ones and product-invention based ones. However, the roles of technology at the time of the establishment of the corporation were many and varied among the different corporations regarding product versus process technology, radical versus incremental technological change, and domestic versus foreign technology. Renowned 'classical' product innovations were significant product improvements rather than radically new products. They came into being through the strenuous work of a small inventive and entrepreneurial elite in a context of contemporary technological and industrial development rather than through flashes of genius in radically new areas. The inventors were often well educated and internationally oriented, both regarding markets and science and technology. There were several links to science in early corporate development, the strongest link being to scientific modes of operation rather than to scientific results. A sweeping generalization would be that Swedish technology in its infant stages had close links to industrial management as well as to foreign technology rather than to science.

The rise of large corporations based on product inventions resulted to a large extent from managerial achievements, especially in international marketing, in which direct foreign investment was an early strategy. Integration of inventive and entrepreneurial skills took place on an individual level in a few cases but mostly on a team level. Features of the significant actors, such as a multiproblem orientation and an international orientation, corresponded to some extent to diversification and internationalization in early corporate development. However, different patterns of corporate development could not be aggregated into a general progression of stages. Corporations based on product inventions initially developed around a single product or product line and then rapidly internationalized, while corporations initially based on raw materials or foreign technology rapidly diversified into at least two different product lines. The level of technology does not discriminate between these patterns but rather the size of input and output markets, the distinction between product and process technology, and proprietary conditions pertaining to technology and raw materials. A lead in product technology in combination with a small domestic market, internationally oriented entrepreneurship, and protective trade barriers have contributed to internationalization, while national sources of raw materials and advanced process technology have been associated with domestication, although the export intensity has generally been high.

There has been a great deal of continuity in corporate development as regards diversification on both sector and product area levels. Recently, diversification has been de-emphasized in several corporations, and there is also a definite trend towards increased internationalization. Late internationalizers have a preference for acquisitions and joint ventures. In general, diversification has been accomplished by the corporations through a mixture of strategies ranging from acquisitions of companies and/or technology to internal R&D over intermediate forms with external cooperation.

As the corporations grow, diversify and internationalize, their R&D operations grow, diversify and internationalize in a give-and-take relationship. There has been an important kind of 'grass-roots R&D', the results of which are not as easily recognized and assessed as indisputable innovations. The connections between R&D and corporate growth consist of both a long, increasing and technology-dependent time lag between R&D and sales and a contemporary coupling through budgeting. The time lag between R&D work and a significant degree of diversification is still longer in a large corporation. Contradictory cases of diversification based on innovations originating internally as well as externally suggest a concept of organizational permeability, pertaining both to the susceptibility of an organization to external ideas and impulses and to the elasticity of an organization in the event that internal ideas and impulses lead to product areas outside the present ones.

In the corporations studied, ratios of R&D to sales in 1975 were positively correlated with internationalization (0.48) and size of sales (0.42) while negatively correlated with diversification (−0.28) as approximated quantitatively. Corporate strategies emphasize growth, internationalization and R&D, while diversification is de-emphasized in half of the corporations. The highly internationalized product-invention-based corporations have entered a stage of multinational co-ordination, which reinforces a strong coupling between R&D, size and multinationality.

Corporations also internationalize their R&D, although there has been a tendency to domesticate the 'R' part. Initial internationalization of R&D was, in general, not part of a corporate strategy but often resulted from acquisitions and local ambitions. There is a current trend towards a break-up of traditional patterns of internationalization and increased emphasis on technological and managerial knowledge. More pluralistic and temporary forms of organizing and managing R&D are being employed, and internal R&D is acquiring additional roles of creating access to, and capabilities for, utilization of external R&D. Models of orderly patterns of internationalization, innovation and diffusion are of limited relevance and apparently increasingly so. The supply versus demand oriented theories behind the growth of technology appear in the context of a corporation to be reconcilable in a dynamic pull–push pattern when seen over an extended period of time. A process of 'first pull, then push' was found in several cases, which means that a period in which a technology is developed as a response to an originally perceived demand is followed by a period in which the areas of application for the developed products and knowledge are extended beyond the demand initially aimed at.

Differences in emphasis of corporate policies on profit, growth, diversification, internationalization and R&D were found—especially with respect to diversification and R&D, both over time and among the corporations. There is a complex inter-relatedness between matters and people in policy making, which is far from the picture of a stable consensus about a specific hierarchical means–end structure. Evolutionary expansion of corporate technologies into adjacent areas, considered as 'naturally' connected to existing ones, was commonly emphasized. To varying extents, policies confirmed historical corporate development, and to varying extents they resulted from action and reaction at different levels in the corporations. A combination of policy-evasive behaviour at the top management level and policy-seeking behaviour at lower organizational levels was found in several cases regarding R&D and innovation. Four reasons for policy-evasive behaviour were indicated, namely attitude towards specificity of control through policies, stage of maturation in a policy matter, attitude towards especially political risks, and selective and sequential management attention. A general conclusion is that a need exists for a closer coupling between corporate and R&D policies through interaction in the policy-making process and consideration of patterns of technological development and sources of innovation.

Also R&D and corporate strategy were loosely coupled by means of strategic decisions made with respect to R&D. A strategic decision was by definition determined by the size of a concentrated decision-making effort as well as by the size of the effect of a decision. However, due to an increased interdependence in decision making, there was a limited applicability of the subdivision of decisions by three—into strategic, tactical, and operative decisions, based on notions of importance. To design a decision-making process by interspersing concentrated decision-making efforts in the series of decisions (here called 'strategizing') appears to be important in embryonic stages of R&D and innovation as well as in late stages. Diffuse alternatives, lack of deadlines and underestimation of cost/benefit ratios of R&D in combination with rising profitability of costs of completion are among features in R&D decision making, which tend to yield incrementalism and omissions in the decision-making process.

Corporate boards play virtually no direct role in R&D, and the room left for top management to exercise influence on R&D is on an average utilized to a low degree. Top managers differed regarding their behavioural, financial and technological orientations. Rather than have a general manager, who may be good at many things but not very good at anything, different orientations in top management could be balanced through the composition of teams and—as a long-term complementary alternative—through a balanced succession of managers with different orientations.

The working role of R&D managers above the project level fell in the following categories with approximate frequencies. Management of R&D personnel (41 per cent); management of ideas, information, and projects (30 per cent); management of critical relations (15 per cent); Fayol managerial roles (13 per cent). Roles in the Fayol typology are difficult to separate, but in particular they do not emphasize crucial roles in R&D management, such as the handling of conflicts or deviant behaviour.

The R&D managers did not emphasize the entrepreneurial role, although some of their roles in managing critical relations may be interpreted as having entrepreneurial elements. It is hypothesized here that fear of failure is a barrier to entrepreneurship in large corporations. A climate more benevolent to failure could stimulate corporate entrepreneurship, but at what level is an open question. In general, the problem of managing R&D could to a larger extent be approached with the same philosophy of experimentation that has found application in R&D itself.

The late, but rapid adoption of a divisionalized structure in this sample of corporations was not a consequence of an adopted strategy in the preconceived behaviour sense. Rather, rapid changes in size and diversity of operations paved the way for adopting a newly recognized organizational concept, the diffusion of which was aided by external organizational consultants.

Major structural variations in the outer R&D organization appear to depend especially on the interpretation and implementation of general organizational ideas by top management in addition to manning considerations. R&D intensity was found to correlate significantly neither with a particular structure nor with a diversity of employed organizational means for conducting innovative work.

Some of the organizational ideas in divisionalization are hazardous to R&D when carried to an extreme. The uncertainty associated with sources of, and barriers to, innovation suggests the use of mixed organizational solutions in the form of pluralistic and temporalistic R&D organizations.

Similarly, the idea of top management resorting to strategic considerations (while excluding themselves from operations) is hazardous. 'Diving' in the organization was, however, practised by some corporate managing directors as an information-seeking exercise as well as to motivate behaviour.

With respect to R&D and innovation top management was evasive regarding strategy but active regarding structure and manning. Technical and R&D managers played a minor role in divisionalization. This reorganization into product divisions rearranged interdependencies and relegated the conflict potential arising from sequential dependence of functional managers to lower organizational levels at the expense of a conflict potential arising from a pooled dependence of divisions and tensions between corporate and divisional perspectives.

There was a high frequency of conflicts of various kinds in connection with R&D and innovation. In general, explanations given referred to the characteristics of large corporations, characteristics of R&D and innovation and characteristics of people involved in this kind of work. Typically, significant conflict relations were relations among significant actors, relations associated with a traditional part of the corporation, functional relations, relations between central and local authorities and relations among professionals. While a number of tensions surrounding R&D are natural and may be beneficial to some extent, personal conflicts among significant actors generally have severe effects. The ubiquity, complexity, dynamics and mixed effects of conflicts suggest that conflicts in connection with innovation in large corporations cannot be resolved but at most regulated, and to some extent they are desirable.

Conflicts among professionals were often associated with the formation and change of subcultures. The tensions between a business culture and a science and technology culture were apparent in many cases. However, the culture associated with science and technology is heterogeneous, and the formation of professional subcultures is strongly connected with the structure of graduate education. The subcultures also tend to produce intermittent re-orientations in corporations and sectors of industry.

A subculture may constitute a means of co-ordination as well as a barrier to change. Through a period of conflicts and disordered co-existence, a state of a dominant culture in a corporation may be transformed into one of the following:

(a) a state of amalgamation of cultures;
(b) a state of dominance of a new culture;
(c) regression to the old culture; and
(d) a state of ordered cultural coexistence.

Several factors account for the transformation of different cultures in a corporation. The role of top management as a kind of cultural entrepreneur is important, although cultural change cannot be managed at will. Instruments are, among other things, corporate strategy, recruitment and promotion. A general conclusion is that treating technological change as an autonomous or exogenous variable in relation to cultural change is incorrect.

A diversity of sources of and barriers to both radical and incremental innovation were found both internally and externally. Sources of ideas among people were generally skewly distributed. Moreover, top management, as well as higher R&D management, was more selective than generative. Among a wide variety of perceived barriers to innovation, the most frequently indicated ones were related to management and organizational and human attributes rather than to, for example, the resource situation or the business environment. This emphasizes behavioural skills as an additional dimension of entrepreneurship in large corporations. Internal competition among individuals on both operative and managerial levels appears as a barrier in innovative work, while internal competition on a project or R&D unit level as well as external co-operation appears to have a positive effect on the rate of innovation. A general conclusion would be that the age and ageing of organizations rather than the size of an organization, create barriers to innovation — size being primarily a matter of a chosen form of management and organization.

13.2 CONCLUSIONS REGARDING TECHNOLOGY, MANAGEMENT AND MARKETS

The synthesizing discussion in Chapter 12 has proceeded along two inter-related themes:

(a) technology and management;
(b) management and markets.

Conclusions

While the technology factor has gained an increasing interest in explaining economic change, so far the management factor has not. Lack of empirical insight and lack of analytical tractability appear to disfavour the recognition of the management factor. Neo-classical economic theory disregards, in particular, a skew distribution of managerial talent, a skewness possibly contributed to by managerial innovations and their varying rates of diffusion.

Viewing the state and change of technological and managerial knowledge in parallel produces a set of analytical questions, which highlight the possible interdependencies. Managerial innovations, such as scientific management, multivisional structure and linear programming, show similarities to technological innovations regarding patterns of innovation and diffusion. Among dissimilarities we may mention the impossibility of patenting managerial innovations, which makes such innovations comparable to unpatentable but diffusable process innovations.

To the extent that both technology and management matter in economic development, a case could be made that the management of R&D and technological innovation in particular ought to matter. Examples of managerial innovations in these areas can be found, although they are not frequently conspicuous, possibly due to the intangible nature and degree of professionalization of management of R&D and innovation. Concerning the relative importance of technological and managerial knowledge and skills in corporate development, the empirical findings call for an up-grading of managerial achievements relative to technological ones. At the same time several failures and limitations of management of R&D and innovation were indicated. The presence of multinational corporations rather than national conglomerates, and the connections between R&D and internationalization rather than between R&D and diversification, show that technology differentials rather than regional market differentials limit the economizing of managerial capacity. A general conclusion would be that the management factor deserves increased recognition, empirically as well as analytically, relative to the technology factor.

By taking R&D and innovation into account, two kinds of qualifications of the hypothesis that internal organization is superior to a market organization result. Aspects of R&D and innovation modify the arguments pertaining to superiority in general, but also the general arguments behind a claimed superiority apply to a modified extent to superiority with respect to innovativeness, in particular. The present study partially supports Williamson's hypothesis in several respects, such as the realization of transactional economies through inter-individual joining of inventive and entrepreneurial skills, the rise of hierarchies — their imperfections at the top notwithstanding — internalizing of R&D, comparative advantages of a range of managerial functions relative to market functions, and the rise of product-invention-based multinational corporations. To a limited extent diversification may be explained by transactional considerations since managerial efficiency may have been sacrificed for managerial security in spreading business risks among different product areas, which is not necessarily efficiency inducing in overall respects.

The present study also offers indications of management failures and limitations regarding R&D and innovation, such as failures in radical diversification, incremental R&D decision making, conflicts and barriers to innovation in large corporations. Limitations derive from human and organizational attributes as well as from the recombinant and non-consumable nature of technology, yielding latent economies to be realized. The heterogeneity of an inventive and managerial elite, moreover, implies limitations of internal organization relative to a market organization.

Empirical as well as analytical evidence indicates the emergence of quasi-integrated forms in connection with R&D and innovation, such as external R&D co-operation, reliance upon innovation takeover and semi-autonomous innovation companies. Regressions to organizational forms intermediate to internal organization and market organization indicate the existence of quasi-integrated forms, which are the most conducive to technological innovation. Experimentation with organizational forms and managerial as well as technological innovation will make an arrival at stable, optimally quasi-integrated forms unlikely.

REFERENCES

Ansoff, H.I. (1968), *Corporate Strategy, An Analytical Approach to Business Policy for Growth and Expansion*, Harmandsworth, Penguin Books.
Asplund, G. (1975), *Strategy Formulation—An Intervention Study of a Complex Group Decision Process*, Stockholm, The Economic Research Institute at the Stockholm School of Economics.
Babbage, C. (1832), *On the Economy of Machinery and Manufactures*, London, Charles Knight.
Baranson, J. (1980), *Technology and the Multinationals. Corporate Strategies in a Changing World Economy*, Lexington, Lexington Books.
Birney, R.C., Burdick H. and Teevan, R.C. (1969), *Fear of Failure*, New York, Van Nostrand-Reinhold.
Blake, S.P. (1974), *A Manager's Guide to Research and Development*. Stanford Research Institute, Menlo Park.
Bohlin, H. (1976), A review of technical functions in the industrial corporation. Paper presented (in Swedish) at a seminar 7-9 January 1976 at *Institutet för Företagsledning*, Stockholm (unpublished).
Bolin, E. and Dahlberg, L. (1975), *Dagens Storföretagsledare*, Stockholm, Studieförbundet Näringsliv och Samhälle (in Swedish).
Braybrooke, D. and Lindblom, C. (1963), *A Strategy of Decision. Policy Evaluation as a Social Process*, London, The Free Press of Glencoe.
Bright, J.R. (1964), *Research, Development and Technological Innovation: An Introduction*. Richard D. Irwin, Inc. Homewood, Illinois.
Burns, T. and Stalker, G.M. (1961), *The Management of Innovation*, London, Tavistock Publications.
Carlson, S. (1951), *Executive Behavior. A Study of the Work Load and the Working Methods of Managing Directors*, Stockholm, Strömbergs.
Carlson, S. (1979), *Swedish Industry Goes Abroad. An Essay on Industrialization and Internationalization*, Lund, Studentlitteratur.
Chandler, A.D. Jr. (1969), *Strategy and Structure. Chapters in the History of the Industrial Enterprise*, Cambridge, Mass., MIT Press.
Channon, D.F. (1973), *The Strategy and Structure of British Enterprise*, Basingstoke, Macmillan.
Clarke, T.E. (1974), 'Decision-making in technologically based organizations: a literature survey of present practice', *IEEE Transactions on Engineering Management*, Vol. EM-21, No. 1, February 1974, pp. 9-23.
Dahmen, E. (1970), *Entrepreneurial Activity and the Development of Swedish Industry, 1919-1939*. Richard D. Irwin, Inc. Homewood, Illinois. (Title of the original: *Svensk industriell företagarverksamhet. Kausalanalys av den industriella utvecklingen 1919-1939*. Band 1-2. Industriens Utredningsinstitut, Stockholm, 1950.)
Dantzig, G.B. (1963) *Linear Programming and Extensions*, Princeton, Princeton University Press.
Dobrov, G.M. (1978), 'The management of R&D technological progress as an object for applied systems analysis', *R&D Management*, Vol. 8, Special Issue, 1978.
Drucker, P.F. (1977), *People and Performance: The Best of Peter Drucker on Management*, New York, Harper & Row.
Fayol, H. (1949), *General and Industrial Management*. Sir Isaac Pitman & Sons, Ltd., London. (Title of the original: *Administration industrielle et generale*. First published in *Bulletin de la Société de l'Industri Minérale* 1916.)
Finch, F. (1976), *A Concise Encyclopedia of Management Techniques*, London, Heinemann.
Freeman, C. (1974), *The Economics of Industrial Innovation*, Harmondsworth, Penguin Books.
George, C.S. (1968), *The History of Management Thought*, Englewood Cliffs, Prentice-Hall.
Gerstenfeld, A. (1977), 'Interdependence and innovation', *Omega*, Vol. 5, No. 1, 1977, pp. 35-42.
Gluck, F.W. and Foster, R.N. (1975), 'Managing technological change: a box of cigars for Brad', *Harvard Business Review*, September-October 1975, pp. 139-150.

Hanson, W.T. (1971), 'Multinational R&D in practice. Eastman Kodak Corporation'. *Research Management*, Janaury 1971, pp. 47-50.
von Hippel, E., (1977), 'Successful and failing internal corporate ventures: an empirical analysis', *Industrial Marketing Management*, No. 6, 1977, pp. 163-174.
Hlavacek, J.D. and Thompson, V.A. (1973), 'Bureaucracy and new product innovation', *Academy of Management Journal*, Vol. 16, No. 3, September 1973, pp. 361-372.
Horváth, D. (1973), Divisionalisering i Sverige, Umeå Universitet, Avd. för företagsekonomi, Umeå (mimeograph, in Swedish).
Jantsch, E. (1967), *Technological Forecasting in Perspective*, Paris, OECD.
Jewkes, J., Sawers, D. and Stillerman, R. (1969), *The Sources of Invention*, Basingstoke, Macmillan (2nd edn.).
Johansson, J. and Wiedersheim-Paul, F. (1975), 'The internationalization of the firm — four Swedish cases', *Journal of Management Studies*, October 1975, pp. 305-322.
Kamien, M. and Schwartz, N. (1975), 'Market structure and innovation: a survey', *Journal of Economic Literature*, Vol. 13, 1975, pp. 1-37.
Kast, F. and Rosenzweig, J. (1970), *Organization and Management. A Systems Approach*, New York, McGraw-Hill.
Krech, D., Crutchfield, R.S. and Ballachey, E.L. (1962), *Individual In Society, A Textbook of Social Psychology*, New York, McGraw-Hill.
Lawrence, P.R. and Lorsch, J.W. (1967), *Organization and Environment*. Harvard University, Boston.
Leroy, G. (1976), *Multinational Product Strategy. A Typology for Analysis of Worldwide Product Innovation and Diffusion*. New York, Praeger Publishers.
Levitt, T. (1960), 'Marketing myopia', *Harvard Business Review*, Vol. 38, No. 1.
Little, et. al. (1973), *Barriers to Innovation in Industry. Opportunities for Public Policy Changes: Report to the National Science Foundation*, Cambridge, Mass., Arthur D. Little Inc.
Lundström, R. (1974), *Alfred Nobel som Internationell Företagare. Den Nobelska Sprängämnesindustrin 1864-1886*, Uppsala, Uppsala Studies in Economic History (in Swedish).
Mansfield, E., Teece, D. and Romeo, A. (1979), 'Overseas research and development by US-based firms', *Economica*, No. 46, pp. 187-196.
March, J. and Simon, H. (1958), *Organizations*, New York, John Wiley.
Markowitz, H. 1952, 'Portfolio Selection.' *Journal of Finance*, Vol. VII, No. 1, March 1952, pp. 77-91.
Marquis, D.G. (1969), 'The anatomy of successful innovations', *Innovation Magazine*, November 1969.
McClelland, D.C., Atkinson, J.W., Clark, R.A. and Lowell, E.L. (1953), *The Achievement Motive*, New York, Appleton-Century-Crofts.
Merton, R.K. (1957), *Social Theory and Social Structure*. Revised and enlarged ed. Glencoe, The Free Press.
Mintzberg, H. (1973), *The Nature of Managerial Work*, New York, Harper & Row.
Mintzberg, H., Raisinghani, D. and Theoret, A. (1976), 'The structure of "unstructured" decision processes', *Administrative Science Quarterly*, Vol. 21, June 1976, pp. 246-275.
Nelson, R. and Winter, S. (1974), 'Neoclassical vs evolutionary theories of economic growth: critique and prospectus', *Economic Journal*, Vol. 84, December 1974, pp. 886-905.
Nelson, R. and Winter, S. (1977), 'In search of useful theory of innovation', *Research Policy* Vol. 6. 1977, pp. 36-76.
Nyström, H. (1979), *Creativity and Innovation*, New York, John Wiley.
Osers, J. (1972), 'The financing of R&D in some socialist countries of Eastern Europe', *R&D Management*, Vol. 3, No. 1, 1972, pp. 29-33.
Papo, M. (1971), 'How to establish and operate multinational labs', *Research Management*, January 1971, pp. 12-19.
Penrose, E.T. (1959), *The Theory of the Growth of the Firm*, Oxford, Basil Blackwell & Mott.
Phillips, A. (1980), 'Organizational factors in R&D and technological change: market failure considerations', in Sahal (1980), *op. cit.*
Pratten, C.F. (1976), *A Comparison of the Performance of Swedish and U.K. Companies*, Cambridge, Cambridge University Press.
Price, D. de S. (1963), *Little Science, Big Science*, New York, Columbia University Press.

References

Price, D. de S. (1973), 'The relations between science and technology and their implications for policy formation', in Simons and Strasser (eds): *Science and Technology Policies*. Cambridge, Mass., Ballinger Publ.

Quinn, J.B. (1977), 'Strategic goals: process and politics', *Sloan Management Review*, Fall 1977, pp. 21–37.

Ronstadt, R. (1978), *Research and Development Abroad by U.S. Multinationals*, New York, Praeger Publishers.

van Rumker, R. (1971), 'Multinational R&D in practice. Chemagro Corporation', *Research Management*, January 1971, pp. 50–54.

Sabin, S. (1973), 'At Nuclepore, they don't work for G.E. anymore', *Fortune*, Vol. 88, December 1973, pp. 144–153.

Sahal, D. (1978), 'The distribution of technological innovations', International Institute of Management. Discussion Paper 78-61, 1978.

Sahal, D. (ed.) (1980), *Research, Development and Technological Innovation*, Lexington, Lexington Books.

Salveson, M.E. (1959), 'Long-range planning in technical industries', *Journal of Industrial Engineering*, Vol. 1959, pp. 339–346.

Schmookler, J. (1966), *Invention and Economic Growth*. Cambridge, Mass., Harvard University Press.

Schon, D.A. (1967), *Technology and Change. The New Heraclitus*, New York, Delacorte Press.

Schumpeter, J.A. (1939), *Business Cycles, A Theoretical, Historical and Statistical Analysis of the Capitalist Process, Vol. I–II*. New York, McGraw-Hill.

Schumpeter, J.A. (1951), *Essays of J.A. Schumpeter* (Edited by R.V. Clemence) Cambridge, Mass., Addison-Wesley Press.

Schumpeter, J.A. (1976), *Capitalism, Socialism and Democracy*. London, George Allen & Unwin.

Singh, P. (1971), 'Management styles and philosophies abroad', *Research Management*, January 1971, pp. 64–69.

Sloan, A.P., Jr. (1963), *My Years with General Motors*, New York, Doubleday.

SOU (1975), Internationella koncerner i industriländer. Samhällsekonomiska aspekter. Betänkande av Koncentrationsutredningen, Industridepartementet, Stockholm, 1975. (In Swedish).

Steele, L.W. (1975), *Innovation in Big Business*, Amsterdam, Elsevier North-Holland.

Steindl, J. (1965), *Random Processes and the Growth of Firms*, London, Griffin.

Stern, N. (1979), 'In the beginning the ENIAC', *Datamation*, May 1979, pp. 229–234.

Taylor, F.W. (1964), *Scientific Management*, London, Harper & Row.

Twiss, B.C. (1976), 'A study of the diffusion of management concepts and techniques amongst R&D managers', *R&D Management*, Vol. 6, No. 2, 1976, pp. 87–92.

Vernon, R. (1966), 'International investment and international trade in the product cycle', *Quarterly Journal of Economics*, May 1966.

Williamson, O.E. (1975), *Markets and Hierarchies: Analysis and Anti-trust Implications. A Study in the Economics of Internal Organization*, London, The Free Press.

Winkofsky, E.P., Mason, R.M. and Souder, W.E. (1980), 'R&D budgeting and project selection, a review of practices and models', *TIMS Studies in the Management Sciences*, No. 15, 1980, pp. 183–197

Wrapp, H.W. (1967), 'Good managers don't make policy decisions', *Harvard Business Review*, September–October 1967, pp. 91–99.

Wright, R.V.L. (1973), *Strategic Centers — A Contemporary Managing System*, Cambridge, Mass., Arthur D. Little.

Yoshino, M.Y. (1976), *Japan's Multinational Enterprises*, Cambridge, Mass., Harvard University Press.

INDEX

Achievement, need for, 113
Acquisition, 66, 81-82, 203
Administration, 178
Administrator, 92
Alfa-Laval, 12, 14, 16, 21-28, 32-39, 41-44, 47-53, 57-58, 62-68, 74, 80-82, 94-101, 105, 118-122, 133-137, 140, 143, 155, 161-166
Ansoff, H.I., 79
Appropriability, problems of, 188, 193, 196
Astra, 21-28, 30-36, 41-44, 47-53, 57, 62-70, 80-84, 94-100, 106, 118-122, 131-132, 140, 143, 148-150, 155, 161-163
Astra-Hässle, 30-31, 33, 38, 43-44, 69-70, 97, 102, 107, 108, 131-132, 148-150, 164

Babbage, C., 181-182
Baranson, J., 58
Barriers to innovation, 127, 180, (definition) 159, 162-174
Bayer, 57
Blake, S.P., 183
Bohlin, H., 118
Boliden, 12, 21-28, 32-36, 44, 49-51, 62-68, 80-82, 94-101, 106, 118-122, 132-133, 140-143, 161-163, 170
Bounded rationality, 178, 186, 188, 194, 199
Braybrooke, D., 79
Budgeting decisions, 65, 84
Burns, T., 157, 183

Capitalist, 7
Carlson, S., 55, 111
Centre concept, 51-52
Central R&D budget, 120-122
Central R&D laboratory, 120-122, 127-128
Chandler, A.D. Jr., 124-125, 181
Channon, D.F., 126
Collective R&D, 120, 201
Competition, 185
    Internal, 201
Conflict, (definition) 145
    Groups of, 146-147
    Dynamics of, 147-154
    Effects of, 154-155
Consumer markets, 136-137
Coordination, multinational, 52-54, 56
Corporate board, role of, 93, 109-110
Corporate entrepreneurship, 112-115, 209
Corporation, definition, 8
Cultural change 140-143

Cultural structure, 139-140
Culture, (definition) 130
Cost overruns, 89-90

Dahmen, E., 11, 12
Decision making, strategic, 80-85
Decision making, R&D, 85-91
Decisions
    Administrative, 79
    Operative, 79
    Strategic, 79
    Tactical, 79
Decentralization, 54, 67, 204
Development, 4-6
Development centre, 51, 54, 121
Deviant behavior, 103-104
Diffusion, 7-8
Diversification, (definition) 16-17, 20, 22-25, 32-37, 43-44, 50, 62, 124, 126, 184, 192
    of R&D, 27-28, 35-37
Diving, 100, 110-111
Division, definition, 118
Divisionalization, 67, 118, 124-128, 187
Drucker, P.F., 182
Du Pont, 125, 181

Eastman Kodak, 57
Elites, heterogeneity of, 194-196
Embryonic decision making, 90
Engineering industry, 133-135
England, 18, 48, 126
Entrepreneur, (definitions) 6-7, 15-17, 92, 157-158
Establishment chain, 55-57

Fayol, H., 111, 114, 208-209
Fear of failure, 113, 115, 209
Forestry, 135
Freeman, C., 4

General Electric, 183
General Motors, 125, 181-182
Germany, 18, 48, 57, 163
Gerstenfeld, A., 88
Graduate education, 139-141
Grassroots R&D, 25-26, 39, 184
Growth, definition, 20
Goal interrelatedness, 63-64

Hierarchy, 186-187, 190-192

217

von Hippel, E., 128
Horizontal integration, 20, 188

IBM, 57
Idea, (definition) 159
Iggesund, 2, 13, 21-28, 32-36, 44, 49-51,
    62-68, 80-82, 94-101, 118-122, 135,
    161-163, 170
Industrial Research Institute, 172-174
Industrialization, 10-11
Information, 178-179, 186-187, 190, 194-195.
    See also Knowledge
Information impactedness, 186, 188
Innovation by invasion, 74, 140, 172
Innovation definition, 7-8
    Embryonic, 201
    Financial innovation, 7, 11, 12
    Incremental, 13-14
    Managerial innovation, 7, 177-186, 198-200, 205
    Organizational, 181
    Technological innovation, 177-186, 198-200, 205
    Radical, 13-14, 201, 205
Innovation chain, 127
Innovation company, 198, 120-122
Innovation, system for, 187, 197
Innovation take-over, 197
Innovator, 7, 157-158
Invention, 14
Inventor, 15-18
Invention based corporations, 12-15, 54-55
Integration, 187
Inter-organizational relations, 187
Inter-organizational decision making, 88
Integration, 8, 20, 126-127, 190, 196, 198, 204
Interaction, 196, 201
International marketing, 15, 18-19, 51
International product life cycle theory, 57
Internationalization, (defintion) 16-17, 46,
    47-53, 62, 124, 126, 184, 192
Internationalization of R&D, 53-54, 56-58

Jantsch, E., 5, 183
Japan, 2, 90-91, 179, 184
Jewkes, J., 4, 171, 182
Johansson, J., 55
Joint ventures, 66

KemaNobel, 14, 16, 17, 21-28, 32-38, 44,
    49-51, 62-68, 80-82, 94-101, 106,
    118-122, 135-136, 161-163, 170
Knowledge, 4-5, 179-180. See also Information
Kreuger, Ivar, 14

Latent economies, 195
Levitt, T., 73-74

Licensing, 8, 66, 191, 203
Lindblom, C., 79
Little, A.D., 172-174

M form. See Multidivisional structure
Management (definitions) 6-7, 92, 116, 160,
    163-165, 177-205, 186
Management composition, 110
Management, limitations of, 184-185, 192-196
Management succession, 110
Management science, 205
Manager (definition) 92, 179, 190
Managerial control, 180
Managerial economies, 180
Managerial implications, 155, 172-173, 200-205
Manning decisions, 84, 88, 96, 127
Mansfield, E., 56
March, J., 145
Market, (definition) 8, 136-137, 172-173, 186-200
Marketing, 17-18, 26-27, 51, 99, 105-106,
    136-139, 147, 161, 166, 172-173
Marx, K., 6
Military markets, 137-139
Mintzberg, H., 79, 111-112
MNC, 46
Multidivisional structure, 118, 124-126, 181,
    185, 187, 198-199
Multinational R&D, (definition) 46, 186
Multinationality, 46

Need for achievement, 113
Nelson, R., 178, 198
NIH (Not-invented-here), 44, 167
Nobel, Alfred, 15, 16, 17, 182, 185
Nyström, H., 127

Opportunism, 186, 188, 194, 199
Organization (definition) 116, 186-200
    Divisional definition, 116, 118
    Functional definition, 116, 118
    Inner definition, 116
    Outer definition, 116

Patent, 180, 183, 191
Penrose, E.T., 180
Permeability, 44, 127
PERT, 183
Pharmaceutical industry, 131-132
Philips, 2, 21-28, 34, 37, 47-54, 57-58, 62-68,
    118-122, 135-136, 163
Phillips, A., 187-189, 193, 196
Philips-Sweden, 2, 62, 80-85, 101, 106,
    138-140
Pluralism, 126, 171-173, 201-204
Pluralistic R&D organization, 201-204

Index

Policy, (definition) 60
Policy conflicts, 71
Policy-evasive behavior, 71-73, 75-77
Policy making, 67-77
Policy-seeking behavior, 71-73, 75-77
Politicizing, 90-91
Price, D. de S., 5, 199
Process technology, 13-14
Producer markets, 136-137
Product area, definition, 20
Product line, definition, 20
Product technology, 13-14
Production function, 177-178
Professionalization, 92, 130
Profit centre, 51, 128, 200

Quasi-integrated forms of organization, 196-200
Quinn, J.B., 75-78

Raw material based corporations, 12-15, 54-55
Raw material based industries, 132-133
Recruitment, 102-103
Research, 4-6
R&D, (definitions) 4-6
R&D management, (definition) 77, 92, 101-109, 111-114
Ringi system, 90
Roles of R&D managers. See R&D management
Roles of top management. See Top management
Romeo, A., 56
Ronstadt, R., 56
Russia, D., 18, 48

Sahal, D., 198, 199
Satellite organization, 106, 201
Sawers, D., 4, 171, 182
Schmookler, J., 42-43
Schon, D.A., 128, 140, 172
Schumpeter, J.A., 6-7, 184-185
Science, 4-5
Scientific advisory board, 100, 121-122
Scientific management, 181, 185
Sector, (definition), 20
Significant actors relations among, 150-154
  roles of, 15-18
Simon, H., 145, 186
Size, effects of on R&D, 37-39, 124, 165-166, 173
SKF, 2, 12, 14, 16, 21-30, 32-39, 43-44, 47-54, 57-58, 62-68, 80-87, 90, 94-101, 118-122, 142, 155, 161-166, 170
Sloan, A.P., 128
Smith, A., 180
Sources of ideas (definition), 159, 159-162, 171

S&T, 5
Stalker, G.M., 157, 183
Steele, L.W., 55-56, 90, 112-114, 127
Stillerman, R., 4, 171, 182
Strategy, (definition), 60, 124-125
Strategic decision, definition, 79
Strategic planning, 68
Strategy/structure-hypothesis, 124-125
Strategizing, 87-91
Structural variety, 126. See also Pluralism
Structure, (definition) 116, 124-125
Subculture, (definition) 130, 147
  within science and technology, 131-136
  within marketing, 136-139
  professional, 139-143
Sweden, 1, 2, 9-18, 137

Taylor, F.W., 181-182
Technical ventures operation, 183
Technological forecasting, 183
Technological innovation. See innovation
Technological levelling, 1
Technological substitution, 74
Technologists, 179
Technology, (definitions) 4-5, 177-186
Technology based companies, 13
Technology exploitation strategies, 66
Technology procurement strategies, 66
Technology sharing, 1
Technology transfer, (definition) 8, 127, 200
Technology trade, (definition) 8
Teece, D., 56
Temporalistic R&D organization, 204-205
Top management, 75-77, 92-101, 109-111
Transaction, 186-189, 194-196

Uncertainty, 141, 157, 178, 186, 194
United States, 1, 18, 48, 56, 124-125, 137, 179, 185

Venture development company, 201-204
Venturism, 128
Vernon, R., 57
Vertical integration, 20, 25, 187-188, 201
Volvo, 2, 14, 16, 21-28, 31-39, 47-54, 62-68, 70-71, 80-84, 94-101, 118-122, 136-137, 161-163
Volvo Flygmotor, 32-33, 38, 44, 137-138

Wiedersheim-Paul, F., 55
Williamson hypothesis, 186, 200
Williamson, O.E., 175, 181, 183, 186-200, 211
Winter, S., 178, 198
Wrapp, H.W., 75-78

Yoshino, M.Y., 90, 184

Zeitgeist, 161